TAIWAN

Taiwan

A POLITICAL HISTORY

Denny Roy

CORNELL UNIVERSITY PRESS

ITHACA AND LONDON

First published 2003 by Cornell University Press
First printing, Cornell Paperbacks, 2003

Printed in the United States of America

Library of Congress Cataloging-in-Publication Data
Roy, Denny
   Taiwan : a political history / Denny Roy.
     p. cm.
   ISBN 0–8014–4070–X (colth : alk. paper) — ISBN 0–8014–8805–2 (pbk. : alk. paper)
    1. Taiwan—Politics and government—1945– I. Title.
DS799.816 .R69 2003
320.95124'9'09045—dc21

2002012235

Cornell University Press strives to use environmentally responsible suppliers and materials to the fullest extent possible in the publishing of its books. Such materials include vegetable-based, low-VOC inks and acid-free papers that are recycled, totally chlorine-free, or partly composed of nonwood fibers. For further information, visit our website at www.cornellpress.cornell.edu.

Cloth printing   10 9 8 7 6 5 4 3 2 1
Paperback printing   10 9 8 7 6 5 4 3 2 1

＊

To Jinzhen, Meihua, and Meitai,
daughters of Taiwan

CONTENTS

✳

PREFACE

While many books on Taiwanese politics are clearly biased either for or against the Kuomintang or Taiwan independence, I am beholden to no particular political organization in Taiwan and have aimed for a balanced assessment. My hope is that the people of Taiwan choose their own destiny for themselves, free of compulsion or duress.

First, I should make a few remarks on terminology: in general I have used the Wade-Giles system for romanizing names and terms associated with Taiwan, and the Pinyin system for those associated with mainland China. I depart from Wade-Giles in some cases where place names have well-known but nonconforming spellings and where individuals have their own preferred ways of spelling their names. I accept the premise that Taiwan and the PRC are de facto separate countries. Accordingly, I use the terms "Taiwan" and "The Republic of China (ROC)" to refer to the subject of this book, while "China" refers strictly to mainland China except in the few instances, clearly indicated in the text, where I discuss China as an abstract, nongeographic notion.

I am grateful for the generous support of the Chiang Ching-kuo Foundation for International Scholarly Exchange, which helped make this book possible. The foundation never made even the slightest hint of attempting to influence my analysis. I also sincerely thank Ms. Chung Ju-yu for helping me compile some of the photographs used in this book. Finally I thank my family for their support.

The views expressed herein are mine alone and do not represent the opinions of the U.S. government, the U.S. Department of Defense, or the Asia-Pacific Center for Security Studies.

D.R.

CHRONOLOGY OF MAJOR EVENTS

15th century	First known Chinese contact with Taiwan, already inhabited by aborigines
1544	Portuguese explorers encounter Taiwan and call it *Ilha Formosa*
17th century	Heavy Chinese migration to Taiwan
1624	Dutch build Fort Zeelandia near Tainan
1662	Ming loyalist Cheng Ch'eng-kung seizes Taiwan from the Dutch
1683	Qing forces from mainland China capture Taiwan
1885	Qing government makes Taiwan a province of China
1895	Treaty of Shimonoseki cedes Taiwan to Japan; organized, armed resistance to Japanese occupation persists until 1902
1898	Japanese administrator Goto Shimpei begins modernization program
1921–34	Taiwanese political activists repeatedly but unsuccessfully ask Tokyo to establish a Taiwan parliament
1930	Japanese retribution follows aborigine uprising in Musha village
1937–45	Japanese armed forces accept Taiwanese recruits
1945	With Japan's surrender, Taiwan reverts to control of Chinese government under Chiang Kai-shek's Kuomintang (KMT); Chen Yi becomes governor of Taiwan
1947	February 28 uprising leads to KMT counterattack and massacres
1949	KMT, defeated on the mainland by Chinese Communist Party (CCP) forces, moves its government and remaining military units to Taiwan; government places Taiwan under martial law
1949–53	Taiwan implements successful land reform program
1950	With outbreak of the Korean War, U.S. government decides to block impending Chinese invasion of Taiwan

1951	KMT government creates Taiwan Provincial Assembly
1952	Republic of China signs a peace treaty with Japan
1954	United States and Taiwan establish Mutual Defense Treaty; National Assembly approves indefinite extension of Temporary Provisions of the Constitution
1954–55	First Taiwan Strait Crisis
1955	Chiang arrests General Sun Li-jen
1958	Second Taiwan Strait Crisis
1960	Liberal activist Lei Chen and his colleagues arrested; Taiwan dissidents in Japan begin publishing *Taiwan Seinen*
1964	Peng Ming-min arrested for questioning KMT's reunification philosophy
1966	First export processing zone opens in Kaohsiung
1971	United Nations General Assembly expels the Republic of China
1972	Tokyo severs diplomatic relations with Taiwan
1975	Chiang Kai-shek dies during fifth term as ROC president; Chiang Ching-kuo becomes chairman of KMT Central Committee
1977	Alleged KMT ballot tampering triggers riot in Chungli
1978	Chiang Ching-kuo is elected ROC president
1979	United States switches diplomatic relations from Taipei to Beijing and gives notice it intends to terminate Mutual Defense Treaty; Congress balances this move by passing Taiwan Relations Act; large anti-KMT riot in Kaohsiung
1980	Dissident politician Lin Yi-hsiung's family members murdered
1981	Chen Wen-cheng, university professor and critic of the KMT, found dead under suspicious circumstances; Beijing offers Nine-Point Proposal for reunification
1984	Assassins linked to the KMT murder writer Henry Liu in California
1986	Opposition politicians form Democratic Progressive Party (DPP) in defiance of ban on new parties
1987	KMT-controlled government lifts martial law
1988	Chiang Ching-kuo dies; Lee Teng-hui assumes the presidency and becomes head of the KMT
1989	DPP wins enough parliamentary seats to propose legislation
1990	National Assembly elects Lee president
1991	Lee announces formal end to war with China; all National Assembly members resign and election refills their seats
1992	Government relaxes sedition law and abolishes Taiwan Garrison Command; renewal elections held for Legislative Yuan
1993	Semiofficial representatives of China and Taiwan meet in Singapore; conservatives split from the KMT and form New Party

1995	Chinese president Jiang Zemin offers Eight-Point proposal for reunification; Lee travels to United States; China carries out missile tests near Taiwan
1996	China holds military exercises, including missile launches off Taiwan's coast; Lee wins first direct presidential election
1997	National Assembly dismantles provincial level of government
1999	China suspends cross-strait dialogue over Lee's remark that Taiwan and China have "special state-to-state relations"
2000	DPP candidate Chen Shui-bian is elected president; KMT politicians meet with CCP officials in China
2001	KMT expels Lee after he begins organizing support for Chen; DPP replaces KMT as largest party in the legislature

※

TAIWAN

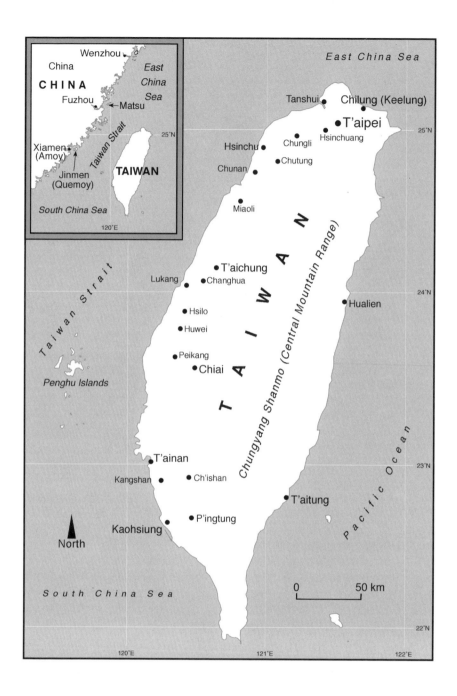

※

Introduction

Beautiful, Beleaguered Island

Taiwan's present circumstances are peculiar and intriguing. This small country has made tremendous economic and political progress in the last half century. Damaged by wartime bombardment and further dragged down by the turmoil and pressures that came with a new government in the midst of losing a civil war on the Chinese mainland, postwar Taiwan became known as one of Asia's economic success stories, its per capita gross national product rising from two hundred dollars after World War II to more than thirteen thousand dollars by 1999. Taiwan was equally famous for evolving from an authoritarian police state to a multiparty democracy with a popularly elected president.

Yet this admirable and seemingly harmless country finds itself the target of continuous military threats by its huge and powerful neighbor, which aims hundreds of ballistic missiles at the island. Taiwan's own people are divided over whether or not their island is part of China. Diplomatic battles, curious and sometimes confusing to foreign observers, rage between the Republic of China (Taiwan, also known by the acronym ROC) and the People's Republic of China (mainland China or the PRC).

Heated disputes result from the usage of particular words and phrases. Athletes from Taiwan have participated in the Olympic Games, for example, under the odd banner of "Chinese Taipei." In publicly describing himself, ROC president Chen Shui-bian may use one of two terms that mean "Chinese." Yet one of these terms (*Huaren*) would please his party and anger the authorities in Beijing, while another (*Zhongguoren*) would have the opposite effect. The reigning hegemonic power in Asia, the United States of America, and the rising potential regional superpower,

1

China, recognize that Taiwan may drag them into a Sino-American war, which both deeply hope to avoid.

These circumstances call for explanation, and a complete explanation is possible only through a review of Taiwan's political history. Hence this book, which seeks to tell Taiwan's story in a way that illuminates the origins of Taiwan's present domestic and international political situation. Accordingly, while this book examines selected events from the last several centuries of Taiwan's political history, more recent periods are studied in greater depth.

The government officially known as the Republic of China controls not only the main island of Taiwan, but also the Penghu (Pescadores) island group in the Taiwan Strait, a few small islands in the seas near Taiwan, the Jinmen (Quemoy) and Matsu islands near the coast of the Chinese mainland, and Tungsha (Pratas) Island in the South China Sea. The Taiwan Strait, ranging in width from 100 to 150 miles, separates the main island from the coast of Fujian Province on the Chinese mainland. The island of Taiwan is 240 miles long and 85 miles wide, with a shape often compared to a tobacco leaf (incidentally, nearly half of Taiwan's male population smokes). At fourteen thousand square miles, Taiwan is about one-third the size of the U.S. state of Ohio, or slightly smaller than the Netherlands.

Mountains or hills cover most of the island, leaving only about a third of its land arable. The highest peaks rise over 3,000 meters above sea level—the highest is Jade Mountain at 3,952 meters (13,114 feet)—and are covered with snow in the winter despite Taiwan's subtropical monsoon climate. In the densely populated lowlands, the average temperatures are 64 degrees Fahrenheit in January and 82 in July, with average humidity of 80 percent and about 100 inches of rainfall annually. Unfortunately for its 22 million inhabitants, Taiwan is subject to earthquakes and typhoons.

Taiwan's rapid postwar economic development earned it recognition as one of the Asian "tigers" or "dragons." Famous as an efficient producer of textiles, Taiwan has developed strong capital- and technology-intensive manufacturing sectors that export petrochemical products and electronics, particularly computer hardware. Service industries, including finance, insurance, and real estate, have become the largest sector of Taiwan's economy. Once accounting for more than 90 percent of the population, Taiwan's farmers now make up only 8 percent of the work force. The island's main crops are rice, vegetables, fruit, and tea. Taiwan's fishing industry boasts over twenty-seven thousand vessels and catches over a million metric tons of fish annually. Over a quarter of Taiwan's exports go to the United States, and another 20 percent go to China/Hong Kong. Japan is the leading source of Taiwan's imports, mostly agricultural goods and industrial raw materials and secondarily manufactured goods, followed by the United States.

The largest religious tradition on Taiwan is a blend of Buddhism and Taoism, given expression in the island's many temples and in the shrine shelves commonly found in homes and places of business. Christianity has perhaps a million adherents in Taiwan and Islam some fifty thousand. The newer religions of I-kuan Tao and Tien Te Chiao claim another million members.

As in mainland China, Mandarin is the official language of Taiwan, although other Chinese dialects and indigenous tongues are common first languages among Taiwan's people. This reflects Taiwan's considerable ethnic diversity, which deserves elaboration in some detail.

It is appropriate to begin with Taiwan's first inhabitants, the aborigines. Although the aborigines are frequently discussed as a single group of people, there are important differences in culture, customs, language, and ethnicity among the nine major tribes, which are the Ami, Atayal, Bunun, Paiwan, Puyama, Rukai, Saisiyat, Tsou, and Yami.[1] Some of the aborigines are thought to have migrated from Northeast Asia (China or Japan), but most are classed ethnographically as Malayo-Polynesian and show strong biological and linguistic similarities to Malay peoples in some parts of the Philippines, Malaysia, and Indonesia. Some observers see cultural similarities between Taiwan's aborigines and groups of Indians in the Americas as well. The three largest tribes—the Ami, Paiwan, and Atayal—account for 85 percent of all Taiwan's aborigines. The oldest groups of aborigines on Taiwan were primarily hunter-gatherers and many were seminomadic. Some groups that arrived later were agricultural. Intertribal warfare and head-hunting have been common during most of Taiwan's history. Aboriginal religions are generally polytheistic and animistic. Chinese immigrants generally considered the aborigines subhuman savages, although they distinguished between the *shengfan* ("raw savages") and the *pepohuan* ("ripe"). The latter, the Chinese thought, could be civilized and to some degree assimilated. The overall regard of the aborigines as a primitive race left them susceptible to atrocities at the hands of the Chinese and, later, the Japanese. At the time Chinese settlers began arriving, some aboriginal communities farmed the lowlands, leading to continual clashes over the possession of farmland. The Chinese were notorious for trickery and hard bargaining as well as outright violence in their dealings with the aborigines. Over time, most of the lowland-dwelling, aborigine farmers were assimilated into Chinese society, killed off, or driven into the

---

[1] One of the major studies on this subject is Emily Martin Ahern and Hill Gates, eds., *The Anthropology of Taiwanese Society* (Stanford, Calif.: Stanford University Press, 1981).

forests, where they gradually integrated with the more ancient mountain-dwelling peoples.

Those aboriginal communities that lived in more mountainous areas from the outset and subsisted through hunting and gathering were less affected by Chinese settlement and the Japanese occupation. This explains why, until recently, Taiwanese aborigines were known colloquially as *Shandiren* ("Mountain People"; today, the more politically correct term is *Yuanzhumin*, or "original inhabitants"). The majority of aborigines continue to reside in the countryside of the central mountains and the east coast, areas that were less attractive to Chinese settlers. The Yami tribe inhabits Lan Yu Island off Taiwan's southeast coast.

In recent years the ROC government has recognized the aborigines as a disadvantaged group and funded many programs designed to raise their socioeconomic status and preserve their cultures. Nevertheless, Taiwan's aborigines as a group continue to manifest the classic signs of social distress—poverty, alcoholism, and lack of education.

Several distinct groups of people migrated to Taiwan from China during recorded history. These groups were all classified as Han Chinese, or the ethnic group to which over 90 percent of China's present population belongs. Distinctions among the Han Chinese should arguably be termed "subethnic." For simplicity and clarity, however, this book will refer to the three major groups of Han Chinese people on Taiwan as separate ethnic groups: the Fujianese, Hakkas, and Mainlanders.

The Fujian (or Hokkien in the local dialect) Chinese, who make up about 70 percent of the population, are the largest ethnic group in present-day Taiwan. Their ancestors immigrated to Taiwan from China's Fujian Province, just across the Taiwan Strait. Fujianese retain much of the culture and lifestyle of southeastern China, including their religion, their language (a dialect called *Minnanyu* or the southern Min language), and their use of the lunar calendar. Also known as Hoklos (pronounced "Ho-lo's," with the "k" silent), Fujianese began arriving in Taiwan about a thousand years ago. Migration was heaviest from the fourteenth to seventeenth centuries, especially after the fall of the Ming dynasty in 1644.

Economic opportunity beckoned the Fujianese to Taiwan. Mostly farmers and fishermen, they occupied the bulk of Taiwan's western plain. Their relatively large numbers often allowed them to displace the Hakkas who had preceded them. With various groups of outsiders from the Dutch to the Japanese to the newly arrived Mainlanders controlling the prime positions in government and the military, the Fujianese pursued success through commerce and land ownership. Today ethnic Fujianese dominate Taiwan's business community.

Originally the Fujianese lacked a strong sense of unifying identity (in contrast, for example, to the Hakkas). They were more likely to think of themselves first as natives of either Zhangzhou or Quangzhou, two major cities in Fujian. Their experiences under Japanese colonial rule and Mainlander-dominated postwar Republic of China government, however, forged a strong "Taiwanese" identity among the Taiwan Fujianese. Indeed, members of other groups with deep roots in Taiwan have often complained about Fujianese appropriating the term *Taiwanese* to refer narrowly to the people, culture, and language of Taiwan's Fujianese community, excluding the Hakkas and aborigines. (In this book, "Taiwanese" refers more broadly to all the ethnic communities established in Taiwan before the postwar Mainlander immigration.)

Decades of official repression of local language, culture, and history contributed to a huge increase, following the liberalization that began in the mid-1980s, in outward expressions of Taiwanese nationalism. Because of the size of the Fujianese community, the line between broad Taiwanese pride and narrow Fujianese chauvinism was sometimes unclear. It has been common in recent years, for example, for Fujianese taxi drivers to refuse service to riders who cannot speak the Minnanyu dialect. Taiwanese businesses such as the corporate giant Evergreen Marine Corporation have been accused of discriminatory hiring in favor of Minnanyu speakers (a charge Evergreen denies).[2]

Sometimes compared to Europe's Gypsies, the Hakkas are a Chinese minority group that might have originated in Mongolia and was driven out of northern China by persecution some fifteen hundred years ago. Landowners systematically mistreated Hakka peasants, and the central government forbade them from participating in the civil service examinations until Emperor Kangxi revoked this policy in the seventeenth century. This background helps account for their reputation as a tough, assertive, and clannish people.

Harassed into leaving Henan Province during the Qin dynasty, the Hakkas settled in Anhui and Jiangxi provinces. Purged from there in A.D. 419, they moved into Guangdong Province and the mountains of Fujian. From there many Hakkas took to the sea, migrating to Southeast Asia and Taiwan. Hakka settlements appeared in Taiwan as early as a thousand years ago. About a third of Guangdong's Hakkas sailed to Taiwan in the latter part of the thirteenth century. The latest large wave of Hakka migration followed the defeat of the Taiping Rebellion, a major uprising in China led by a Hakka, in 1864.

Called *Kejiaren* ("guest people," i.e., "strangers") by other Chinese, the

---

[2] "Blurring the lines of ethnic division," *Taipei Journal*, Mar. 10, 2000, online at http://www.taiwanheadlines.gov.tw/20000319/20000314f1.html, accessed Oct. 30, 2001.

Hakkas are known for holding firm to their distinctive customs despite their long migrations. In contrast to the Fujianese, Hakka women worked in the fields along with the men and did not bind their feet. With the desirable western lowlands dominated by the more numerous Fujianese, most Hakkas in Taiwan settled in hillier areas between the coast and the aboriginal communities. Hakkas therefore had greater early association with the aborigines than did the Fujianese. Hakka intermarriage with aborigines was not uncommon; neither was warfare between Hakkas and native tribes, as Hakkas often forced agricultural aborigine tribes off their land and native tribesmen returned the favor by hunting for Hakka heads.

Resistance to Japanese rule was particularly strong in areas heavily populated by Hakkas. Conversely, however, Hakkas tended to have a comparatively amicable relationship with the recently arrived Mainlanders, creating among some Fujianese doubts about whether or not the Hakkas could be trusted to support "Taiwanese" causes opposed by the Mainlanders. Hakkas today are heavily concentrated in certain professions for which land ownership is not a prerequisite (such as railroad workers, police, and commercial fishing), largely as a result of their forebears having lost their land to encroaching Fujianese. Many Hakkas, such as former president Lee Teng-hui, have become successful politicians. Some cities have disproportionately large Hakka communities, such as Hsinchu, where they are the majority ethnic group.[3] The total number of Taiwanese Hakkas today is about 2 million.

Governed by Japan for fifty years, Taiwan reverted to the control of the Republic of China on Japan's defeat in 1945. Ethnic Chinese who settled in Taiwan after the war are referred to collectively as the "Mainlanders" (*Waishengren*, literally "outside province people," as opposed to *Benshengren*, or "local province people"). Since their arrival, Mainlanders have dominated the high-ranking positions in government, the military, and education, and live mostly in the cities. Their concentration in the capital Taipei is especially high. Mainlanders came to Taiwan from all parts of China, but most hailed from the southern and central provinces. In the early postwar years, natives of Zhejiang Province (the home province of Taiwan's first ROC governor, Chen Yi, and of ROC president Chiang Kai-shek) dominated the government. Speaking the Mandarin Chinese dialect, considered in China the language of the educated, they brought with them an air of superiority. Mainlanders also considered themselves more Chinese than the native Taiwanese, who had isolated themselves

---

[3] John F. Copper, *Taiwan: Nation-State or Province?* (Boulder, Colo.: Westview Press, 1996), 12.

from the heart of Chinese civilization and had been further tainted by fifty years of Japanese rule.

The Mainlanders are far more anti-Japanese than native Taiwanese. As an ethnic minority, the Mainlanders have also been generally less enthusiastic about democratization than the Taiwanese because this weakens the Mainlanders' relative power. Despite their high representation in the socioeconomic elite, Mainlanders have felt insecure inasmuch as their exile to Taiwan cut them off from their ancestral properties, while they lacked large land holdings on Taiwan.

Taiwan's ethnic politics raise the question of whether the members of various groupings act politically as individuals or as nations (i.e., ethnic groups).[4] Put another way, are they primarily motivated by the objective of security for themselves and their families, or do they seek security for their nation as a whole? Circumstances often bring about an overlap of individual and national interests. For instance, if my ethnic group is threatened with genocide, the ultimate danger to national security, by definition my own personal security is endangered as well. To the extent that it is possible to distinguish between individual and national interests, I will argue that while members of these groups have sometimes acted on the basis of national identity, they have more often been motivated mainly by a desire to protect and advance their individual interests. The chapters that follow describe contentions between Chinese settlers and aborigines, rebellions of the local population against the Dutch or Japanese colonial governments, and strife between Taiwanese and the postwar Mainlander administrations. For the most part, these can be characterized as struggles among individuals grouped according to political and/or ethnic affiliation rather than struggles between nations per se. While a Taiwanese nationalism eventually emerged, this arguably stemmed from the more fundamental desire of individuals to protect themselves from systematic exploitation and mistreatment by their officials.

The list of important historical players includes not only individuals and nations but also states and regimes, beginning with the Dutch, under whose control Taiwan fell during part of the seventeenth century. Dutch colonialism in Asia was geared toward enriching and strengthening the home state, creating opportunities for Dutch businesses, and sheltering the work of Dutch missionaries. Dutch administration of Taiwan reflected these goals. As part of building a viable economic base on the island, the

---

[4] *Nation* is a flexible term. I use it sometimes as a synonym for ethnic group, but also to refer to a coalition of ethnic groups—for instance, Taiwanese nationalism versus Mainlander nationalism.

Dutch developed Taiwan in ways that not only benefited the inhabitants in some ways, but even encouraged more Chinese to emigrate there. Yet the Dutch administration's chief concern was protecting the interests of the colonials rather than the locals, resulting in conflict between the administration and Taiwan's permanent residents, principally over economic issues. This conflict generated several uprisings before the eventual ouster of the Dutch.

Another important player is the Chinese government. While China's rulers had knowledge of and some contact with Taiwan from ancient times, premodern Chinese officials considered the island barbarian territory in which they had little interest. The imperial capital finally sent a token administration to the island less because of perceived opportunities than because of the problems Taiwan caused: it had become home to a large community of settlers who had illegally migrated there; pirates and political and military enemies of the Beijing government found haven there; and foreign powers threatened to claim it as a colony, which would have further compromised China's strategic position vis-à-vis the imperialist powers. Once it took responsibility for Taiwan, the Qing government's interests were to contain these problems and to show the imperial flag. Officials sent to Taiwan were often arrogant and corrupt and rarely committed to improving the lives of the Taiwanese. Unhappy with these officials, the Taiwanese frequently rebelled. Even Governor Liu Ming-ch'uan, remembered as an extraordinarily capable and dedicated public servant, had to endure protests over the taxes he levied to raise funds for the island's modernization.

Much like its Dutch predecessor, the Japanese colonial government sought to extract from Taiwan benefits for its own citizens and empire. Possession of a colony such as Taiwan, a prize won by Japan's victory over China in the 1894–95 Sino-Japanese War, gave Tokyo prestige and international recognition as a great power. Japan also gained the financial and agricultural surplus Taiwan produced, while certain well-placed Japanese citizens found in Taiwan the opportunity to make their fortunes. As their country became a cog in the Japanese empire, Taiwan's people shared in the fruits of further development and modernization, but at the cost of forced assimilation, political suppression, and being made second-class citizens in their own country.

Policies of the ROC's ruling Kuomintang (KMT) regime toward Taiwan changed from the immediate to the later postwar years, reflecting always the KMT's interest in defending its claim to be the legitimate government of China. After inheriting Taiwan from the defeated Japanese, the KMT administration first tried to strip it of all wealth and resources that might be transported to the mainland to strengthen Chiang's campaign against the Communists. Much of these confiscated assets were diverted toward enriching corrupt officials and their relatives. The administration of Chen Yi, Taiwan's first Chinese governor of the twentieth century, saw an intensification of the worst aspects of Japanese colonialism, with the added disadvantages of the official arbitrariness and indiscipline that replaced the comparative orderliness of the Japanese administration.

This approach had to be reversed when Chiang's forces were defeated on the mainland and forced to flee to Taiwan in 1949. Chiang brought not only the remnants of his army and government, but even the government's collection of national art treasures, as Taiwan became the depository of Chinese civilization, the temporary seat of the Republic of China, and the base from which he would regroup for an expedition to recapture the mainland from Mao Zedong's Communist regime. Thereafter, Taiwanese were forced to bear the burden of the KMT's vision for the future ROC, which included supporting an oversized military and government apparatus. Political liberalization on Taiwan beginning in the late 1980s greatly eased the conflict between Taiwanese society and the state/regime. But a consequence of democratization was to discontinue the suppression of Taiwanese nationalism, which some aspects of KMT rule had unintentionally fostered through the decades.

As nationalism became more prominent in Taiwan's politics, a rival regime weighed in as an influential player. The Chinese Communist Party (CCP) government's legitimacy rested partly on the claim that it was more patriotic than its predecessors. The Qing monarchy had given away much Chinese territory to the imperialist powers, CCP propagandists said, while Chiang's KMT government had tried harder to appease the Japanese invaders than to drive them out of China. The Communist regime, by contrast, committed itself to restoring Beijing's rule over all territories that rightfully belonged to China. Taiwan's aloofness was a double political challenge to the CCP: the island was not only a formerly Chinese-administered territory that had been lost to foreign imperialism, but it also sheltered the KMT government, thereby denying the Communists their complete victory in the Chinese Civil War.

The CCP thus took the position that the eventual incorporation of Taiwan into the PRC was a vital state interest. This made the recovery of Taiwan a vital regime interest as well; the ruling leadership could not be expected to survive the perception that it was so seriously failing to do its job. But just as Beijing was prepared to wait until conditions were "ripe" before recovering Hong Kong, the CCP leadership from Mao Zedong through Jiang Zemin has indicated a willingness to be patient provided Taipei observed the minimum requirement of honoring the principle that Taiwan is part of "China." An independent Taiwan, however, is not acceptable. The interest of Taiwanese opposition politicians, and allegedly of Lee Teng-hui's administration, in proclaiming Taiwan independent alarmed the CCP and prompted Beijing to issue warnings that have included both public statements and military exercises. Through the process of political liberalization, therefore, Taiwanese found their security threatened less by their own government and more by the PRC. Consequently, Taiwan's democratization, further consolidated in the peaceful regime change that came with the election of Chen Shui-bian as president in 2000, progressed amidst the hostility of Taipei's large, inescapable neighbor. The details of this story, remarkable in many respects, are in the chapters that follow.

❇

Taiwan's Early History

Through most of antiquity, the Chinese government considered Taiwan beyond the pale of Chinese civilization. In the eyes of Chinese elites, Taiwan's inhabitants were savages who possessed nothing of interest to China and who were unwilling to pay tribute or learn Chinese ways. The first mention of Taiwan in official Chinese historical records concerns the emperor's dispatch of a ten-thousand-strong expedition to explore the island. The famous Chinese voyager Cheng Ho also made an unplanned visit to Taiwan in 1430 when he was shipwrecked while returning to China from Southeast Asia. He reported to the government he had associated with the aborigines and discovered some useful medicinal herbs, but he evidently did not encounter any Chinese settlements while on the island.

Imperial China not only made no territorial claim to Taiwan, it had no interest in colonizing Taiwan. Indeed, during much of the period of Chinese settlement in Taiwan, the Chinese central government forbade emigration on pain of execution by beheading. There were social, ideological, and political reasons for this policy. The government presumed that those who desired to go abroad were merchants, a class despised and often persecuted by Confucian officials. The imperial court in Beijing would find it difficult to comprehend why any honorable Chinese citizen would want to leave China, the heart of civilization, for barbarian territory. Chinese rulers were opposed to the development of large Chinese settlements abroad, fearing these would become havens for pirates and rebels, leading to more banditry and insurrection on the mainland. Thus premodern China's conception of state and regime security called for distancing China from Taiwan, a departure from the mindset of the typical great power or of present-day China.

In contrast to imperial China, the Japanese government under the Tokugawa Shogunate sent a force of several thousand men led by the governor of Nagasaki to attempt to conquer Taiwan in 1598, but aboriginal warriors drove the Japanese off. Other than aborigines, the island's first settlers were likely Japanese pirates and traders, as Taiwan lay close to trade routes linking Japan with China and Southeast Asia. Japanese established a community on the southwest coast called Takasago, and for some time controlled the northern coast, but under the Tokugawa Shogunate's policy of isolation Japanese settlers left Taiwan in 1628.

The Ming dynasty had outlawed Chinese maritime activity, but these restrictions were abrogated in the late 1500s, resulting in increased fishing and seaborne trade in the Taiwan Strait. Prior to the 1600s, there were comparatively few permanent Chinese settlements on Taiwan, although Chinese fishermen and pirates sometimes camped on the island. There was less Chinese activity on Taiwan than on the much smaller Penghu Island group lying between Taiwan and the mainland.

Early Chinese Settlement of Taiwan

During the seventeenth century, however, Chinese settlement on Taiwan grew exponentially. Chinese immigrated to Taiwan in the hope that their chances of economic success would be better there than on the mainland. For many Fujianese peasants, prospects at home were not bright. Fujian Province, of which mountains and hills take up some 95 percent, had a small amount of cultivable land relative to its population, and each of its frequent poor harvests meant disaster for many farming families. Hakkas in Guangdong and other provinces faced persistent discrimination and had often been forced off desirable land. For all its hardships, Taiwan offered hard-pressed Chinese a chance to cultivate their own land, be their own boss, find a new opportunity to get rich, or leave behind the restrictions of the station in life they had been born into on the mainland. The high taxes and insurrection of the late Ming dynasty, which ended in 1644, convinced thousands of Chinese to migrate to Southeast Asia and Taiwan.

Earlier groups of Chinese settlers were predominantly young men who planned to live and work on the island only temporarily. Accordingly, they built simple houses of bamboo and thatched grass. Chinese farmers usually stayed on Taiwan from the spring planting season through the fall harvest, returning home to the mainland during the winter. Most Chinese farms produced crops for sale on the mainland, where they could bring good prices. There was limited trade with Japan as well, as Taiwan served as a meeting place for Chinese and Japanese traders. Other Chinese came to Taiwan to fish, hunt, log, or work as traders. Fishermen lived on Taiwan during the fishing season, drying and salting the fish they caught in nearby waters. Chinese communities outside the mainland found the opportunity to develop alternative forms of government; villages on Penghu evidently selected their own leaders, and the same practice might have prevailed on Taiwan.[1]

Significantly, Taiwan became a haven for antigovernment intellectuals as well as the economically dispossessed. A large number emigrated in the eighteenth century, for example, to escape a purge of the literati on the mainland by the Qing emperor Qianlong, who had deviously asked his people to contribute books for a government-sponsored compilation project, then hunted down the authors of writings he found offensive.

With seafaring a large part of the lives of the Chinese who settled on Taiwan, the Buddhist/Taoist deity Matsu became perhaps the single most important personage in the religion of Taiwan's Chinese community. Known as "goddess of the sea" and the patron saint of fishermen, Matsu's veneration is based on the legend of Lin Mo-niang, a fisherman's daughter born in 960 on Meichou Island near the coast of Fujian Province. Lin reputedly used her supernatural powers to save seafarers in danger of drowning. Gradually promoted in religious status during the Sung and Yuan dynasties, she became the object of worship in hundreds of temples throughout Taiwan.

With Chinese settlement of Taiwan came the interaction of the Chinese and aborigine communities. A mixture of conflict and cooperation, the relationship on balance was a struggle between the individual security of Chinese and that of the aborigines in Chinese-penetrated areas. Some aborigines inhabited Taiwan's western plains, the region most desirable to Chinese farmers. There was little Chinese compunction about pushing the aborigines, at best seen as an inferior people and at worst as wild animals, off this land. For their part, aborigines sometimes attacked and plundered Chinese settlements.

Certain aboriginal communities engaged in some farming, using methods that in the opinions of the Chinese and the Europeans were backward, and also hunted using bows and arrows, spears, nets, and traps. Visitors found the aboriginal practice of head-hunting lurid and barbaric, although beheading was a common form of execution in the Chinese penal

---

[1] John E. Wills, Jr., "The Seventeenth-Century Transformation: Taiwan under the Dutch and the Cheng Regime," in Murray A. Rubinstein, ed., *Taiwan: A New History* (Armonk, N.Y.: M. E. Sharpe, 1999), 86.

system, and it was reportedly not uncommon for Chinese to use the body parts of dead aborigines for food and the making of medicine.[2] Aboriginal head-hunting of enemies, traditionally members of rival tribes and later Chinese, had religious as well as political significance. Tribesmen offered heads as a sacrifice to various gods of nature in the hope of gaining more successful hunts or harvests.

Many of the first contests with aborigines over living space involved Hakka settlers. As Hakkas filled the southwest plain and drove off the aboriginal farming communities there, aborigines were reported to have crossed the Taiwan Strait on bamboo rafts to raid villages on the Fujian coast of iron and armor. The tribes wanted metal to better arm themselves for clashes with the Hakkas, whose iron swords and pikes gave them an advantage against the bamboo spears of the natives.[3] Hakka homes reflected the insecurity of living within striking distance of disgruntled aborigines. Rather than using timber, which was vulnerable to fire, the Hakkas built the walls of their houses with hardened earth, formed by filling the space between bamboo frames. Typically, several such houses were grouped together and surrounded by an earthen wall that created a small fortress.

The camphor industry was a major impetus to Chinese-aborigine conflict because it drew Chinese woodsmen into forests often inhabited by the "raw" aborigine communities that were not reconciled to the Chinese presence on the island. Camphor was traditionally used in medicines or as an insect repellent. Later, in the late 1800s, manufacturers of celluloid film and smokeless powder used camphor as a component. The evergreen trees that produce camphor grew abundantly along the base of the central mountain range. After the camphor trees were cut down and chopped up, the camphor crystals were distilled from the wood chips while still in the forest. Chinese entering an area near an aborigine community to gain access to the trees would often offend or mistreat the natives in the process; aborigines would ambush some of the Chinese loggers; and the Chinese would retaliate by raiding and destroying nearby aborigine villages.

Nevertheless, aborigines living in mountainous areas faced less of an immediate threat to their livelihoods than plains aborigines from the Chinese, who usually wanted to extract resources from the woods rather than clear it for farmland and living space. Some forest-dwelling aborigines reached accommodations with the Chinese that allowed for economic co-

---

[2] George Leslie Mackay, *From Far Formosa: The Island, Its People and Missions*, 4th ed. (New York: Fleming H. Revell, 1900), 276.

[3] W.G. Goddard, *Formosa: A Study in Chinese History* (West Lansing: Michigan State University Press, 1966), 26.

operation. By the 1600s, the paths through many aboriginal communities were well-trodden by Chinese traders seeking to acquire deer skins and meat for resale. Chinese could lodge cheaply in aboriginal villages, bartering with mainland-imported salt, which was useful as a preservative as well as a seasoning. In time many mountain aborigine communities would suffer economically because the Chinese overhunted deer, a staple of the aboriginal diet.

The Dutch Administration

The Dutch East India Company sought a base for trade with China and Japan. They originally targeted Penghu, building a small fort on one of the islands. The Ming government insisted the Dutch leave Penghu, which was Chinese territory, and suggested they move to Taiwan instead. The Dutch established a settlement in the Tainan area, building the Casteel Zeelandia on a sand bar at the mouth of the harbor and a fort named Provintia on the shore. Spain, which ruled the Philippines to the south, made an attempt to counter the Dutch move by building outposts at the north end of the island in Keelung and Tansui in 1626 and 1629, respectively. But the Spanish abandoned the unproductive Tansui settlement in 1638, and in 1642 the Spanish fortress in Keelung, its garrison weakened by disease and the opposition of local aborigines, fell to Dutch soldiers.

Although brief (1624–1663), the Dutch presence was important because the Dutch undertook the first serious effort at developing Taiwan. Establishing a government over much of the island, the Dutch organized labor, created mines and plantations, and introduced new crops and tools. Dutch administration and infrastructure facilitated trade as well as the immigration of more Chinese to Taiwan. Taiwan's Chinese population might have risen as high as fifty thousand under Dutch rule, while Dutch residents numbered only two to three thousand, mostly soldiers. The island became a profitable operation for the Dutch East India Company. Taiwan exported dried fish and deer meat to China and sugar and deerskins to Japan, while the Dutch administration collected taxes from Taiwan's residents. Ignoring the Chinese government's ban on immigration, the Dutch recruited Chinese settlers in Fujian and provided tools, oxen, and seed to help them establish successful farms on Taiwan. The Dutch required a 10 percent cut of all production that took place in their zones of control, including fishing and hunting as well as agriculture. Commercial deer hunting, which peaked in Taiwan during Dutch rule, was particularly profitable, as Dutch administrators sold licenses to hunters from mainland China, collected 10 percent of the hides, antlers (used in making

Chinese medicine), and meat the hunters took as a tax, and bought much of the remainder for export to Japan.

Chinese and aborigines alike had grievances against Dutch rule, largely because of the economic burden imposed by the Dutch administration's heavy taxes. These included taxes on staples such as butter and alcohol, plus a head tax on all Chinese over the age of six. Prior to Dutch administration, Chinese on Taiwan had traded with Japan without taxation. The Dutch government did not allow Chinese farmers to buy the land they worked; the Dutch East India Company owned all real estate. Dutch soldiers created further resentment through bullying and extortion. There were major Chinese uprisings against the Dutch in 1640 and 1652. On the latter occasion, which involved a few thousand poorly armed Chinese peasants, aborigine warriors joined with Dutch soldiers armed with muskets in a slaughter of several thousand of the rebels.

Such instances of Dutch-aborigine cooperation should not obscure the fact that Dutch governance faced considerable aboriginal opposition and the Europeans carried out a military campaign against some tribes in the region around Tainan in 1635–36, culminating in the surrender of many villages to Dutch control. A similar campaign took place in the north beginning in 1644 after the Dutch captured the Spanish settlement and then worked to pacify aboriginal villages from Tansui southward. In conquered villages, the Dutch appointed local leaders and helped mediate disputes. They also carried out moderately successful education and missionary programs. In some villages most of the inhabitants converted to Christianity, although in these cases deep-seated animistic beliefs and practices often persisted. The Dutch developed romanized writing systems for some aboriginal languages, and Dutch missionaries provided basic schooling for aboriginal children in many villages. All things considered, the aborigines probably had a better relationship with the Dutch than with the Chinese.

Dutch efforts to "civilize" the aborigines inevitably involved hostility toward some aspects of traditional local culture. On some occasions Dutch authorities expelled female shamans from villages. In general, the Dutch discouraged head-hunting and certain customs connected with sex and marriage. Among the Siraya people of the Tainan region, for example, abortion (by massage) was mandatory for the wives of men participating in hunts for animals or heads because a pregnant wife was thought to bring bad luck to a hunter. The Dutch worked to abolish this practice, succeeding in some areas.[4]

---

[4] John Robert Shepherd, *Marriage and Mandatory Abortion Among the Seventeenth-century Siraya*, American Ethnological Society Monograph Series, No. 6 (Arlington, Va.: American Anthropological Association, 1995).

Characterizations of the Dutch East India Company as a statelike entity notwithstanding, this period of Taiwan's history mainly involved three groups of individuals, the Chinese, aborigines, and Dutch, striving to advance their economic and physical security vis-à-vis each other and their natural environment. Although the Dutch soon left the scene, competition and conflict between Chinese and aborigines and between subdivisions within the Han community would persist under two subsequent ethnic Chinese governments.

The Cheng Dynasty

In 1661, a half-Chinese, half-Japanese merchant named Cheng Ch'eng-kung (Zheng Chenggong in Pinyin; known to Europeans as Koxinga, a derivative of Kuo Hsing-yeh, the name given him by the former Ming dynasty) led an overthrow of the Dutch authorities. Cheng's father Cheng Chih-lung, a wealthy trader and pirate, had fought against the new Manchu regime in China in support of the outgoing Ming dynasty. Foreshadowing Chiang Kai-shek, the younger Cheng carried on this futile campaign, eventually making Taiwan his base of operations in a twelve-year effort to defeat the Manchus and reestablish the Ming dynasty on the mainland.

While Cheng was still based in Xiamen (Amoy) on the mainland coast, the Manchu government in 1659–61 ordered all settlements along the southern coast moved inland several miles to deny the rebels logistical support. This destruction of homes and livelihoods turned many more southern Chinese into impoverished refugees, some of whom would immigrate to Taiwan.

After a costly defeat while attempting to conquer the mainland city of Nanjing in 1658–59, Cheng in 1661 turned his large force of between twenty-five thousand and thirty thousand troops on the Dutch presence in Taiwan. Ho Pin, who served the Dutch as a guide, told Cheng the locations of Dutch-built ports and roads. Cheng besieged the heavily outnumbered Dutch garrison in Casteel Zeelandia until the Dutch agreed to withdraw from Taiwan. A Dutch force returned the next year and captured Keelung, but soon thereafter abandoned it, permanently ending Dutch influence on Taiwan. Before his death in 1662 at age thirty-eight (possibly from malaria), Cheng established a government modeled after Ming China, with Tainan as his capital.

The Cheng dynasty was racked with scandal and family political intrigue. Cheng and his son Cheng Ching had a falling out over the latter's affair with his younger brother's nurse, who bore Cheng Ching's son Cheng Ko-tsang. The elder Cheng ordered his brother Cheng Tai to kill

Cheng Ching, an order Cheng Tai refused to carry out. Defeating a competing faction to assume the throne after his father's death, Cheng Ching had Cheng Tai thrown into prison, where he soon died. Cheng Ko-tsang was Cheng Ching's eldest son, but owing to the circumstances of his birth the Cheng family would not accept him as successor to the throne after his father died in 1681.

Many more Chinese emigrated from the mainland to Taiwan under the auspices of the Cheng government, increasing the island's productivity. The Chinese population during the Cheng dynasty might have reached 100,000, with emigration boosted by the Qing's policy of dismantling settlements on the southern coast. The Cheng government encouraged Chinese settlers to push inland and bring additional wilderness areas under cultivation. Cheng awarded his supporters with land and also established a system of military farms on which soldiers labored part-time to support themselves. Cheng's Taiwan continued to trade with Japan, Okinawa, and the Philippines. Like the Dutch before them, Cheng administrators sponsored rudimentary education among the aborigines, but also required aborigines to pay a head tax and to supply corvee laborers. Turmoil within the court notwithstanding, Cheng's kingdom was sufficiently stable that he sought to expand it. He sent a Spanish friar to the Philippines carrying the demand that the Spanish pay Cheng annual tribute. He succeeded only in prompting a Spanish massacre of ethnic Chinese living in Manila. At the time of his death Cheng was preparing to invade the Philippines.

The Cheng Ching regime's attitude toward the mainland was ambivalent. A sizable proportion of the Cheng military had defected to the Qing government, including Shih Lang, a politically shrewd naval commander who would later lead the Qing's conquest of Taiwan. Although the regime killed his mother and father and desecrated the graves of his ancestors, Cheng himself had negotiated with the Qing and was evidently willing to accept the status of an autonomous tributary state. Cheng allowed continued trade with the mainland. From Beijing's standpoint, all Chinese were subjects of the emperor; as John E. Wills writes, "The late imperial political tradition gave no support to any idea of 'one empire, two systems.'"[5] Taiwan still represented a possible staging area for attacks against the mainland. Indeed, Cheng took advantage of the Rebellion of the Three Feudatories in 1673 to reestablish a position on the mainland coast until Qing forces drove him back to Taiwan in 1680.

Shih Lang described Taiwan as "a defense shield for several southeastern provinces. If abandoned, it will be occupied by either the natives or

[5] Wills, "Seventeenth-Century Transformation," 97.

bandits [i.e., Cheng's followers]."[6] Concurring, the Qing dispatched a large force in 1683 under Shih's command to wrest Taiwan from the Cheng government. After winning a decisive naval battle around Penghu, Shih sailed with his forces to Taiwan and opened negotiations from a position of strength. He further weakened Cheng resistance by welcoming Cheng soldiers to surrender and join his army, which enjoyed more reliable pay. The Tainan government agreed to accept magistrates and a garrison from the mainland in return for a comfortable exile in Beijing for the third Cheng king, Cheng Ch'eng-kung's young grandson Cheng Ko-shuang. Soon after Shih Lang's mainland troops entered the Cheng capital, they confiscated the homes of its wealthy residents and extorted their property—a scene that would be repeated three centuries later. Admiration and even veneration of Cheng Ch'eng-kung are common among today's Taiwan people, who see him as one of the country's principal forefathers.

Taiwan Absorbed into the Chinese Empire

Since Taiwan had not previously been part of the Chinese empire and evoked no patriotic stirrings in the hearts or minds of mainland Chinese elites, its post-Cheng status was a matter of some debate. Shih Lang asked the Dutch if they were interested in buying Taiwan back; they were not.[7] One school of thought was that Taiwan should be abandoned and its Chinese population shipped back to the mainland. The argument that prevailed, however, was that unless the Chinese government took charge of it, Taiwan would remain a thorn in the mainland's side, a threat to state and regime security either as a base for a foreign power or a haven for Chinese undesirables. In 1684, therefore, negative security considerations moved China to incorporate Taiwan—not as a province, but as a prefecture of Fujian Province, which lay across the Taiwan Strait. Thus began two centuries (1683–1895) of nominal Qing dynasty rule over Taiwan.

The Qing's principal concerns for Taiwan were to keep it out of the hands of foreigners; to preclude anti-Qing movements from emerging there; and to prevent the island from being too great an economic drain on the Chinese Empire. Judged against these minimum criteria, the govern-

---

[6] Masahiro Wakabayashi, "Fifty Years of Tension Across the Strait," *Taipei Times* Online, Sept. 29, 1999, online at http://taiwansecurity.org/news/TT-Fifty-Years-of-Tension.htm, Oct. 10, 2000.

[7] John E. Wills, Jr., *Embassies and Illusions: Dutch and Portuguese Envoys to K'ang-hsi, 1666–1687* (Cambridge, Mass.: Harvard University Council on East Asian Studies, 1984), 148, 151.

ment's performance was barely satisfactory. A numerically inferior French force seized and held a foothold on northern Taiwan for nearly one year in 1884–85. Until the last few years of its rule, the Qing claimed responsibility for only part of the island, which worked to encourage the intervention of foreigners who had grievances against "raw" aborigine tribes. Local officials were unable to rein in several major uprisings that required thousands of reinforcements from the mainland to put down. Taiwan was subsidized by the central government until the year it passed to Japanese control. The challenge of effectively governing Taiwan was beyond the Qing's ability and commitment.

Although the Qing garrisoned the island with approximately ten thousand troops (the number rose by several thousand during times of crisis) drawn from the army in Fujian and rotated every three years, it could be argued that the Chinese central government did not actually exercise effective control over Taiwan during this period. The areas settled by Chinese constituted less than half the island's territory, and the Chinese did not become the majority ethnic group on Taiwan until the nineteenth century.[8] The real power in most of the Chinese-settled areas lay with powerful families. Significantly, the irrigation systems that greatly increased Taiwan's agricultural productivity and made the island a major supplier of foodstuffs to China, Japan, and Southeast Asia were for the most part privately financed and constructed. Conflicts festered throughout the island under Qing rule—between villagers and outlaws, between differing Chinese clans, and between Chinese and aborigines.

Uprisings during Qing Rule

Several factors made Taiwan difficult for the Chinese central government to rule. Taiwan's polity was more cosmopolitan and ruggedly individualistic than that of the mainland, with many families making their livelihood through hunting, fishing, and trading, and without the need for the huge public works projects that required extensive organization among the mainland Chinese. Taiwan was also a hotbed of communal antagonism, not only bringing Chinese into close contact with aborigines, but also mingling groups from the mainland between whom there was bad blood. Serious ethnic strife was common, especially between Fujianese and Hakkas. The Qing administration worsened the situation by

[8] James W. Davidson, *The Island of Formosa: Past and Present* (New York: Oxford University Press, 1988), 561; John F. Copper, *Taiwan: Nation-State or Province?* (Boulder, Colo.: Westview Press, 1996), 11.

frequently employing Hakka militiamen to help put down rebellions led by Fujianese, deepening suspicions between the two groups. There were major fault-lines within these groups as well, such as between Fujianese from the rival cities of Chang-chou and Ch'uan-chou, that sometimes led to communal violence. Vestiges of loyalty to the Ming and opposition to Manchu rule persisted well into the Qing dynasty. These sentiments contributed to uprisings in Taiwan as well as on the mainland. Finally, Qing emigration policies and the frequent shortage of cultivable land relative to available labor contributed to a large pool of unemployed young men on the island, many of whom became drifters who were easily incited to riot.

The character of Qing rule often eroded the population's loyalty and confidence in their public officials. A backwater on the fringe of the Chinese Empire, Taiwan was not a prestigious post for mainland administrators. Consequently the quality of many officials sent to Taiwan by the central government was low, resulting in cases of unwise decision-making, corruption, injustice, and inefficiency, combined with brutal punishments to keep public order. Not surprisingly, insurrections against the mainland authorities were frequent—a total of 159 sizable rebellions during the period of Qing rule, including three particularly large "Great Rebellions" in 1714, 1787, and 1833. Mainlanders commonly said of Taiwan, "Every three years an uprising, every five years a rebellion."[9]

Some outbreaks of public disorder clearly stemmed from or were exacerbated by official misconduct. An example was the Chu Yi-kuei uprising of 1721. Antagonized by the harsh rule of the local magistrate and his son, Fujianese duck farmer Chu led a group of rebels in raids on two military outposts south of Tainan in April 1721 to obtain weapons. Chu's rebel force, at first less than a hundred, grew to several thousand. First a Hakka bandit leader, Tu Chun-ying, allied his men with Chu. Then a tactical blunder turned more residents against the government. Officials offered rewards to aboriginal warriors for the heads of rebels, leading to indiscriminate killing, destruction, and panic among innocent settlers. The enlarged group of rebels commanded by Chu and Tu defeated government troops and sent Qing administrators fleeing to the mainland. In two weeks they captured the prefectural capital of Tainan and gained control of two of the island's three counties. The rebellion's stunning success was short-lived. Predictably, rivalry between self-styled "kings" Chu and Tu and preexisting ethnic tensions led to fighting between the Fujianese and Hakka rebel factions. The inevitable Qing retaliatory response came after the government had raised some twelve thousand troops, who began

---

[9] George H. Kerr, *Formosa Betrayed* (Boston: Houghton Mifflin, 1965), 4.

landing near Tainan in June. Assisted by Hakka fighters who had formerly been allies of Chu and by aborigine guides, the government forces quickly put down the rebels and captured their two principal leaders.

Other uprisings had communal origins or overtones. In 1832, for example, after a drought led to a reduced rice crop, residents in the Chiayi area determined to retain their rice stocks rather than export it. Corrupt local officials, however, made a secret deal with traders to ship the rice out anyway. When the farmers discovered the scheme, Fujianese Chang Ping led them in a riot. As others joined in and the movement spread across the island, however, it turned into an anti-Hakka campaign. Even when they had the opportunity to intervene at an early stage, officials often lacked sufficient force or expertise to contain such incidents of communal violence. An initially minor dispute between Chang-chou and Ch'uan-chou natives in two villages in 1782 escalated because local leaders were unable to satisfactorily settle the matter and the parties to the dispute called in allies among their ethnic kinsmen in surrounding villages. Thousands were killed and more than four hundred villages destroyed as the conflict ran its course unhindered.

Another case of violence that strayed from its original goal as it escalated was the 1786 rebellion led by Lin Shuang-wen. Lin's campaign began in Tali near Taichung as an attempt to overthrow the Qing administration and reinstate the Ming. As they moved north, Lin's followers carried out wonton destruction, murder, and looting as underlying ethnic hatreds gushed forth. Lin captured settlements of Ch'uan-chou Fujianese and attacked two Hakka villages to seize their store of grain. Eventually Hakka, Ch'uan-chou Fujianese, and aborigine volunteers joined with government troops to defeat Lin's band.

In the main, the authorities relied on either calling in overwhelming force or attempting to preempt future uprisings by implementing policies based on lessons learned from a previous incident. After the Lin Shuang-wen rebellion, for example, the Qing government ordered Chinese in central Taiwan resettled to separate Chang-chou and Ch'uan-chou natives. Some officials in Taiwan tried to forestall trouble by requiring wealthy individuals and organizations to provide money, food, or employment for transients.

Ad Hoc Emigration Policies

The Qing's vacillating emigration policy was emblematic of the lack of vision in Beijing's Taiwan policy. Qing officials initially decided to keep the island's population low, since it was presumed a large proportion of

Taiwan's residents would be dissidents, pirates, and other troublemakers. Taiwan's Chinese population greatly decreased as Qing regulations required all Chinese residents on Taiwan who did not have their wives with them or own property on the island to return home to the mainland. Because the government feared that many of them were pirates, Guangdong residents were banned from applying for permission to travel to Taiwan. As Guangdong immigrants to Taiwan were predominantly Hakkas, this restriction contributed to the numerical superiority of Fujianese over Hakkas. The Qing also forbade future immigration to Taiwan by any Chinese other than unmarried males. The result, as John R. Shepherd notes, was "a volatile, bachelor-dominated society in Taiwan that was prone to brawling and rebellion."[10] Some Qing officials later lobbied for a reversal of these policies that limited Taiwan's growth. Instead of a small population and a minimal administrative presence, they argued, Taiwan would create fewer problems and eat up less funding if the state promoted further development and greater, more balanced colonization along with a stronger government. According to this view, married men should be allowed to bring their wives to Taiwan, as families would stabilize the Chinese communities and reduce outbreaks of public disorder. Clearing more land in Taiwan for cultivation would bring more of the aborigines and their former lands under Chinese control. The larger population and increased economic development would generate greater tax revenue, enabling the government to station more soldiers and civil servants on the island. The Qing moved gradually in this direction. Particular impetus came from the aborigine rebellion of 1731–32 and a simultaneous, opportunistic Chinese uprising in Feng Shan County to the south, which were interpreted as evidence that the state should promote rather than restrict colonization. In the 1730s the Chinese emperor Yongzheng lifted the restrictions on families immigrating to Taiwan. With greater Chinese immigration, however, strife on the island, and consequent administrative costs, increased. The government found it more difficult to control illegal Chinese encroachment on aboriginal land. As Chinese settlers cleared more land, conflicts between them and aboriginal communities increased. Communal conflict within the Chinese population increased as well.[11] The administration reversed course again as Taiwan's governor-general Hao Yu-lin moved in 1738 to discontinue further clearing of aboriginal land and in 1739 to reinstitute the restrictions on families immigrating to Taiwan. It was by now impossible, however, to turn back the clock. Taiwan's

---

[10] John R. Shepherd, "The Island Frontier of the Ch'ing, 1684–1780," in Rubinstein, ed., *Taiwan*, 113.

[11] Ibid., 127.

Qing-administered population continued to grow apace—from 415,000 in 1735 to over 2.5 million in 1895[12]—because of illegal migration and because a substantial number of Chinese women were now on the island. Trade with the mainland, particularly in rice and sugar, also flourished despite government opposition, paralleling somewhat the situation in the 1980s and 1990s. After an uprising in 1786, restrictions on immigration changed yet again, and Chinese were allowed to move to Taiwan if they had relatives already on the island.

Independent Landlord Kingdoms

The pursuit of economic and physical security by individual families within a political vacuum of largely ineffective Qing government led to the rise of small quasi-kingdoms built up by powerful landlords. Most of Taiwan's "landlords" were actually not the primary owners of land, but were property managers who paid rent for the land to absentee landlords. These property managers enjoyed the right of permanent tenancy, and their annual rent payments to their landlords, typically 10 to 15 percent of the harvest, could not be raised. The property managers in turn sublet the land, on short-term leases if they wished, and charged their tenants 50 percent rent. Moreover, unlike the landlords, they were able to supervise and guide development of the land and to monitor the harvests to ensure they received the full share of profits owed to them. Successful property managers became local elites.

The top priority of Taiwan's garrison of Qing soldiers was guarding the government's administrative offices and major ports of entry into the island. While there were military posts in the countryside, these forces were stretched too thin to guarantee the safety and order of the agricultural communities. Furthermore, because of the weakness of the Qing administration in many parts of Chinese-settled Taiwan, rival landlords were often left to fight out for themselves competing claims over land and water usage. For these reasons of individual security and interest, the more powerful landlords raised private militias, recruiting militiamen from among their tenants and sometimes drawing on the support of local religious organizations. Not only was the Chinese administration often ineffective in preventing or resolving local disputes, but corrupt officials often demanded payoffs for their services, giving local communities an incentive to govern their own affairs. Local authority devolved to individ-

[12] John R. Shepherd, *Statecraft and Political Economy on the Taiwan Frontier, 1600–1800* (Stanford, Calif.: Stanford University Press, 1993), 161–162, 169.

uals with wealth (e.g., landlords) or prestige within the clan or village. The system of government was reminiscent of mainland Chinese feudalism, but without the overarching central government.[13] To keep the peace, competing communities had to work out and respect territorial boundaries. Violations of these agreements resulted in interclan feuds that might last for generations.

Along with evading government controls, some Taiwanese elites pursued their interests by courting the government's favor, which could lead to a bureaucratic appointment for a family member. An official position added political power to a wealthy family's economic power. A member of the wealthy Lin clan,[14] Lin Wen-ch'a, exemplified this point. The authorities considered Lin a criminal after he led his house militia in a revenge attack on a rival family to kill his father's murderer. To regain the government's favor, he successfully employed his militia against the Small Sword Society (Hsiao Tao Hui), a group of rebellious landowners, and later led three thousand Taiwanese soldiers on the mainland who helped the Qing put down the large-scale Taiping Rebellion. He returned to Taiwan in 1863 to fight another uprising by local landlords, this time in his hometown of Wufeng. Through these loyalist efforts, Lin earned accolades and rewards from the government, and his family acquired the lands of defeated rebel landlords at discounted prices.

Qing Policies toward the Aborigines

The growth of the Chinese population on Taiwan inevitably forced changes in the culture and lifestyles of aboriginal tribes as the Chinese overhunted the deer population and converted plains and forests to farmland. The Qing government made a considerable effort to preserve the livelihood of aborigines and to protect them from abuse and exploitation by Chinese settlers. The government valued the aborigines as taxpayers, conscripted soldiers (sent to punish outlaw tribes or to intervene in inter-Chinese communal battles), and corvee laborers, and hoped to avoid the economic costs of aborigine uprisings. It recognized aborigine land ownership rights and required Chinese who used aboriginal land to pay rent to the natives. On occasion the Qing rewarded tribes that assisted in mili-

---

[13] Goddard, *Formosa*, 30.

[14] The Lin family's history is well documented. See Huang Fu-sun, *The Rise of the Lin Family of Wu-Feng: From Crossing the Straits to Opening the Land, 1729–1864* (Taipei: Independent Evening Post, 1987); Huang, *The Downfall of the Lin Family of Wu-Feng, 1861–1885* (Taipei: Independent Evening Post, 1992); Johanna Meskill, *A Chinese Pioneer Family: The Lins of Wu-Feng, Taiwan, 1729–1895* (Princeton, N.J.: Princeton University Press, 1979).

tary campaigns against outlaw or rebellious tribes with lands taken from the defeated enemy. Some aborigines eventually joined the landlord class.

To reduce conflict between Chinese and aborigines, Qing officials tried to prevent movement between the Chinese-settled plains and the mountainous homelands of the unassimilated *sheng fan* by establishing a boundary marked by trenches and lined with military guard posts. This was not solely to prevent Chinese settlements from aborigine raids. The government also wanted to limit Chinese penetration into aboriginal lands, which the authorities realized was a major reason for aborigine discontent and thus an indirect cause of violent conflict between aborigines and Chinese.

The Qing administration encouraged lowland aborigines to become part of Chinese society. A gradual, limited reconciliation between the Chinese and some aborigine communities was reflected in a myth concerning a Chinese official named Wu Feng. Wu was reputedly a fair and honest man who on the one hand defended the aborigines in his jurisdiction against being mistreated by other Chinese and on the other hand tried to persuade the tribesmen to give up their traditional practice of head-hunting. The story holds that Wu managed to secure a forty-year moratorium on head-hunting, after which the tribe told him their rituals demanded a new supply of heads. Wu helped them by revealing that a man wearing a red hood would pass by a certain spot the next morning and would serve as an easy victim. The tribesmen found the red-hooded man as Wu had predicted and chopped off his head. Only then did they learn, to their horror, that they had killed their friend Wu. Grief-stricken, they renounced head-hunting forever, and Chinese and aborigines in that region thereafter lived in peace out of respect for Wu's sacrifice. This myth would persist into the next century, revived by a Japanese administration facing the same challenges governing the aborigines.[15]

Incorporated, "ripe" aborigine communities were required to pay the government a head tax, sometimes in the form of grain. Those who refused were subject to being forced off their land and into the mountains. Government administrators and their agents also requisitioned aborigines to provide menial labor as porters, couriers, and so on. This practice was sometimes abused, with aborigines forced to work as the personal servants of Chinese, creating resentment and occasionally a violent backlash from aborigine communities.

The potential for Chinese to exploit aborigines was expanded by "tax farming": a Chinese merchant paid an aboriginal village's taxes in ex-

[15] Sinkichi Eto, "An Outline of Formosan History," in Mark Mancall, ed., *Formosa Today* (New York: Praeger, 1964), 46–47.

change for monopoly rights to sell goods to the village and to market the village's products. Mismatches often arose in the deals struck between the natives and these crafty Chinese businessmen. A late-seventeenth-century Chinese observer noted that the tax farmer's agents

> take advantage of the simple-mindedness of the barbarians and never tire of fleecing them, looking on whatever they have as no different from their own property. In connection with the activities of daily life, great and small, all of the barbarians—men, women and children—have to serve in their homes without a day of respite. Moreover, they take the barbarian women as their wives and concubines. Whatever is demanded of them they must comply; if they make a mistake they must take a flogging.[16]

A major revolt, centered in the aborigine village of Ta Chia Hsi, near present-day Taichung, broke out in 1731. Moving to expand their administrative structure in the northern part of the island, Chinese officials relied heavily on forced aborigine labor, triggering a series of incidents of abusive treatment that culminated in the beating of a group of village women who had refused a work assignment. In retaliation, aborigine men attacked and burned the subprefectural office, killing some officials and driving away the rest. The aborigines then killed and destroyed the homes of some of the Chinese settlers in the area. Qing troops marched in from the south, but were unable to defeat the rebellious aborigines, their numbers swelled by tribesmen formerly considered loyal to the government. In May 1732 they came close to capturing the city of Chang Hua, the county seat. The rebels were eventually beaten and their remnants chased into the mountains later in the year, but only with the assistance of Hakka warriors and several thousand reinforcement troops shipped in from Fujian. The uprising of 1731–32 spurred the Qing to move toward improved relations with the aborigines. The government established forty-seven schools for aborigine youth and dramatically lowered the tax rate for aborigine settlements.

The government's policy was more aggressive during the last twenty years of Chinese rule, as Qing officials determined that for both economic and security reasons it was necessary to establish control over the mountains in central and eastern Taiwan. These years thus saw more frequent military campaigns against aborigine settlements, construction of roads from the plains into the mountains, more schooling and other attempts to Sinicize "pacified" aborigines, and a program to subsidize Chinese will-

---

[16] Quoted in Laurence Thompson, "The Earliest Chinese Eyewitness Accounts of the Formosan Aborigines," *Monumenta Serica* 23 (1964): 195–196.

ing to settle in newly opened areas. Under Liu Ming-ch'uan's leadership, the Qing forces on Taiwan sometimes employed their latest weapons, including cannon, machine-guns, and warships, in fierce campaigns against the aborigines. The Chinese forces nevertheless suffered huge casualties—perhaps one-third out of their total number of 17,500.[17]

Development on Taiwan in the Late Qing

Several administrators sent in the waning years of the Qing government tried to promote development and modernization on Taiwan, partly out of a desire to make the island more defensible in the likely event of war with Japan. Shen Pao-chen, director of the Fuzhou Navy Yard in Fujian Province, was on Taiwan in 1874–75 to oversee work to strengthen its defenses. This he did, organizing militias and building heavy gun emplacements on the coast, but Shen's agenda was much broader. He sought to Sinicize Taiwan's mountainous regions by clearing more land for cultivation, encouraging new Chinese settlements, building more roads from the lowlands into the highlands, and extending efforts to assimilate aborigine communities. Shen also promoted coal mining in the Keelung area using Western techniques and called for telegraph cable links between northern and southern Taiwan and between Taiwan and the mainland.

As governor of Fujian, Ting Jih-ch'ang supervised Taiwan's development in 1875–78. His government made further contributions to Taiwan's infrastructure, laying railroad tracks and telegraph lines. Ting even dreamed of building a 350-mile railway along the entire length of Taiwan, from Keelung in the north to Hengch'un in the south, a plan that in his day proved financially unfeasible. Ting hoped to increase Chinese settlement on Taiwan by opening mines and expanding the cultivation of cash crops such as tea. He also favored pacifying the aborigines by drawing them into the Han economy rather than through military suppression.

The most notable administrator of the Qing period was Taiwan's first governor (1884–91), the capable and progressive Liu Ming-ch'uan. Seeking to develop and modernize Taiwan and demonstrating a willingness to tackle difficult challenges that was uncharacteristic of the risk-averse, loss-cutting Qing administration, Liu carried out important tax and fiscal reforms and improvements of Taiwan's economic infrastructure. He also distinguished himself by treating dissidents who complained about high taxes with remarkable leniency. Some of Liu's projects proved too ambi-

[17] William M. Speidel, "Liu Ming-ch'uan in Taiwan, 1884–1891" (Ph.D. diss., Yale University, 1967), 298–303; Robert Gardella, "From Treaty Ports to Provincial Status, 1860–1894," in Rubinstein, ed., *Taiwan*, 191.

tious, but he is honored in Taiwan as a national hero. Qing officials in Beijing, generally conservative, feared Liu's seemingly radical agenda and were dismayed by his wasteful wars against the aborigines and his attempts to make Western investors partners in Taiwan's mining industry. Liu was recalled and retired in 1891.

Taiwan's Foreign Relations under the Qing

Taiwan's economy became strongly oriented toward production for international markets in the latter years of Qing rule, an era inaugurated by the opening of the west coast ports of Tanshui and Anping to Western traders in 1860 in accordance with the Treaty of Peking. International trade had important political and social effects on Taiwan, both positive and negative. Taiwan began growing rice and tea while under Qing administration. The island found a niche in the production of tea, which became a major export. The export price of camphor rose in the late 1800s, benefiting Taiwan, which was the world's leading supplier. The growth of trade for tea and camphor helped Hakka and Chang-chou natives in northern Taiwan gain ground on the Ch'uan-chou natives in southern Taiwan who had previously been the most economically successful social group.[18] Gaps in wealth between the richer and poorer classes increased. Opium became, in terms of monetary value, Taiwan's dominant import, with tens of thousands of Taiwanese becoming addicts. Western missionaries such as the Canadian George Mackay helped promulgate Western-style education and particularly Western medical practices on Taiwan. Mackay offered free dental services to win trust and attract potential converts. He claimed he personally extracted over twenty-one thousand Taiwanese teeth.[19]

The U.S., British, French, Japanese, and Prussian governments each considered acquiring Taiwan, either by purchase or seizure, at some time during the nineteenth century. These major powers viewed Taiwan as barbarian territory, a haven for pirates and for "wreckers" who robbed shipwrecked vessels and murdered their crews, often with the cooperation of local authorities. About fifty Western ships were wrecked off the Taiwan coast between the opening of Taiwan to Western trade in 1860 and Taiwan's ascension to provincial status. For many years the central government in Beijing failed to satisfy foreign demands to curtail these activities. As a result, British, French, and Japanese naval forces were drawn

[18] Lin Man-houng, "Maoyi yu Ch'ingmou T'aiwan te Ch'ingchi shehui piench'ien 1860–1895," *Shihhou Yuehk'an* 9, no. 4 (July 1979): 26–27.
[19] Chang Chiung-fang, "Remembering George Lesley Mackay," *Sinorama* (May 2001): 68.

into clashes in and around Taiwan. In an 1867 case, aborigines massacred the crew of a shipwrecked American vessel. Beijing answered the U.S. government's complaint with the excuse that Taiwanese aborigine lands were not under China's jurisdiction. In 1871, Botan tribe aborigines killed fifty-four members of the crew of a ship from the Ryukyu Islands, over which Japan claimed sovereignty, that had wrecked off Taiwan's southern coast. The Japanese government protested to Beijing, which again responded that China could not be held responsible because the atrocity was committed outside the territory occupied by Chinese. The Chinese also restated their position that the Ryukyus were a Chinese tributary state, not a Japanese territory, and therefore Tokyo had no basis to become involved. Japan took matters into its own hands, dispatching a military expedition that attacked the Botan in 1874. Fearing war with Japan, the Chinese agreed to a settlement that included payment of indemnity money to Tokyo and tacit recognition of Japan's claim on the Ryukyus. Fearing its neglect was inviting foreigners to colonize Taiwan, China changed its position and declared Chinese jurisdiction over all of Taiwan, including areas inhabited by aborigines.

The French landed forces in Keelung and threatened after the Franco-Chinese War of 1884 to take Taiwan as reparations. But unable to advance inland against tough resistance by Liu's forces and wracked by disease, the French withdrew in 1885. That same year Beijing approved upgrading Taiwan's status from a dependency of Fujian Province to a province in its own right, a change motivated by the Qing's desire to strengthen Taiwan against these mounting foreign pressures.

A Distinct Chinese Community

This historical background provides balancing perspective to the attitude of more recent Chinese governments, which have viewed Taiwan as the jewel of the Chinese empire and asserted strong claims to ownership of the island. To be sure, from the beginning, Taiwan's proximity to China framed the island's destiny. With the Japanese opting out, it was inevitable that Chinese settlers would challenge and eventually displace the aborigines as Taiwan's dominant civilization. Similarly, the Dutch administration yielded to a Chinese warlord who was able to transport a force of overpowering size across the strait from its base in China. Cheng Ch'eng-kung himself was compelled to submit when the Chinese government decided to take over Taiwan.

Yet while growing within China's shadow, Taiwan remained distinct from China. The island was originally a problem for the Chinese government: an unauthorized refuge for Chinese citizens of dubious character, an unruly place that consumed administrative resources and caused friction between China and foreign powers. The people who became known as the Taiwanese came to Taiwan to get away from conditions in China. Taiwan became a place where Chinese individuals and communities could make a fresh start. This was the beginning of Taiwan's divergence from the mainland in social, economic, and political development. From here foreign influences would play an important role as well—first the Dutch and then, more profoundly, the Japanese.

❋

The Japanese Occupation

Military success against China in the 1894–95 Sino-Japanese War heralded Japan's emergence as the first modern Asian great power. Although the immediate object of the war was control over Korea, Japan would press for possession of Taiwan as part of the postwar settlement. Besides affirming Japan's new status as a peer of the European imperialist powers and America, colonization of Taiwan had potential military and economic benefits for Tokyo. The island's location made it suitable as a base for expanding into Southeast Asia or defending the home islands from threats originating in the south (where the Europeans had colonies). Inoue Tsuyoshi, advisor to Prime Minister Ito Hirobumi, wrote to Ito, "Taiwan . . . can control maritime rights in the Yellow Sea, the North China Sea and the Sea of Japan. It is the door to Japan's defense. If we lose this good opportunity, the island of Taiwan will be taken by other powerful countries within two to three years."[1] Control of a productive source of food and raw materials was highly desirable for a crowded, resource-poor country with big ambitions. With further development, Taiwan might also serve as a profitable market for Japanese exports. Thus the Japanese, who had already seized the Penghu Island group, were insistent during negotiations with China after the war that Taiwan change hands, despite the efforts of Li Hung-chang, the leader of the Chinese delegation. Li tried to resist or at least delay ceding Taiwan by arguing, among other things, that Taiwan was rife with malaria and opium addiction.[2]

---

[1] Masahiro Wakabayashi, "Fifty Years of Tension Across the Strait," *Taipei Times* Online, Sept. 29, 1999, online at *http://taiwansecurity.org/news/TT-Fifty-Years-of-Tension.htm*, accessed Oct. 10, 2000.

[2] W.G. Goddard, *Formosa: A Study in Chinese History* (West Lansing: Michigan State University Press, 1966), 143.

Under the terms of the Treaty of Shimonoseki, ratified by the Chinese and Japanese governments in May 1895, along with the payment of reparations equivalent to twice China's national income, China agreed to permanently cede Taiwan and the Penghu Islands to Japan. Beijing sent Taipei a brief telegraphic message after the treaty had been signed saying Taiwan was no longer Chinese territory and instructing Chinese officials to return to the mainland. Understandably, the general perception of Taiwan's Chinese residents was that China had sold them out. Local elites grabbed Governor T'ang Ching-sung before he could slip away and expressed their indignation. His office informed Beijing, "The literati and people of Formosa are determined to resist subjection by Japan. Hence they have declared themselves an independent Island Republic, at the same time recognizing the suzerainty of the sacred Tsing [Qing] Dynasty."[3] Nanjing governor Chang Chih-tung replied to T'ang that resistance on Taiwan could not be linked to the Qing government, which feared Japanese retaliation against China. Taiwan's government named T'ang president of the Republic of Taiwan (Taiwan Minzhuguo), but as the message to Beijing indicated, this government was primarily interested in "independence" only from Japan, not China. The new Taiwanese government attempted, unsuccessfully, to persuade the British to take over the island, then hoping to rally international support for blocking the Japanese occupation, declared independence in May 1895. Many Westerners, however, welcomed a Japanese administration in Taiwan, hoping this would help tame and modernize the island and thus facilitate trade. And indeed, under Japanese rule piracy in the waters around Taiwan would be greatly reduced, lighthouses would be built on the coastline, and Taiwan's ports made more efficient.

Local support for independence, as well, was less than universal; some of Taiwan's inhabitants felt resistance to Japan was futile and hoped Japanese rule would reduce crime and warlordism on the island.[4] Those who did oppose cession to Japan included intellectuals who feared Chinese culture and civilization were in jeopardy. The Declaration of Independence read in part, "If we, the People of Taiwan, permit [the Japanese] to land, Taiwan will become the land of savages and barbarians."[5]

T'ang's government had a force of fifty thousand Chinese troops re-

---

[3] J. W. Davidson, *The Island of Formosa: Past and Present* (London: Macmillan, 1903), 273.

[4] John F. Copper, *Taiwan: Nation-State or Province?* (Boulder, Colo.: Westview Press, 1996), 29.

[5] Goddard, *Formosa*, 144–145.

cruited from the mainland. These troops, however, had little motivation to die for Taiwan and lacked confidence in the new republic's ability to pay their wages. Many of them headed for the ports seeking passage to the mainland, looting and marauding as they went, instead of making a stand against the Japanese. The first contingent of twelve thousand Japanese soldiers that landed at Keelung on May 29 established control over the city and its environs within three days. In Taipei, the self-proclaimed local government fled, leaving an angry mob to burn the governor's offices. T'ang, visiting the port of Tamsui on the pretext of conducting a military inspection, boarded a German merchant ship bound for Xiamen just ten days after his inauguration, earning the epithet "the Ten-Day President."[6] The nerve of the defenders collapsed, and a small Japanese unit took the capital in one day. Subduing the southern part of the island proved more difficult. Taiwanese nationalists rallied in the historical capital of Tainan and named Liu Yung-fu, a general with about thirty thousand troops under his command, the new president. Liu tried to get the Japanese to agree to a plebiscite after two years to decide Taiwan's political future. The Japanese, however, did not need to make such concessions. Their advance continued, and Liu fled to the mainland disguised as a refugee. The Japanese capture of Tainan in October 1895 marked the official end of organized Taiwanese resistance, although a more troublesome anti-Japanese guerrilla campaign, in which Hakkas in southern Taiwan featured prominently, would continue until 1902. Six major uprisings would occur in the next two decades, along with continued fighting between the Japanese and aborigines.

The Japanese established a two-year period after their takeover of Taiwan during which its ethnic Chinese residents could relocate to China rather than stay on as citizens of the Japanese Empire. About a quarter of the island's population took advantage of the opportunity to leave. Many Taiwanese who had the means to leave stayed on, believing life under a Japanese colonial government offered more hope than prospects on the mainland, where the Qing dynasty was in its dying days and the coastal provinces were especially poor.

Like many would-be conquerors in the region who would follow them, Japanese forces in Taiwan had a particularly difficult time stamping out guerrilla activity in the rural areas, where many farmers were part-time irregular fighters who could count on the support of local villagers. They carried out sabotage of some government-built facilities, and Japanese po-

---

[6] Interview with historian Lin Cheng-rong of Tamkang University in "The Taiwan Republic: The First Ever Taiwan Independence Movement?" online at http://www.etaiwannews.com/History/2001/05/28/991018022.htm, p. 3, accessed Sept. 18, 2001.

lice or soldiers who camped or traveled in the countryside were at risk of attack. The Japanese styled the guerrillas as "bandits." Some were indeed outlaws, but this group was comprised of Taiwanese from many walks of life, from prominent citizens to drifters. By one count there were ninety-four partisan attacks against the Japanese from late 1892 through 1902. Japanese reprisals were merciless; some six thousand Taiwanese died in the Yun-lin Massacre of June 1896. About twice as many "bandits" were killed during this guerrilla war (twelve thousand) as during the five-month Japanese campaign to secure their takeover of the island.[7] The bitterness of the guerrilla war was reflected in the harsh penalties prescribed by the 1898 Bandit Punishment Ordinance and the 1904 Fine and Flogging Ordinance, laws that were applied only to Taiwanese.

The story of Houbiling, a Taiwanese stronghold in the Kaohsiung area that has been compared to the American fortress Alamo, illustrated the Japanese administration's ruthless and uncompromising attitude toward organized resistance. Beginning in 1897, a group led by guerrilla Lin Shao Mao based in Houbiling beat back attempts by Japanese soldiers to dislodge them. In 1899 Lin offered the Japanese a deal: he would surrender the fort if the Japanese would pay him a substantial indemnity, release his relatives from prison, and allow his followers to live in the area free of tax obligations or Japanese police. The Japanese, who had suffered high casualties fighting Lin, agreed. For three years Lin's people prospered. In 1902, however, an enlarged force of Japanese troops suddenly attacked, massacring Lin's people and burning their fields. Lin and most of the other inhabitants, probably about two hundred Taiwanese, died and Houbiling disappeared from the map.[8]

The frequent failure of the Japanese forces to distinguish between the rebels and the rest of the populace often generated additional resistance. Occasionally the rebels challenged Japanese forces in or near major cities. Armed rebels attacked Taipei and its suburbs in early 1896, killing about two hundred Japanese troops and civilians. Another attack on Taipei in May 1897 involved two thousand rebels. Japanese teachers massacred at a school near the Taipei suburb of Shihlin were found to have been tortured and mutilated. The Japanese reacted with their own campaign of murder and torture in brutal reprisals against Hakka villages for six weeks after-

---

[7] Weng Chia-in, *T'aiwan Hanjen Wuchang K'angjih shih yenchiu* (Taipei: National Taiwan University, 1986), 92–95. Taiwan Historian Lin Cheng-rong says Taiwanese deaths in the six months after Japanese troops landed might have exceeded 14,000, against 278 Japanese killed. Interview with Lin, online at http://www.etaiwannews.com/History/2001/05/28/991018022.htm, p. 4, accessed Sept. 18, 2001.

[8] Gung Fei-tao, "Lin Shao Mao," Taiwan Lishih Chihliao, online at http://taiwan resources.com/info/history/crazy.htm, accessed Sept. 18, 2001.

ward. An insurrection led by a Hakka in part of Tainan in June 1896 led to the indiscriminate destruction of some thirty nearby villages by Japanese security personnel. Even civilian politicians in Tokyo complained that this was an excessive use of violent force, and the Japanese Imperial Household donated money for reconstruction.[9]

When the initial policy of brute force and terrorism against Taiwanese partisans produced poor results, the Japanese administration changed tactics in 1898 and offered economic incentives and amnesty for guerrillas who renounced their life of "banditry" and swore allegiance to the Japanese emperor. The government soon found, however, that many who had accepted amnesty and its rewards were still assisting other rebels. A heavy-handed military approach was resumed, including massacres of villagers suspected of supporting guerrillas. Concentrating on the Taichung area, the government announced it would hold responsible the families of fugitive rebels, but that it would also offer surrendering rebels amnesty and rewards as in 1898. The authorities invited the 360 who accepted the offer to a banquet in Taichung's Taulok assembly hall on May 25, 1902. Once the guests were inside, the hosts locked the doors and slaughtered the former rebels.

The Colonial Administrative System

As a colonial territory, Taiwan was under a different system of governance than the Japanese home islands. In theory, Taiwanese, as subjects of the Japanese Empire, had claim on the rights and privileges granted by the Meiji constitution. But under Law 63, enacted in 1896, executive orders given by the governor-general had the same force as law, which in effect put Taiwan under a military dictatorship. The governor-general's broad powers included authority to appoint most of those who filled powerful positions in government, including provincial governors. If he was a military officer, as was the case in 1895–1919 and 1926–45, he was also commander of all military forces on the island.

To blunt local discontent, which threatened the efficiency of their operations on the island, the Japanese made significant political reforms over the course of the occupation. These reforms gave some Taiwanese a greater, though never decisive, voice in public affairs. The Japanese divided Taiwan into five provinces (*shu*), plus three additional subprovin-

---

[9] George H. Kerr, *Formosa: Licensed Revolution and the Home Rule Movement, 1895–1945* (Honolulu: University Press of Hawaii, 1974), 29–30.

cial units for less-populated areas.[10] The five provinces had their own provincial assemblies with Taiwanese representatives, but typically only half were elected, the other half being appointees of the government, and the governor-general had the power to veto or cancel their initiatives. In the 1920s, there were meaningful elections for many local political offices. The government moved to reduce the role of the police in civil administration and dropped most of the severe penalties that had arisen from the guerrilla war period. In 1921, the Japanese established the Advisory Council (Hyogikai) to the governor-general, ostensibly to allow for local input. Most of the members were Japanese, and a large proportion of the minority Taiwanese membership were collaborators. In 1935, the Japanese administration began allowing elections for half the seats in provincial, country, and town assemblies. The government appointed the other half. By the end of the decade about three thousand Taiwanese held elected offices. This gave elected Taiwanese substantial input into local government. Still, voting requirements limited the franchise to males who were at least twenty-five years of age, paid at least five yen in local taxes annually, and obtained clearance from the police, keeping a disproportionate share of influence in the hands of the Japanese. In 1935, for example, only 3.8 percent of the Taiwanese population was qualified to vote, compared to 14.6 percent of the Japanese community in Taiwan.[11] The Japanese leadership also retained the power to overrule decisions made by these elected Taiwanese officials.

Even if they did not shift the imbalance of power from the Japanese to the Taiwanese community, these electoral procedures had long-term consequences for Taiwan's political development. They helped atomize the movement for Taiwanese autonomy by creating incentives for politicians to focus on local issues and cultivate local power bases rather than work to support national organizations and national goals such as the establishment of a Taiwan parliament. Local elites were now more likely to compete against each other rather than cooperate. The Kuomintang (KMT) would continue to employ the electoral system of single-vote, multiple-member districts that the Japanese introduced. Finally, these reforms acclimated the Taiwanese to orderly democratic participation.[12]

[10] Edward I-te Chen, "Japanese Colonialism in Korea and Formosa: A Comparison of the Systems of Political Control," *Harvard Journal of Asiatic Studies* 30 (1970): 141–142.

[11] Chen Ming-tong and Lin Jih-wen, "Taiwan Difang Hsuanchude Ch'iyuan yu Guochia Shehui Kuanhsi Chuanpien," in Chen and Zheng Yungnian, eds., *Liangan Chits'eng Hsuanchu yu Chengchi Shehui Bianch'ian* (Taipei: Yuedan Chubanshe, 1998), 34.

[12] Shelley Rigger, *Politics in Taiwan: Voting for Democracy* (London and New York: Routledge, 1999), 37–39.

Two institutions extended Japanese control to the grass-roots level: the police and the *hoko*. Beside the island's military garrison, the administration fielded a police force of about twelve thousand officers, a special police contingent of five thousand in the aboriginal districts, and an additional six thousand military police.[13] In rural villages the Japanese policeman, who might be the colonial regime's only representation in the community, had broad responsibilities and powers that might, for good or ill, involve them in the personal matters of the locals.

The Japanese administration continued to employ the traditional Chinese *baojia* system of collective responsibility to help suppress crime, dissent, and organized Taiwanese nationalism. Under the *baojia* system, rendered *hoko* in Japanese, a neighborhood leader had responsibility over a group of households. The government relied on the *hoko* leaders to ensure the community met its obligations, including the payment of taxes and the supply of labor for state projects. The leader and the rest of the group could also be called into account for any crime committed by a member of one of their households, which gave the whole group an incentive to suppress troublemaking. If a suspected criminal fled, the authorities might punish his relatives and neighbors. The *hoko* system required all Taiwanese (with the exception of unassimilated mountain-dwelling aborigines) to register, but Japanese and foreign nationals did not have to register. If this system was unjust, its more efficient employment in Japanese hands was a major reason why organized violence in Taiwan decreased greatly under Japanese rule without a commensurate increase in the size of the colonial police force.[14] The Japanese also used networks of informants and two kinds of ostensibly voluntary groups, village associations (*burakukai*) and the Youth Corps (Seinendan), which mobilized additional labor for government projects and campaigns, to regiment Taiwanese society.

Japanese Policies and Their Impact

Economic development was an area in which the interests of Taiwanese individuals, Japanese individuals, and the Japanese state/regime found considerable convergence. The Taiwanese gained in general and absolute terms, even if the system allowed some Japanese to gain more. Achieving their purposes on the island required the Japanese to undertake substan-

---

[13] Joseph W. Ballantine, *Formosa: A Problem for United States Foreign Policy* (Washington, D.C.: The Brookings Institution, 1952), 28–29.

[14] Hui-yu Caroline Ts'ai, "One Kind of Control: The *Hoko* System in Taiwan Under Japanese Rule, 1895–1945" (Ph.D. diss., Columbia University, 1990), 46–47.

tial expansion and modernization of Taiwan's infrastructure. The Japanese constructed roads and railroads, built hospitals and harbors, established irrigation systems for the countryside and sewage systems and an electric power supply for cities, modernized Taiwan's banking and monetary systems, and established news media. There were some 164 kilometers of major roads in Taiwan in 1899, shortly after the Japanese takeover, and 4,456 kilometers by 1935.[15] New sanitation practices and government-sponsored campaigns against rats and unclean water supplies greatly reduced the incidence of diseases such as bubonic plague, cholera, smallpox, malaria, and dysentery. The huge Chianan irrigation system, completed in 1930, produced one of the largest reservoirs in East Asia and turned tens of thousands of acres into fertile farmland. Hydroelectric plants such as that near Sun Moon Lake, finished in 1937, made it possible for the island to build heavy industries.

It was not clear at the outset that Japan's colonization of Taiwan would be profitable in strictly economic terms. Tokyo heavily subsidized the first few years of its administration in Taiwan. After 1904, however, Taiwan was financially in the black. The Japanese vision of Taiwan's economic role within the empire changed through the occupation period. Up to the mid-1920s, Japanese efforts toward Taiwan's economic development focused on agriculture. The island's principal contribution was to be supplying rice and sugar. The industrial sector saw some growth thereafter, with a few large Japanese projects and a large number of light industries that were mostly Taiwanese owned. During the Pacific War, however, Japanese planners consciously built up Taiwan's heavy industries so the island could process raw materials from Japanese-occupied Southeast Asia.

Under the Fujianese land policy imported to much of Taiwan, tenants had co-ownership rights with landowners; after many decades, much confusion had developed over the ownership of farmland throughout the island. The Chinese administration had not resurveyed the land in the two centuries prior to the Japanese takeover, so it was unclear how much land tax revenue was due the government. In the first decade of their rule in Taiwan, the Japanese conducted a new survey, discovering Taiwan had more taxable farmland than previously thought. Then they instituted a land reform program similar to that carried out earlier in Japan: the government took ownership title away from primary landowners, giving them bonds as compensation. The Japanese also permitted the Taiwanese to form farmers' associations, albeit under strict controls. While the original impetus for these associations was the desire to protect the rights and

[15] Sinkichi Eto, "An Outline of Formosan History," in Mark Mancall, ed., *Formosa Today* (New York: Praeger, 1964), 52.

reduce the rents of tenant farmers, the Japanese administration used them primarily to promote the implementation of advanced agricultural techniques to improve production[16] as well as to steer farmers toward producing the particular crops the authorities wanted according to the schedule the authorities desired. Another avenue through which the Japanese controlled Taiwanese farmers was manipulation of the supply of water available for irrigation. In Kerr's assessment, "The Formosan farmer ceased to be a free agent, becoming instead a small cog in a vast machine, obliged to turn at the speed and in the direction dictated by the government."[17] The amount of cultivated land more than doubled under Japanese rule. Accordingly, rice production also greatly increased. Although more than half the rice Taiwan produced was exported to Japan, by the 1920s the average Taiwanese was better fed than his counterpart in any province of mainland China.[18]

The Japanese authorities shifted a large proportion of Taiwan's rice fields to sugar production for reasons of narrow economic interest. Japanese companies came to dominate Taiwan's sugar industry because they got preferential treatment from the colonial administration and because it was easier for them than their Taiwanese counterparts to raise large amounts of capital. While the rice farmer could eat his crop or sell it at the consumer marketplace, the only option a sugar farmer had was to deliver his cane to the (usually Japanese-owned) sugar mill, accepting whatever price the mill was willing to pay. The owners of the Japanese-controlled sugar industry in Taiwan thus enjoyed the high profits made possible by supplies of raw materials kept artificially cheap.

A Forestry Bureau established in 1915 proved more effective than the previous Chinese administration in protecting Taiwan's forests, including the valuable camphor-producing trees, from uncontrolled and illegal harvesting.

Throughout the period of their rule in Taiwan, Japanese policymakers wrestled with the issue of assimilation. In principle, assimilation meant Taiwan's people would give up their heritage and traditions to enjoy the progress and prosperity enjoyed by subjects of the Japanese emperor. For Japanese, the superiority of their culture and civilization were self-evident. If this was less the case for Chinese and aborigines, abandoning parts of their traditional culture and identity were the price of affiliation with a modern, industrialized Asian great power and the chance to gain access to its benefits. The issue had important implications for the indi-

[16] Ballantine, *Formosa*, 35–36.
[17] Kerr, *Licensed Revolution*, 93.
[18] Copper, *Taiwan*, 30.

vidual security of Taiwanese. If the government's policies aimed for and achieved the conversion of Taiwan's people from colonial subjects to more fully fledged Japanese, the systematic exploitation and discrimination they underwent would be harder to justify. The proassimilationist view was that Taiwanese were increasingly alienated from China and could therefore become Japanized just as the Okinawans had. The opposing view was that Taiwanese could never develop the mind-set or patriotic spirit of the ethnic Japanese. Thus their destiny was to remain under a military government indefinitely. Different Japanese administrations throughout the occupation period varied in their attitudes, and consequently their policies, toward assimilation. Contrasting views played themselves out in 1914, when a prestigious retired Japanese politician, Itagaki Taisuke, traveled to Taiwan to promote assimilation. He founded the Taiwan Dokakai, which quickly enrolled about three thousand Taiwanese members along with a few resident Japanese. Governor-General Sakuma Samata waited until Itagaki left Taiwan, then moved against the Taiwan Dokakai, disbanding it and arresting its leaders.

In the 1930s, the Japanese administration began a policy called *Kominka* (literally "Imperial-subjectization"). As part of this policy, the government legalized Taiwanese-Japanese intermarriage, opened the Imperial University in Taipei to Taiwanese students, and banned Chinese-language radio broadcasts. The authorities also ordered discontinuation of the Chinese-language sections of newspapers, made changes in the education system to diminish the study of Chinese in favor of Japanese, and sponsored campaigns to supplant Chinese cultural and religious practices with their Japanese versions. Starting in 1940, the authorities began urging both Chinese and aborigines to adopt Japanese names. Although name-changing was promoted as an honor and an important step in attaining the privileges of Japanese nationality, only about 7 percent of Taiwan's Chinese community complied.[19] In connection with the *Kominka* policy, the government encouraged both the Japanese and Chinese communities to refer to the aborigines as "Takasago people" (Takasago was an archaic Japanese name for Taiwan) instead of "savages" (*seibanjin*).

Assimilating Taiwan into the Japanese Empire was one of the reasons the Japanese administration made several attempts to encourage more Japanese to immigrate to Taiwan. Other reasons were to alleviate overpopulation in the Japanese home islands and create Japanese communities that were acclimated to the tropics in preparation for the Japanese Empire's southward expansion. Because of unexpectedly high costs, natu-

[19] Wan-yao Chou, "The *Kominka* Movement: Taiwan Under Wartime Japan, 1937–1945" (Ph.D. diss., Yale University, 1991), 57.

ral disasters, and the large numbers of Japanese immigrants who decided to change jobs or return home, these programs, which involved incentives such as giving land to new Japanese immigrant farmers, failed to reach their goals.

The Japanese educational system was designed to teach the Taiwanese population the basic skills necessary to make them productive workers and to inculcate in them an attitude of loyalty toward the government, Japan, and its emperor. The curriculum reinforced Japanese patriotic and jingoistic themes. The government required all teachers and students in Taiwan's schools to ritualistically bow toward the emperor in Tokyo every Monday morning. Making Japanese the medium of instruction was of course partly designed to strengthen the bond between the colonial subjects and Tokyo. An unintended consequence of the primary school system that expanded under Japanese administration was the growth of a sense of Taiwanese nationalism, as schooling brought together the children and parents of different Chinese clans and ethnic groups. Literacy in general also greatly improved throughout Taiwan under the Japanese administration.

Japanese residents maintained their own system of elementary schools, which were Taiwan's best, and which Taiwanese students could attend only if they obtained special permission. The system was less openly discriminatory after 1922, when the authorities officially opened government schools to Taiwanese as well as Japanese students. Admission, previously based on ethnicity, was thereafter to be based on Japanese language proficiency. In theory, Taiwanese students had the same opportunities for higher education as students from the resident Japanese community; in practice, however, the Japanese language requirement was a natural barrier, and Japanese students far outnumbered Taiwanese in the universities even though Japanese comprised only 5–6 percent of the island's population. The authorities systematically channeled Taiwanese students toward technical specialties and away from the social sciences, which might be politically sensitive. Taiwanese students had access to several schools that had been established by Christian missionaries. These, however, were classed as "private schools" by the Japanese administration, a designation that disadvantaged them relative to government schools. Moreover, the missionary schools were constantly under investigation by the state because of their foreign connections.

The Japanese administration sought to weaken some aspects of Taiwan's culture while promulgating Japanese culture. The most far-reaching of these policies involved language. Japanese was the language used in the schools, banking, and the civil service. The authorities discouraged the use of Chinese, especially after 1937, when Chinese-language newspapers were forbidden. Taiwanese who wanted to study their native language had to do so on their own time. During the war, the colonial government offered incentives to the Taiwanese to learn Japanese, which was thought to promote pro-Japanese patriotism. Families that were certified as having learned a small amount of Japanese earned an emblem for display on the front gate of their house that brought small privileges from the local administration.

The colonial authorities sponsored campaigns and organizations that discouraged some practices because they were distinctly Chinese, such as men wearing their hair in a long queue. Similarly, the Japanese government suppressed Taiwan's popular Taoist religion because it was a Chinese faith, and therefore associated with Chinese nationalism. The operators of many Taoist temples registered them as Buddhist temples to protect them. The anti-Taoism campaign culminated in the late 1930s, when authorities began ordering the destruction of Taoist temples. After an outcry in both Taiwan and Japan, Governor-General Hasegawa Kiyoshi, who took office in late 1940, halted this extreme policy. The corollary to suppressing Chinese religion was the promotion of Japan's state religion, Shinto. Taiwanese were required to profess reverence for the emperor. When a member of the Japanese royal family visited Taiwan, onlookers were expected to stand at attention and bow as the visitor passed by. Every home was also required to maintain a Shinto *kamidana* household shrine, even though this was an alien religion to the Taiwanese.

The colonial government discovered that performers of traditional Chinese puppet theater were lampooning the Japanese government and military during their performances. These were therefore suppressed in 1939 and replaced with the Japanese cardboard-cutout *kamishibai* story-telling medium. Unlike the Chinese puppet shows, which appealed to young and old alike, the *kamishibai* only held the interest of children, and its saturation with jingoistic Japanese propaganda made it an even poorer substitute in the eyes of Taiwanese audiences.[20]

The Japanese observed that the high expenses associated with traditional social obligations were plunging many Chinese families into debt or even bankruptcy. The authorities therefore imposed ordinances to cut back on Chinese holidays and to limit the expenditures connected with marriages, births, deaths, and religious ceremonies. They encouraged Taiwanese to adopt Shinto wedding customs and to cremate rather than bury their dead to save land space and prevent disease. According to Chinese custom, the dead bodies of family members were kept in coffins in the family home until the determination of a proper place for burial, which

[20] Kerr, *Licensed Revolution*, 196–197.

sometimes took many days. Families in this circumstance often ran afoul of Japanese police attempting to enforce public health regulations. Out of safety and security concerns, the government banned fireworks and the burning of fake money at funerals. The Japanese administration banned indentured servitude, which was then common in Taiwan, along with foot binding and other customs that kept certain groups permanently disadvantaged.

The administration's policies toward Taiwanese culture were clearly designed to make Japanese rule stronger or more efficient, without regard to the best long-term interests of the Taiwanese, unless one accepts the dubious Japanese-centric view that Taiwan could achieve its greatest prosperity and security by consolidating its position as a Japanese territory. It does not necessarily follow, however, that the impact of these policies on the interests of individual Taiwanese was relentlessly negative. This raises a difficult philosophical issue. If the presumption is that all aspects of all cultures are equally good and entitled to preservation, any changes wrought by an alien power are indefensible cases of "cultural imperialism." If this presumption is dropped, however, it becomes possible to inquire whether in some instances the imperialist policy had the effect of doing the locals a favor by eliminating a "bad" cultural practice they were better off without. The elimination of foot binding, head-hunting, and perhaps other traditional Taiwan practices would seem to support the latter view.

Fascist Japan used narcotics as a means of unconventional warfare as well as a revenue-generating enterprise, distributing drugs to soften-up the opposition in areas or among populations over which the Japanese government sought political control. Northern China was one of the principal target areas. The Japanese administration on Taiwan also evidently made narcotics available to young, middle-class Hakka men, a group that produced a relatively high proportion of anti-Japanese activists. Taiwan played an important role in Japan's drug warfare. The government sanctioned the cultivation of coca on plantations in south-central Taiwan. Taiwan was reputedly one of the world's leading producers of cocaine during the Japanese occupation. The Japanese also recruited Taiwanese to deal drugs on the mainland. Some Taiwanese convicts were offered this duty as an alternative to imprisonment. On Taiwan itself, the authorities maintained a monopoly over certain goods, including opium as well as tobacco, alcohol, salt, and camphor, which allowed the government to sell these items for more than the world market price. In the case of opium, the government argued trafficking had to be restricted to limit opium addiction on the island. The policy indeed kept opium use on Taiwan low, but it also facilitated the production of opium for distribution overseas, such as the illegal trafficking in China. The lid on Japan's drug operation was blown off in 1930 when, in connection with its obligations as a member of the League of Nations, the Japanese government allowed the league's Narcotics Control Commission to convene an open hearing in Taiwan as part of its investigation of the narcotics trade in Asia. To the embarrassment of the Japanese, 117 Taiwanese stepped forward to discredit the official line that the administration's drug policy in Taiwan had no interest other than reducing addiction among the island's residents.[21]

Taiwanese Reactions to Japanese Authority

Collaboration with the Japanese government was one strategy of maintaining or promoting individual security in occupied Taiwan. There were ample financial incentives to pursue this course, although there was also a risk of suffering retaliation by Taiwanese guerrillas. Supporting the Japanese regime did not necessarily imply a sellout of national aspirations for personal gain; some Taiwanese intellectuals believed Taiwan should denounce China for its backwardness and betrayal and welcome Japanese rule as an opportunity for the island to be modernized by administrators from Asia's most advanced country.

Compulsion is costly and inefficient, even in an authoritarian system. Despite the pervasiveness and effectiveness of Japanese control in Taiwan's Chinese communities, the Japanese made a considerable effort to win the support of the Taiwanese elite. Governor-General Nogi Maresuke began in 1897 to recognize certain eminent Taiwanese as *Shinsho* ("gentlemen") and award them medals. His successor Kodama Gentaro courted the favor of Taiwanese elites by attending several ceremonies honoring their family members. Although the Japanese authorities banned many publications they deemed subversive, their censorship policies were tempered by the desire to minimize antagonism of educated Taiwanese. In the early 1930s, for example, the government tolerated the newspaper *Taiwan Shin Mimpo* (*Taiwan New People's News*), which was an outgrowth of the nationalistic *Formosa Magazine* that had been published in Japan but banned on the island. (The magazine's fairly moderate political line was that Taiwan should be treated the same as other prefectures of Japan proper and that Taiwan's distinct culture and identity should be preserved.) Those Taiwanese elites who cooperated with the government often became rich by taking advantage of the special business privileges with which the government rewarded them.

[21] Ibid., 146–149; Ballantine, *Formosa*, 40.

For various personal and nationalistic reasons of their own, many other Taiwanese worked against the Japanese authorities either through political activism or armed rebellion. If their immediate circumstances were not enough to motivate Taiwanese activists, there was the additional impetus provided by Chinese nationalist thought and activities on the mainland, knowledge of which spread to Taiwan. The revered nationalist leader Sun Yat-sen even visited Taiwan in 1900. Lin Hsien-t'ang and the umbrella Home Rule Association (HRA) represented agitation for political change through open and peaceful means. Although considered a moderate, Lin called for greater Taiwanese representation and decision-making power within the regime. The Japanese authorities mainly tolerated the HRA's activities, although on certain occasions when political relations between the Japanese and the Taiwanese were particularly tense, the police raided and broke up HRA meetings. Lin, originally named a member of the first Advisory Council, often found his activities constrained by Japanese harassment and threats. To counter the HRA, the Japanese authorities sponsored the Public Interest Society (Koekikai) led by Advisory Council member and wealthy collaborator Ku Hsien-yung. Ku and his society supported assimilation, arguing the pro-Japanese position that Chinese nationalism was misplaced, since China had abandoned Taiwan while Japanese rule had brought modernization and economic benefits.

In November 1924, Lin sent to the Taiwan governor-general a list of twelve demands for the reform of the colonial administration. These included: more opportunities for Taiwanese to serve in local government; an end to discrimination in favor of Japanese; curtailing police abuse; outlawing and eliminating opium smoking; protections of freedoms of speech and of the press; abolition of collective responsibility; more local input into industrial and agricultural policies; allowing travel between Japan and Taiwan without passports; and a halt to prosecuting all criticism of the government as sedition.[22] The efforts of Lin and others bore some fruit. Home Rule activists were largely responsible for the modest political reforms Japan made in 1935. The last of the Home Rule organizations, however, was disbanded under Japanese pressure in 1936. Lin was one of the Taiwanese appointed to the upper house of the Diet during the desperate reforms shortly before Japan's surrender and divestiture of its captured territories.

Taiwanese students and activists in Japan in the 1920s found far greater freedom of political discussion there than on their home island, although their families back in Taiwan were subject to police harassment, as were they themselves on returning home. A group of Tokyo Taiwanese began

[22] Kerr, *Licensed Revolution*, 136–137.

publishing the monthly journal *Formosan Youth* (*Taiwan Seinen*) in 1920. Under various names in subsequent years, the publication was an important forum for Taiwanese political activists for more than a decade. The most important nationalist group on the island was probably the Taiwan Bunka Kyokai (Taiwan Cultural Association), founded in 1921 by Taipei physician Chiang Wei-shui. In accordance with its innocuous-sounding name, the association claimed its interest was in promoting local culture rather than a political agenda. Nevertheless, it consistently supported home rule and its members expounded on the theme of Taiwanese nationalism in published articles and public lectures. Members of another nationalist association, the Taiwan Gikai Kisei Domeikai (League for the Establishment of a Taiwan Parliament), annually submitted petitions to the Japanese Diet from 1921 through 1934 asking for a representative form of government on Taiwan. These petitions, bearing up to two thousand signatures, were buried by committee action and were never discussed publicly on the floor of the Diet. Several petitioners were arrested in 1924, and the group eventually broke up.

While some Taiwanese opposed Japanese authority by working within the system, Japanese records show that insurrection persisted throughout the occupation, although its frequency gradually declined over the course of Japan's rule. There were a total of nineteen major uprisings. In a single 1934 case, police arrested 425 Taiwanese who allegedly planned to overthrow the Japanese regime and restore Taiwan to the rule of the mainland government. The Japanese colonial government imprisoned or executed 109 of those arrested.[23] Between 1895 and 1920, the authorities arrested no fewer than 8,200 people annually on the charge of attempting to overthrow the government. During the 1920s there were at least 6,500 such arrests per year, and from 1931 to 1940 at least 3,450. The long-term declining trend reflected both Japanese policing efforts and the realization of Taiwanese society that violent revolts "all met with tragic failure. Consequently there developed among the Taiwanese a feeling that. . . . to resist the Japanese by force not only resulted in great sacrifices and little results, but it was also against the nature of the times."[24] Beginning in the 1920s, notes Chen Shao-hsing, the "resistance of the people changed gradually from revolt by force to organized political and social movements."[25] After hostilities between Japan and China began in 1937, the Japanese authorities on Taiwan intensified their efforts to hunt down and imprison or exe-

[23] Ibid., 155–156.

[24] Wu Cho-liu, *Chuang-pa Chi*, vol. 1 (Taipei: n.p., 1963), 196.

[25] Chen Shao-hsing, "Population Growth and Social Change in Taiwan," *Bulletin of the Department of Archeology and Anthropology*, National Taiwan University, no. 5 (May 1955), 86.

cute Taiwanese nationalist leaders operating outside the limited scope sanctioned by the colonial government. This virtually destroyed the underground nationalist movement.[26]

Harsh, even callous or excessive, Japanese retribution for Taiwanese crimes, especially sedition, was common. On a few occasions, the colonial authorities drew criticism from fellow Japanese in the home islands, pointing up the fact that Taiwan's system of governance was more authoritarian that the system in Japan proper. In May 1909, Japanese police arrested eight Taiwanese while they were gambling in a small Hakka town. While they were under detention, a policeman named Shima whipped them viciously, and three died of their injuries. Townspeople succeeded in taking Shima to court, but the judges, while calling the incident "regrettable," ruled that Shima was not subject to prosecution because he was acting within his official duties when he tortured his prisoners. Angry townspeople attacked the police station, bringing a predictably violent reaction from the police. Later that year, the authorities discovered Lo Fuhsing's attempts to organize Hsinchu Hakkas into a rebel group with plans to seize Taipei. The police arrested hundreds of suspected members of the group, and after superficial trials many were executed and hundreds imprisoned. Both of these cases caught the attention of Japanese media and politicians who argued that despite Japan's noble-sounding official statements about its purposes in Taiwan, the colonial administration's activities were cruel and exploitative.

In a later case, soothsayer Lo Chun recruited a small group of anti-Japanese followers in southern Taiwan based on his claims that he could marshal magical powers to drive the Japanese off the island while protecting the local people from Japanese retaliation. Lo's adherents were involved in a flare-up of violence near Kaohsiung in which a mob killed fifty-one Japanese. When Japanese soldiers arrived, they first randomly pulled fifty-one Taiwanese men, women, and children from an onlooking crowd and executed them, and then went on a rampage through the nearby villages. Large numbers of Taiwanese were arrested, tortured, and summarily executed. An estimated four thousand died. Others entered an adjudication process bent on revenge; of 1,413 detainees who went to trial, 866 were sentenced to death and 500 got long prison terms at hard labor. Governor-General Sakuma tried to maximize the impact of the executions on the Taiwanese public by carrying out a few each day. Japanese residents in Taipei complained that Sakuma's vengeance might cause an islandwide rebellion, and the Japanese media criticized his excess. Ninety-six execu-

[26] Maurice Meisner, "The Development of Formosan Nationalism," in Mancall, ed., *Formosa Today*, 164.

tions had been carried out before Tokyo ordered Sakuma to change the remainder of the death sentences to life imprisonment, using the coronation of the new Taisho emperor as a pretext for granting clemency. After the coronation ceremonies ended, Sakuma's government executed thirty-seven more Taiwanese allegedly implicated in a new anti-Japanese conspiracy before Sakuma was relieved of his post on May 1, 1915.[27]

Japanese Policies toward the Aborigines

The Japanese were much more interested than the previous Chinese administrations in surveying and controlling the entire island and its resources. This required an attempt to pacify the mountain-dwelling aborigines, who viewed the Japanese, as they had learned to view the Chinese, as enemies who sought to take aboriginal land. The preferred strategy of the Japanese authorities was to tame the aborigines through assimilation. This involved, where possible, disarming tribesmen who traditionally relied on hunting for their food supply and forcing them and their families to move down from the mountains into the plains to raise crops and animals. Aborigine families relocating from the mountains to planned agricultural communities often got some government assistance in building their new houses, which were simple huts. Much of the Paiwan and the traditionally agricultural Ami tribes were brought under the Japanese administration. Disarmed aborigines living in sedentary communities in the lowlands were obviously easier for the Japanese to regulate. Japanese success in assimilating aborigines was modest. By the 1930s, only about a quarter of the total aboriginal population of about 200,000 lived in such communities. The rest remained in the rugged mountainous areas, which the Japanese attempted to administer by posting specially trained police there. Spread thinly over a vast area, these policemen were often expected to act as teachers, social workers, and counselors as well as law enforcers to begin the process of preparing the natives to live in a society dominated by Japanese culture. The government built two hundred elementary schools and provided some job training and work opportunities for aborigines. When they resisted, the Japanese administration was inclined to rely on military campaigns and isolation rather than attempting to win aboriginal trust and support. Japanese troops went into the mountains and jungles to fight many battles with aboriginal tribesmen and destroyed scores of aboriginal villages, sometimes employing naval or air bombard-

---

[27] Kerr, *Licensed Revolution*, 106–107, 111–112.

ment. Unable to gain complete control over all the territory inhabited by aborigines, the Japanese sought to contain large tracts of aboriginal land behind deforested buffer zones monitored from guardhouses.[28]

Goto Shimpei, whom Governor-General Kodama Gentaro named director of the civil administration in 1898 and gave broad policy-making authority in nonmilitary matters, commissioned studies of the aborigines and asked for information from the United States about the American Indians. Perhaps the greatest success of Goto's policy was the agreement reached with the eight thousand Ami in the Taitung area, who were sedentary farmers. The Japanese brought in administrators, security personnel, and teachers and agreed to pay the Ami a monthly fee. As for the less accessible and unassimilated mountain aborigines, whose habitat at that time amounted to over half of Taiwan's total area, Goto sought to contain them by establishing a special police force that would limit entry into and exit out of their homelands. Goto intended that this area would gradually be reduced as more aborigines were assimilated.

Under Governor-General Sakuma Samata (1905–15), an army general who had spent much of his career repressing rebellion in Japan and Japanese-occupied China, the Japanese sought to exploit the forests the previous administration had walled off. This required a more aggressive policy against the mountain-dwelling aborigines upon whose homelands this logging would encroach. Japanese work crews were in danger of attack by Bunun and Atayal tribesmen unless they were under heavy guard. Seeking a permanent solution to resistance from the aborigines, Sakuma sent a force of about four thousand soldiers into the forests, concentrating on one region at a time, beginning in 1911. The goal of this campaign was to pacify or exterminate the inhabitants of forests slated for logging within five years. The tribesmen, armed only with simple weapons such as bows and spears and a few crude guns, relied on ambush and on their superior knowledge of the terrain. In some cases they employed avalanches or forest fires against isolated Japanese units. Suffering greater casualties than expected, Sakuma escalated his effort. The number of troops committed to the campaign rose to twelve thousand, and the Japanese attempted to bombard with aircraft and naval gunfire aborigine villages unreachable by troops. Japanese troops tried to terrorize the natives into submission through acts of brutality—hardly a stretch for the Japanese, who considered the aborigines little more than wild beasts. Japanese soldiers on occa-

[28] It is commonly reported that the Japanese authorities built an electrified fence around Taiwan's untamed forest areas to hold back hostile aborigines. Kerr (*Licensed Revolution*, 104–105) asserts that this is a myth based on brief, experimental, and unsuccessful Japanese attempts to protect their camps in east-central Taiwan by surrounding them with electrified barbed wire during Sakuma's antiaborigine drive of 1911–1915.

sion butchered captured and bound aborigine warriors before an audience of villagers. Indiscriminate destruction of entire villages and of all their residents was common. By 1915 Sakuma's campaign had pacified most of the aborigines in accessible areas, although many in remote villages remained defiant.[29]

Even in the areas in which the Japanese established a measure of control, resentment did not disappear. With their unchallenged authority, Japanese policemen often offended villagers by disregarding local language and customs, forcing local men to labor on government projects, and taking sexual liberties with local women. In the higher forest country, Japanese policemen and forest workers still occasionally disappeared, sometimes victims of headhunters. The last major aborigine uprising occurred in Musha village in the mountainous area near Taichung. When the provincial governor and other Japanese dignitaries gathered in the newly built village for a dedication ceremony on October 27, 1930, hundreds of aborigine warriors suddenly attacked, killing the governor and 196 other Japanese. The government responded with the usual military campaign of indiscriminate killing and destruction of aborigine villages implicated in the attack. The Japanese also reportedly used chemical and biological weapons against aborigines after the Musha uprising, foreshadowing the activities of the infamous "731 Unit" in Manchuria during the Pacific War.[30] Press reports in Japan of the atrocities committed by vengeful Japanese troops created enough outrage to force the resignation of both Governor-General Kamiyama Mannoshin and his chief civil administrator, Goto Fumio, in January 1931. But the policy of Kamiyama's replacement, Ota Masahiro, was similarly ruthless. Targeting certain tribes, he first disarmed them and then gave their aboriginal enemies free rein to destroy them. After more negative reports back in Japan, Ota was recalled in March 1932.

In sum, the Japanese administration carried on with its predecessors' twin tactics of assimilation and selective warfare. Some aborigines were simply victims of brutality. Others yielded to assimilation. Whether or not assimilated aborigines were better off depends on value judgments about aboriginal culture. For better or worse, the traditional ways of the more accessible tribes continued to lose ground to a lifestyle brought to Taiwan by outsiders. Many, nevertheless, remained largely unaffected by the Japanese presence, such as those in the rugged mountains of central Taiwan, or the sixteen hundred Yami on Lanyu Island, who were largely left alone,

[29] Kerr, *Licensed Revolution*, 103–105.

[30] Hsu Chieh-lin, "The Republic of China and Japan," in Yu San Wang, ed., *Foreign Policy of the Republic of China: An Unorthodox Approach* (New York: Praeger, 1990), 46–47.

except for a small police post to watch over them and a one-room school to teach a few Yami children some Japanese.

Taiwan during the War Years

Despite the potential damage to Taiwan's economy, the Japanese administration allowed those ethnic Chinese who so desired to leave Taiwan for the mainland after the outbreak of war between Japan and China in 1937, and some forty-six thousand took advantage of the opportunity. For those who remained, the Pacific War brought an intensification of the general effort to squeeze material benefits out of Taiwan. Many Japanese complained that Taiwanese were enjoying relative comfort and plenty while other Japanese were suffering great privations and sacrifice to protect the empire of which Taiwan was a part—an argument that made sense from the point of view of the increasingly hard-pressed Japanese, although absurd from Taiwan's standpoint. Pro-Japan indoctrination and propaganda increased in schools and workplaces. Recruitment of Taiwanese labor expanded through the *hoko* system. The Japanese administration also formed a new organization in 1940 called the Hokoku Seinentai (Patriotic Youth Corps) to generate volunteers for large construction projects. Individual Taiwanese citizens were pressed to contribute money, personal valuables, crops, and animals to the war effort, risking police harassment if they refused. Food and other goods were rationed so Taiwan could export more of its surplus to the Japanese home islands and to troops in the field. The government sent thousands of Taiwanese overseas to serve the empire as soldiers and laborers. Many aborigines were porters for Japanese troops fighting in the jungles of Southeast Asia. At home, the authorities recruited students to perform sentry duties in the countryside and on the coasts, with the result that many contracted dangerous diseases such as malaria and tuberculosis. Because of the stresses of war, including overwork, poorer nutrition, and the degradation of public health services, serious disease in general increased substantially on the island.

To balance against wartime privations and maintain the support of Taiwanese elites, limited political liberalization in 1940 led to most town and village assemblies being completely filled by elected Taiwanese. The Japanese government took more dramatic, though meaningless, steps toward political reform in a desperate attempt to marshal support during the last months prior to Tokyo's surrender to the Allied powers. The government announced Taiwan was to be upgraded from a colony to a prefecture and given representation in the Diet (five seats in the lower house and three in the upper house), and the collective responsibility system was finally abolished.

During the early part of the war, Taiwan was an important basing and staging area for Japanese military attacks against Canton and Hainan Island in China and Luzon in the Philippines. Later, as U.S. forces gained dominance of the western Pacific, Japanese bases and military facilities on Taiwan were subject to bombing, although U.S. planners decided not to attempt an invasion of the island. Several hundred Taiwanese died in U.S. bombing raids. The hope and desperation of the period were distilled in a story passed around the island that the goddess Matsu appeared in the sky during an attack by American aircraft and caught the falling bombs in her uplifted skirt.

Taiwanese responded enthusiastically to the opportunity to serve in the Japanese armed forces, which came with the expansion of the campaign in China in 1937. Indeed, until the Japanese resorted to general conscription on Taiwan in the last few months of the war, many more Taiwanese applied for service in the Imperial army and navy than the Japanese could take in. Many applications reportedly included statements of pro-Japan patriotism and respect for the Japanese military apparently written in the applicants' blood. Over 80,000 Taiwanese served Japan as soldiers and sailors during the war. Another 126,000 Taiwanese were employed by the Japanese military in noncombat roles (nurses, porters, interpreters, etc.). Some 30,300 lost their lives.[31] This enthusiasm for Japanese military service is partly a testament to the success of the colonial education system in inculcating pro-Japan values and attitudes among Taiwanese youth. These young Taiwanese may also have perceived that military service offered a chance to move from the status of colonial subjects to that of equals with the Japanese. And, of course, raised on glamorized stories of Japanese military gallantry and inevitable success, most recruits would not have anticipated the wretched fate that awaited their units during the latter stages and aftermath of the Pacific War.

It is noteworthy that in the weeks between Tokyo's surrender to the Allied forces and the arrival of a new Chinese government on Taiwan, the lame-duck Japanese administration continued to maintain public order aside from a few assaults on Japanese policemen, Japanese civilians, and Taiwanese collaborators.

An Ambivalent Legacy

The Japanese colonial administration's primary aim was to make Taiwan efficiently and productively serviceable to Japanese interests. Its poli-

---

[31] Chou Wan-yao, "Jihpen tsai T'aichunshih tungyuan yu T'aiwanjen ti haiwai ts'anchan chingyen, 1937–1945," *T'aiwan shih yenchiu* 2, no. 1 (June 1995): 93–96.

cies degraded some aspects of Taiwanese individual security, but enhanced others. Although Japanese rule in Taiwan was not as brutal as in Korea or Manchuria, most Japanese saw the Chinese and aborigines as inferior races, and Japanese officials from the military governor-general down were deeply steeped in an authoritarian political tradition. Japanese residents in Taiwan had privileges over the locals in all aspects of life, including employment, education, and lifestyle. Taiwanese had little hope of reaching high positions in business or government. Taiwan's people suffered harsh suppression of dissent, official attempts to destroy some aspects of local culture, general discrimination in pursuit of the good life, and countless individual cases of mistreatment and exploitation. The Japanese punished lawbreakers severely, used the death penalty liberally, and sometimes applied legal decrees retroactively.

Self-serving colonialist intentions, however, did not necessarily preclude mutually beneficial effects in some areas, particularly those related to modernization and economic development. With a view, of course, toward supporting Taiwan's contribution to the Japanese economy, the colonial administration made significant improvements in public order and welfare and provided some Taiwanese with economic and advanced training opportunities. Socioeconomic progress was evidenced by the growth in Taiwan's population during the Japanese occupation from 2.5 million to 6 million, even though the island was closed to immigration from China. The value of Taiwan's agricultural output more than tripled during the Japanese occupation. Although the economic gains of most of this bounty went to Japanese businessmen and other parts of the empire rather than to the Taiwanese, Taiwan's standard of living was higher than that of any province in mainland China. The real value of Taiwan's foreign trade increased sixteenfold between 1897 and 1939.[32] Corruption among high Japanese officials was low compared with previous and future Chinese administrations.

The ambivalence of the colonial era makes it difficult to argue with the assertion some Taiwanese nationalists would later make that Taiwan was no worse off under the Japanese occupation than it would have been as a province of the mainland during the same period. The next phase of Taiwan's history would show that if Japanese authorities could be exploitative and heavy-handed, so could those from China.

[32] Ballantine, *Formosa*, 44.

*

The Return of Mainland Rule

The mainland had undergone tremendous political upheaval during the five decades Taiwan was ruled by Japan. A revolution in 1911 swept away the Qing dynasty regime that had ceded Taiwan to Tokyo and established the Republic of China. The new regime, however, proved unable to control the whole country despite its inclination toward authoritarianism—a bitter disappointment to political activists who had hoped for a revitalized government dedicated to helping China overcome its internal weaknesses and resist foreign intrusions. China devolved into a collection of kingdoms ruled by "warlords," local strongmen with their own armies, while choice areas remained foreign concessions. The nationalist leader Dr. Sun Yat-sen, honored today in both Taiwan and the PRC as one of the founders of modern China, revived the Kuomintang (Nationalist Party or KMT; originally established in 1912) in 1914. Sun called for rejuvenation of China in three stages: (1) reunification of China through a military campaign; (2) a period of "tutelage" under the dictatorship of the Kuomintang; and (3) the institution of a constitutional government. Originally open to Communists as well as noncommunists, the party was reorganized with the assistance of Bolshevik advisors. Ironically, the KMT would retain many structural similarities to the Communist Party of the Soviet Union even after the former became resolutely anticommunist.

After Sun's death in 1925, his deputy Chiang Kai-shek inherited leadership of the KMT. Starting from his base in Canton, Chiang led the KMT's armies on a Northern Expedition that nominally unified the country under his party's rule in 1928. During this campaign Chiang turned against the Communists, purging them from the KMT and expelling the party's Russian advisers. Chiang's next objective was extermination of the nascent Chinese Communist Party (CCP). During the 1930s, KMT troops severely weakened but failed to completely destroy CCP forces before the Japanese invasion forced a suspension of Chiang's "bandit suppression campaigns." Japanese forces conquered the major cities of eastern China. The brutality and atrocities that followed Japanese soldiers and the belief that some Chinese put political or economic self-interest over patriotism made the war all the more bitter. Along with millions killed and vast destruction on the Chinese mainland, the Pacific War intensified anti-Japanese sentiment and reaffirmed the belief that China needed to strengthen itself against molestation from abroad. In this context it is not surprising that Chiang's government insisted that sovereignty over Taiwan, a Chinese territory taken by imperialist Japan at a time of Chinese weakness, belonged to the Republic of China. The other Allied powers then at war with Japan, the United States and Britain, accepted the ROC position. The 1943 Cairo Declaration endorsed by Chiang, U.S. president Franklin Roosevelt, and British prime minister Winston Churchill specified that "all the territories Japan has stolen from the Chinese, such as Manchuria, Formosa, and the Pescadores, shall be restored to the Republic of China."

A Clash of Expectations

The mainland's determination to regain Taiwan did not necessarily imply acceptance of Taiwan's people as full-fledged compatriots. Even when Taiwan was part of the Chinese Empire, Mainlanders had regarded the Taiwanese as semiferal Chinese. More seriously, five decades of heavy Japanese influence created suspicions about the depth of Chinese patriotism on Taiwan. The Japanese campaign in China left Mainlanders deeply hostile toward all vestiges of Japanese influence. Chinese in northern China, which had been occupied by the Japanese for a much shorter period than Taiwan, were treated as "traitors" and "collaborators" by KMT forces reasserting control after the Japanese surrender. In the minds of Mainlanders, therefore, the most salient feature of the Japanese occupation of Taiwan was the systematic effort by colonial authorities to turn the hearts and minds of Taiwanese against China. A representative article in a KMT publication of 1946 noted the need for "re-educating" the Taiwanese, who had been "poisoned intellectually and were forced to accept twisted notions."[1] Mainlanders also found that substantial numbers of Taiwanese elites had prospered economically under Japanese rule, which

---

[1] *New Taiwan Monthly*, September 1946, 1–3; Maurice Meisner, "The Development of Formosan Nationalism," in Mark Mancall, ed., *Formosa Today* (New York: Praeger, 1964), 154.

was easily perceived as evidence of widespread collaboration. Additionally, many Mainlanders had developed negative attitudes toward Taiwanese through personal contact before and during the Pacific War. The Japanese government recruited Taiwanese to operate as agents in southeastern China. Because of Japan's extraterritoriality rights in China, these Taiwanese, officially subjects of the Japanese Empire, could take advantage of virtual immunity for their self-serving activities in China, generating resentment in the communities within which they worked.

Thus while some Mainlanders crossed the strait carrying brotherly and charitable attitudes the Taiwanese would have welcomed, in general Mainlanders brought to Taiwan a sense of superiority, a belief that Taiwan had been corrupted by Japanese thinking, and demands for Taiwanese respect, gratitude, and willingness to help strengthen the Republic of China.

Taiwanese had a different interpretation of the Japanese colonial period's significance. While they resented the discrimination and restrictions on their political power that were part of the Japanese occupation, many Taiwanese also believed Japanese rule had helped Taiwan advance economically, politically, and socially relative to the backward, chaotic mainland. The Taiwanese therefore had their own sense of superiority. Taiwanese often played up the positive consequences of the colonial experience, such as the economic and political development that took place under Japanese rule. The Japanese education system and Japanese economic policies, which promoted a degree of prosperity and urbanization and the beginnings of a Taiwanese middle class,[2] had eroded communal loyalties and thus facilitated the growth of a sense of Taiwanese nationhood. Taiwanese political culture had been refined through exposure to Japanese liberal ideas and Wilsonianism during the 1920s and through the experience of their own campaign of several decades to wrest greater autonomy from the Japanese administration. Their high levels of education and political maturity supported Taiwanese demands for autonomy (although most demanded autonomy under the auspices of the ROC central government, not outright independence). Taiwanese politicians and activists frequently criticized KMT economic and social policies and the prevalence of corruption in the Mainlander government by pointing to favorable Japanese performance. From the perspective of the Taiwanese, Mainlanders were too quick to judge them as having been "Japanized" and underappreciative of Taiwan's anticolonial activism, which often entailed great risks and sacrifices. And as some Taiwanese commentators reminded the Mainlanders, it was the Chinese government that had originally given Taiwan over to Japanese rule. One writer, Wang Pai-yuan,

---

[2] Meisner, "Formosan Nationalism," 153.

cleverly argued that Taiwanese had not been compromised by Japanese rule any more so than had mainland Chinese by two and a half centuries under the Qing dynasty, a regime that was ethnic Manchu.[3] Lin Hsien-t'ang and others continued to campaign for a form of self-rule while attempting to allay the fears of Mainlanders. Lin suggested that China's government be reorganized as a confederation of self-governing provinces, but emphasized that this did not imply an exclusion of Mainlanders from Taiwan.[4]

The Arrival of the Mainland Government

By all accounts, most Taiwanese welcomed the reinstitution of Chinese rule following the Japanese surrender. Although Taiwan had never been part of the Republic of China, only a small minority of Taiwanese favored independence or a United Nations trusteeship immediately after the war.[5] Some elements of the Japanese administration had taken steps during the last days of their occupation to sabotage China's reincorporation of Taiwan, arming groups of Taiwanese nationalists and encouraging them to rally local support for independence from China. After finding little success, these provocateurs fled to Japan.[6]

A large segment of Taiwanese elites had prospered under the Japanese regime and faced the possibility of harder times under the new Chinese government; many of these, nonetheless, voiced support for Taiwan's unification with the ROC. Lin and other prominent Taiwanese formed the Preparatory Committee to Welcome the Nationalist Government. At least some probably hoped their outspoken Chinese patriotism would protect them against being called out as collaborators.

Taiwanese disillusionment with the return of Chinese rule began with the arrival of ROC troops in October 1945. A crowd estimated at 300,000 greeted the soldiers entering Taipei.[7] Over the next several weeks ROC soldiers would disarm the Japanese and move both military personnel and Japanese civilians into camps pending their repatriation. Landing with a small advance group, General Keh King-en betrayed a prevalent Mainlander attitude during a public address, referring to Taiwan as "be-

[3] Wang Pai-yuan, "Kao Waishengren chugong," *Zhengjingbao* 2, no. 2 (Jan. 25, 1946): 1–2.

[4] "Dui Shichu Fabiao Zhengjian," *Taiwan Pinglun* 1, no. 3 (Sept. 1, 1946): 6–9.

[5] Some Taiwanese commentators dispute this, arguing that proindependence sentiment was widespread even at this early stage. See, for example, Peng Ming-min, *A Taste of Freedom: Memoirs of a Formosan Independence Leader* (New York: Holt, Rinehart and Winston, 1972).

[6] W.G. Goddard, *Formosa: A Study in Chinese History* (West Lansing: Michigan State University Press, 1966), 177.

[7] Li Hsiao-feng, *Taiwan Minchu Yundung Ssushih Nien* (Taipei: Tuli Wanbao, 1987), 27.

yond the passes" (*kuan wai*, meaning outside the pale of Chinese civilization) and a "degraded territory" and calling the Taiwanese "a degraded people."[8] The locals found the ROC soldiers, some forty-eight thousand of whom arrived on Taiwan within about a year of the Japanese surrender, generally ill-disciplined, poorly educated, and unkempt. Most were from rural areas in Chinese provinces that were far less economically developed than Taiwan. There were abundant anecdotes illustrating the prevailing Taiwanese view that these troops were *t'u baotse* ("hicks"): crowds of soldiers staring in amazement at an elevator in a downtown Taipei department store, soldiers walking along the roads carrying stolen bicycles strapped to their backs, signals corpsmen laying telephone wires across railroad tracks. Chinese troops were also poorly paid; even with enhanced pay for serving "overseas" on Taiwan, they earned the equivalent of about thirty-three dollars per year. With the effects of postwar inflation, a soldier could not possibly subsist on his official pay. Rather, KMT troops were expected to make their living by scrounging and plundering among the local civilian community, following the pattern of Chiang's armies on the mainland. George Kerr writes that by the end of 1945 "Chinese soldiers had overrun schools, temples and hospitals at Taipei and it took most of the year 1946 to get them out. Any building occupied by KMT troops became a mere shell." An example was the Mackay Mission Memorial Hospital, which was "stripped of its equipment and all metal fixtures, including doorknobs. Many of the wooden doors, door-frames and stair banisters were used by the soldiers to feed cooking fires built on the concrete floors."[9] Casual looting and theft by ROC soldiers was widespread. Their officers had the means to carry out larger-scale pilfering. Gangs under the command of ROC officers forced their way into and looted many private residences. Often these homes were virtually emptied. This practice began among the expatriate Japanese community, which numbered about 300,000 civilians, but soon spread to the homes of native Taiwanese. Some KMT officers organized large-scale removal of confiscated Taiwanese property off the island, including requisitioned Japanese trucks for transport, collection depots, and dockside agents charged with overseeing the loading of these goods on ships bound for the mainland.

Much of this activity clearly fell into the category of "carpet-bagging;" Taiwanese certainly saw it this way. But again, one must bear in mind the Mainlander premises that underlay this behavior: that Taiwan owed a profound debt to the KMT armies that had secured its liberation from the Japanese, and that Taiwanese had a patriotic duty to contribute to the sus-

[8] George H. Kerr, *Formosa Betrayed* (Boston: Houghton Mifflin, 1965), 72.
[9] Ibid., 102.

tenance of Chinese troops on the island and to the reconstruction of mainland China and its defense against Communist insurgents. Such attitudes contributed to a climate of tolerance toward plunder and even blurred the distinction between carpet-bagging and the more legitimate project of transferring resources to mainland provinces where they were badly needed.

The New Administration and Its Policies

Residents of Taiwan expected Chiang would make the island a province of China. To their disappointment, he put Taiwan under military government, a status associated with conquered enemy territory. The first governor-general of the Taiwan Provincial Administration, and concurrent Taiwan garrison commander, was Chen Yi. Like Chiang Kai-shek, Chen Yi hailed from Zhejiang Province. He had won Chiang's patronage during the Northern Expedition while a lieutenant of the warlord Sung Chuan-fang in Zhejiang. In 1927, after negotiating behind Sung's back, Chen Yi defected to the KMT side. Chiang rewarded him with a series of government posts: director of the Shanghai Arsenal, vice minister of war, and in 1934 governor of Fujian Province. In the latter position Chen Yi accepted the ignoble task of hunting down and destroying the "rebel" Nineteenth Route Army. This unit had distinguished itself in combat as perhaps the best in China during a battle with Japanese troops in Shanghai in 1932. The unit's commanders, however, were not Chiang's protégés. He ordered the Nineteenth Route Army to disband. They refused, fleeing into the mountains near the Zhejiang coast, where their isolation from resupply helped Chen Yi accomplish his objective. He had substantial Japanese connections and cooperated with Japanese officials and military officers on several occasions. Chen Yi was a 1907 graduate of the Japanese army's Rikugun Shikan Gakko academy, spoke Japanese fluently, and had a Japanese wife, who became known as the "First Lady of Fujian." In 1935, as a guest of the Japanese government, he attended a celebration in Taipei of forty years of Japanese rule over Taiwan. While governor of Fujian, Chen Yi facilitated economic links between China and Japan, even after the Japanese military campaign against China began in 1937. Prior to occupying the provincial capital, Fuzhou, in 1942, the Japanese forces reportedly allowed Chen and his property safe passage out of the city. Chen Yi's governorship also saw him promote an economic policy termed "Necessary State Socialism," which involved the formation of extensive state-run monopolies and strangled thousands of small businesses. Critics also accused his Fujian administration of pervasive corruption and ruthless suppression of dissent through torture and summary execution. In fairness to Chen Yi, charges such as collaboration with the Japanese, a misguided preference for statist economic policies over the free market, failing to stamp out corruption, and intolerance of dissent have been leveled at many KMT officials of his era.

Chiang named Chen Yi to head the Taiwan Investigative Committee, under the auspices of the Central Statistical Bureau, in April 1944. Chen Yi came to Taiwan as governor-general on October 24, 1945. Whether or not he personally abused his position for financial gain, his administration in Taiwan was infamous for its widespread corruption and nepotism. He also developed a reputation for arrogance among Taiwan's people. Chen Yi insisted on speaking only in Mandarin, for example, even though most of his subjects spoke Japanese well but had a poor grasp of Mandarin. He rarely met with Taiwanese community leaders to discuss their concerns.

Not all Mainlander civil servants on Taiwan were rapacious, of course. Mainlanders disputed their negative stereotyping by Taiwanese just as Taiwanese resented being summarily judged as unpatriotic collaborators. A Mainlander who served as an official on Taiwan remembers, "When the Mainland public servants first came to Taiwan, their purpose was not to make money. The majority had the spirit of performing public service, and they wanted to strive for the reconstruction of Taiwan. . . . The Mainland public servants did not enjoy a good life. . . . Their work, compared with similar duties on the Mainland, was more tension-ridden. They unconditionally gave everything to serve the Taiwanese." Referring to the February 28 incident (details of which are given later in this chapter), he asks bitterly, "Among the thousands of wounded and dead Mainlanders, how many were corrupt officials? How many were villains?"[10]

Nevertheless, Taiwanese found that many of the Mainlander officials and their relatives who followed the ROC soldiers to Taiwan were equally interested in extracting the island's wealth. Ostensibly, much of this activity was designed to speed economic reconstruction on the comparatively poor and war-ravaged Mainland. Taiwanese understandably saw it as state-sponsored looting. A Taiwanese activist complained of this period, "When a Chinese with some influence wanted a particular property, he had only to accuse a Formosan of being a collaborationist during the past 50 years of Japanese sovereignty."[11] Whole plants were dismantled and sent back to the mainland, along with pieces of the island's infrastructure

[10] Huang Hsu-tung, "Erh-erh-pa shih-pien ssu-t'ung-lu," *Erh-erh-pa chen-hsiang* (n.d., n.p.), 191, 64; Lai Tse-Han, Ramon H. Myers, and Wei Wou, *A Tragic Beginning: The Taiwan Uprising of February 28, 1947* (Stanford, Calif.: Stanford University Press), 95.

[11] Peng Ming-min, *A Taste of Freedom: Memoirs of a Formosan Independence Leader* (New York: Holt, Rinehart and Winston, 1972), 54.

that might be transplanted or sold as scrap: telephone wires, pipes, metal roofing, fire hydrants, railroad switches, and so on. Goods and items of nearly every kind could be sold at inflated prices in Shanghai's voracious markets. By November 1945 Chinese officials had commandeered all of Taipei's garbage trucks for hauling confiscated property to the docks, while uncollected garbage piled up in streets throughout the city.[12] Taiwanese observed that Mainlander soldiers and officials sometimes refused to pay for their purchases or stand in lines. Mainlanders tended to settle into the neighborhoods where Japanese had formerly lived, reinforcing the image of Mainlanders as the new colonialists. A common local aphorism of the day was "Dogs go and pigs come." The idea was that dogs, representing the Japanese administration, were fearsome, but at least they protected people's property. The incoming Mainlander "pigs," on the other hand, offered nothing but a large appetite. The old expression "passing the five sections of the Imperial exam" (*wu zi deng ke*) was also jokingly employed as a reference to the five things for which mainland officials in Taiwan lusted: cars, houses, gold, high rank, and women.

Mainlanders dominated Chen Yi's government. Of the first twenty-three mayors and county magistrates in postwar Taiwan, three were Taiwanese. Among the twenty-one most important officials in the first provincial government, only one was Taiwanese.[13] Mainlanders also took over a disproportionate share of medium- and lower-level government jobs. Mainlander officials earned higher salaries than their Taiwanese counterparts. To Mainlanders, their domination of government jobs was justified by the lack of qualified Taiwanese personnel—that is, those who had administrative experience, could speak Mandarin fluently, and were untainted by collaboration. At the same time financial constraints due to China's postwar economic weakness kept the ROC's bureaucracy on Taiwan small; Chen Yi's regime employed only about half the number of officials the Japanese colonial administration had maintained. With fewer posts available and more of them going to Mainlanders, about thirty-six thousand Taiwanese civil servants lost their jobs under the Chen Yi's administration.[14] Compounding the resentment of educated Taiwanese was the fact that despite the general policy of repatriating Japanese residents of Taiwan, Chen Yi's government continued to employ some Japanese administrators and technical experts.

Most of Chen Yi's police force, as well, were Mainlanders. The expecta-

[12] Kerr, *Formosa Betrayed*, 100.

[13] Steven Phillips, "Between Assimilation and Independence: Taiwanese Political Aspirations under Nationalist Chinese Rule, 1945–1948," in Murray A. Rubinstein, ed., *Taiwan: A New History* (Armonk, N.Y.: M.E. Sharpe, 1999), 287.

[14] Lai, Myers, and Wei, *Tragic Beginning*, 65.

tion of bribes made the police an attractive profession to men whose desires had nothing to do with protecting and serving the public. There were countless incidents of police corruption and incompetence. In Taipei, it was clear that the police and *loma* ("tiger eel") criminal gangs often coordinated their activities. The new government also proved less adept at administering the surveillance and registration systems inherited from the Japanese. A few months after the institution of ROC rule, "Citizens' Freedom Safeguarding Committees" began to form in reaction to the ineffectiveness of the police forces run by the mainland authorities. Overall, serious crime greatly increased relative to the Japanese colonial era.

Chen Yi's first director of public health, T. S. King, epitomized several of the faults Taiwanese saw among officials of the KMT regime. King headed a pharmaceutical company in Shanghai but had no prior experience in public health administration. On the side he continued to supervise a drug manufacturing and distribution firm of which Chen Yi was a financial beneficiary. A conflict of interest developed between King's public duties and his private business activities. Drug sales could produce huge profits, especially if the market was manipulated through the powerful controls that went with King's directorate. King restricted, for example, the release of 45 million antimalaria Atabrine tablets, supplied to Taiwan from overseas, to preclude competition with his own company's quinine. King's office failed to maintain Japan's effective quarantine system. Cholera and the bubonic plague had been unknown on Taiwan for decades, but in 1946 they reappeared. During the cholera outbreak, centered in Tainan, government-owned hospitals refused to increase the issue of medical supplies or to treat cholera patients admitted outside the normal working hours of 8:00 A.M. to 5:00 P.M. When United Nations medical personnel discovered sewage from the cholera wards was being dumped into ponds that were commercially fished, they asked King to stop the dumping and suspend the sale of fish from the polluted ponds. He declined, reportedly remarking, "After all, only the poor people are contracting the disease."[15]

Taiwan's postwar economy was in a recession. Damage resulting from overexertion and U.S. bombing raids during the last months of the war had depressed industrial output, causing unemployment that was worsened by the return of about 100,000 Taiwanese from abroad. The islanders hoped the new ROC administration would both revitalize the economy and provide greater opportunities for Taiwanese private enterprise. The Chen Yi government, however, disappointed Taiwanese on both counts.

As he had while governing Fujian, Chen Yi eschewed the free market

[15] Kerr, *Formosa Betrayed*, 179–180.

for a socialist approach that established government-controlled monopolies over most of the island's products. He argued that government ownership of industry was preferable to private ownership because the state would use its profits to increase overall quality of life for the public as a whole, instead of enriching a few upper-class families. Some 90 percent of Taiwan's economy came under the government's control—more than during the Japanese occupation.[16] Chen Yi's socialism left little scope for the Taiwanese business people who had hoped to fill the vacuum in Taiwan's economy left by the departure of privileged Japanese. The Chinese administration placed all major Taiwanese industries and enterprises under the supervision of state commissions, which were inevitably staffed by Mainlanders. This afforded immense opportunities for high-ranking officials to get rich through their control of taxes, regulations, and the sale of licenses. The government's monopolies over a broad range of goods and services also allowed officials to create shortages, which drove up prices. Officials then sold the products they controlled on the black market for a handsome profit. Although ultimately state-owned, firms were run as private businesses, with the commissioners overseeing the formation of boards of directors and other management organs. Officials of Chen Yi's government frequently named themselves, their relatives, and their friends to these positions. Many of the authorities thus held both prestigious public posts and lucrative private management positions. The latter could establish their own salaries and perks, including bonuses for serving "overseas," while enjoying insider trading privileges.

The Mainlanders who flocked to Taiwan hoping to make their fortune were generally concerned with quick profits. Few planned to stay in Taiwan permanently. Numerous factories and businesses, therefore, were liquidated and their assets sold off piecemeal by impatient Mainlander managers.

Price inflation became a serious problem, largely because Chen Yi's attempts to protect Taiwan from the economic turmoil on the mainland (such as continuing to use the older local scrip rather than mainland currency) were unsuccessful, and also because his government increased the money supply to make up a shortfall in tax revenue.

Rice production fell, contributing to rice shortages. Taiwan's agricultural output in 1946 was only slightly more than it had been in 1910.[17] Following the Chinese takeover in October 1945, the amount of cultivated land fell from 2.1 to 1.78 million acres. There were three reasons for the reduction. First, the ROC authorities set aside large amounts of farmland for

---

[16] "Formosa in Transition," *The World Today* 4 (May 1948): 213.

[17] Keith Maguire, *The Rise of Modern Taiwan* (Aldershot, U.K.: Ashgate, 1998), 51

the construction of airfields. Second, irrigation works fell into disrepair due to lack of regular maintenance. Third, fertilizer was no longer being supplied from Japan. The rice crop in 1945 amounted to only 640,000 metric tons, compared to 1.4 million metric tons in 1938.[18] Yet Taiwan continued to export rice to the mainland. Taiwanese sold their rice, along with coal and other primary products, to exporters at relatively low fixed prices. Shipped across the strait to Chinese ports, these products brought huge profits. The Chinese military authorities had inherited large stockpiles of food from the Japanese, but transferred much of it the mainland despite the island's shortfall of rice in 1946. Chen Yi publicly blamed the rice shortage on private hoarding. He began a program of searching private premises for stockpiled rice. Imported gangsters were involved, and many abuses resulted from the enlarged powers of search and seizure the program entailed. Chen also ordered wealthy, educated Taiwanese to serve as heads of the local rice collection committees; this helped divide the population against itself and may have been intended to discredit the Taiwanese middle class, the principal source of articulate opposition to KMT rule.[19]

The disposition of Japanese property in Taiwan confiscated by the ROC government became a major source of Taiwanese resentment. Here, again, Mainlanders and Taiwanese had fundamentally different assumptions. Taiwanese felt this property had been stolen from them, and they expected it to be returned. In the eyes of Mainlanders, this property was spoils of war, and using it to generate income to pay the salaries of Mainlander officials on Taiwan was legitimate.[20] In practice, Mainlanders in powerful positions simply embezzled much of this confiscated property. After the war ended, Japanese in Taiwan had begun selling off their assets to Taiwanese. With the reinstitution of mainland government, however, a court case in Tainan established that transfers of Japanese property made after August 15, 1945, were invalid. The Taiwan High Court reaffirmed this decision in December 1948. Ownership of invalidly transferred property reverted to the ROC government.[21] In February 1947, Chen Yi created further outcry among the locals when he announced a policy for the auctioning off of confiscated Japanese property under terms that severely disadvantaged potential Taiwanese buyers relative to Mainlanders.

In January 1946, Chen Yi announced that the government would begin drafting Taiwanese for military service in the war against the Communist

---

[18] Fred W. Riggs, *Formosa under Chinese Nationalist Rule* (New York: Octagon, 1972), 70.
[19] Kerr, *Formosa Betrayed*, 108–109.
[20] Lai, Myers, and Wei, *Tragic Beginning*, 73, 75.
[21] Phillips, "Between Assimilation," 298.

armies on the mainland. Taiwanese were willing to supply manpower for an island defense force, but strongly opposed their young men being sent far from home to join the ragtag army fighting Chiang Kai-shek's war. The public outcry forced Chen Yi to abandon the idea. At the same time, the ROC government showed little sympathy for the plight of Taiwanese who had worked for the Japanese armed forces, even in noncombat roles, and had been left stranded by the Japanese surrender. Many of these Taiwanese were repatriated only with the intervention and funding of the United Nations Relief and Rehabilitation Administration.

Despite the objections of some of his staff, Chen Yi carried out elections in April 1946 that increased Taiwanese political representation. This might have reflected Chen Yi's interpretation of Sun Yat-sen's doctrine of "democracy," or perhaps was intended to mollify Taiwanese resentment over their reduced opportunities for public sector jobs.[22] All Taiwanese over the age of twenty who registered to vote and took an oath "to support the Kuomintang government" were eligible to vote. To run for office, however, a Taiwanese had to secure approval from the local government office. There was no recourse for appeal in the case of rejected applications. Nevertheless, outspoken Taiwanese nationalists were among those elected to assemblies at the provincial, district, city, and town levels. The number of Taiwanese serving in local government positions tripled as compared with the Japanese occupation period. The first session of the Taiwan Provincial Assembly opened in May 1946 and featured lively debate. Assembly members enjoyed the right to ask probing questions of high government officials. General Ko Yuanfeng of the Taiwan garrison, for example, was bombarded with charges of misconduct by his troops against civilians and reportedly walked out of the meeting in a rage. Mainlanders complained that some of the Taiwanese assembly members behaved irresponsibly, speaking excessively loudly and discourteously and interrupting other speakers. Overall, the Provincial Assembly meetings served more to highlight hostility between the government and the Taiwanese community than to promote reconciliation.

Perhaps as a corollary to his views on implementing grass-roots democracy, Chen Yi allowed the Taiwanese press comparatively broad freedom during the first months of his administration. Vigorous reporting of government corruption and mismanagement thus contributed to Taiwanese discontent with KMT rule. Indeed, reportage critical of the government was often overly simplistic and unbalanced.[23] A relatively restrained ex-

[22] Lai, Myers and Wei, *Tragic Beginning*, 59–60, 67–68.
[23] Ibid., 77.

ample, aimed at gaining the attention and favor of visiting Generalissimo Chiang and his wife, was a *Min Bao* editorial of October 28, 1946:

> Many of [the Governor's] men are corrupt. The increasing number of unemployed indicates that a social crisis is approaching, followed by a political and economic crisis. Every day we see youths looking for jobs while all positions high and low are filled by strangers. News of robbery and theft is ever-present in the papers, and we even hear that some of the brothers from the mainland have organized looting parties.[24]

Arrests and harassment of journalists critical of the government began in mid-1946, and state control of the press stiffened permanently after the February 28 incident.

By early 1947, then, several developments had caused a deep reservoir of Taiwanese discontent with the new regime. These included the perception that Mainlanders were chiefly interested in draining the island's wealth and resources, and by their presence had reduced Taiwanese opportunities for desirable government jobs. Other important contributory causes included Taiwanese dissatisfaction with the government's policy on transferring confiscated Japanese property; the mainland government's inability to address Taiwan's postwar economic problems; corruption and other types of misbehavior by Mainlander officials and soldiers; and sustained criticism of the Chen Yi regime by the Taiwanese press. As in previous episodes of Taiwan's history, when pubic disaffection was high, a small incident could set off an explosion of turmoil and violence.

The February 28 Incident and Its Aftermath

On February 27, 1947, a widow named Lin Chiang-mai was selling cigarettes from a small stand in a Taipei park. Two agents from the Monopoly Bureau seized her goods and cash. When she resisted, drawing the attention of onlookers, one of the agents struck her head with his pistol. An angry crowd formed and menaced the agents. One fired his gun to create an escape route, fatally wounding a bystander. After the agents fled, the crowd burned their truck and its contents. The next day, the date from which the incident (known in Chinese as the "2-2-8 incident") takes it name, a group of about two thousand demonstrators walked from the park to the headquarters of the Monopoly Bureau. They carried placards

[24] Kerr, *Formosa Betrayed*, 218.

and a petition demanding the execution of the agents, the resignation of the bureau director, and revision of the monopoly regulations. Finding the bureau gates closed and heavily guarded, the protestors decided to continue to the governor-general's office. When they approached the gates at around noon, guards fired on them. Two died and several others were wounded. In another part of town, a mob beat to death two Monopoly Bureau agents who had allegedly mistreated two children they caught selling cigarettes, then sacked a nearby bureau office. A radio station reported briefly that a demonstration was taking place, and throughout Taipei crowds took to the streets. Within two days the same was occurring in other cities throughout the island. Some young Taiwanese men who had received Japanese military training took to the streets wearing their old uniforms and singing Japanese martial songs.

With the resumption of the Chinese Civil War, the government had moved badly needed troops from Taiwan back to the mainland. During 1946, therefore, the number of soldiers and police on Taiwan had shrunk from forty-eight thousand to eleven thousand.[25] This was too small a force to control the crowds, who took control of Taiwan's nine largest cities. Chen Yi's administration had effective control over only a few government-owned buildings and compounds. Many Mainlanders, including police and soldiers, came under attack by Taiwanese mobs. Some Taiwanese uncovered civilian Mainlanders by speaking Japanese to people they met on the streets. Threatened by a mob, Hakka writer Tai Kuo-hui reported that since he could not speak the Fujianese dialect, he resorted to singing the Japanese national anthem to prove he was not a Mainlander.[26] About a thousand Mainlanders were killed or injured.[27] Mainland Chinese went into hiding, barricaded themselves inside government buildings and police stations, or relocated to a heavily guarded camp set up in north Taipei. In urban areas throughout Taiwan local elites formed their own committees to temporarily fulfill the functions of government, such as preserving public order and maintaining transportation and communication services, often in cooperation with youth organizations.

Chen Yi was compelled to open negotiations with an unofficial, hastily formed Committee to Settle the Monopoly Bureau Incident, which Lin Hsien-t'ang helped organize. In light of the KMT's subsequent interpretations of the incident, it is notable that that the Taiwanese members of the Committee's Executive Group were all prominent citizens, mainly busi-

[25] Lai, Myers, and Wei, *Tragic Beginning*, 7.

[26] Christopher Hughes, *Taiwan and Chinese Nationalism: National Identity and Status in International Society* (New York: Routledge, 1997), 28.

[27] Lai, Myers, and Wei, *Tragic Beginning*, 141.

nessmen and professionals, and included members of the Taipei City Council, the Taiwan Provincial Assembly, and other government-approved organizations. The demands of Taiwanese elites on the Settlement Committee grew during the course of these negotiations. Initially they called for measures specifically related to the events of the previous few days: punishment of the police involved in the altercation that sparked the rioting, compensation for its victims, and amnesty for Taiwanese who had been arrested. On March 2, Chen Yi publicly agreed to restitution and amnesty and promised just punishment of the guilty authorities.

In subsequent talks, however, the Settlement Committee called for political reforms that would strengthen self-rule. Their escalation culminated on March 7 in what became known as the "Thirty-two Demands." The first ten items called for Taiwan's autonomy as a province within the ROC; Taiwanese filling the majority of the commissioner positions; an electoral procedure over which Taiwanese would have more control; freedoms of speech, the press, and assembly; and the right to strike. The next seven demands stipulated disbanding the independent police forces attached to government agencies, which had an especially notorious reputation for corruption; filling important police leadership posts and judgeships on Taiwan with Taiwanese; and outlawing politically motivated detention. A set of six demands sought economic reforms, including the replacement of a variety of specific taxes with a uniform progressive income tax; Taiwanese directors for public enterprises; greater Taiwanese control over the management of formerly Japanese properties on Taiwan; and abolishment of the Monopoly and Trading bureaus. Further demands aimed to restrict the powers of soldiers over civilians, abolish the ROC garrison command on the island, require the Chinese government to pay for food supplies shipped from Taiwan to the mainland, secure the release from prison of wealthy Taiwanese being held (and extorted) as collaborators, and guarantee the equal rights of aborigines.

Chen reacted angrily to the demands, and a military police commander, Chang Mu-t'ao, warned the Settlement Committee that the central government would regard the attempt to dismantle the Taiwan garrison command as insurrection. At the next day's (March 8) session, the committee softened its position and retracted the boldest provisions. At the same time, however, other Taiwanese were calling for more drastic reforms and even for an armed uprising. But the discussion soon became academic.

Fighting between KMT and CCP forces had resumed on the mainland in early 1947 following the failure of negotiations for a coalition government. By the beginning of March, communist troops were close to capturing the city of Changchun. This context added alarm and urgency to the appearance of an insurrection in a KMT-controlled area. By March 5, Chiang had concluded Taiwan was in the midst of an antigovernment rebellion and had decided to send troops from the mainland to restore central government control. The next day Chen Yi requested reinforcements.[28] In a radio address, Chen Yi denounced the Settlement Committee as "rebellious," reinstituted martial law, and explained that a group of troublemakers had been exploiting the atmosphere created by the February 28 incident to carry out plunder and sedition. The mission of the troops from the mainland was to restore public safety, he said. A speech by Chiang in Nanjing on March 10, which was later printed on leaflets that were airdropped on Taiwan, echoed these themes:

> [S]ome Taiwanese who had formerly been conscripted and sent to the South Seas area by the Japanese and had engaged in the war, some of whom were communists, took advantage of the trouble incidental to the Monopoly Bureau's attempt to control cigarette stall-keepers and agitated the public. Thus they created a riot. . . . Governor General Chen has already declared in compliance with instructions from the Central Government that the Government General of Taiwan should be converted into a regular provincial administration at a certain time in the future, and that the popular election of prefectural magistrates would be held within a certain period. All Taiwanese were very glad to accept this declaration. Therefore, the unfortunate Incident has already been settled. But unexpectedly the so-called Committee for Settlement of the February 28 incident in Taiwan suddenly made impossible proposals which included the request that the Taiwan Garrison Command should be eliminated, that arms should be surrendered to the Committee for safe-keeping, and that Army and Navy personnel in Taiwan should all be Taiwanese. The Central Government naturally cannot consent to such requests which exceed the province of local authority. Moreover, violent actions such as attacking government agencies were committed yesterday. Therefore the Central Government decided to send troops to Taiwan for the purpose of maintaining public peace and order there. . . . I have . . . strictly ordered the military and administrative personnel in Taiwan . . . not to resort to any revenge action, so that our Taiwan brethren may be amicably united and cooperate.

Chiang also called on the Taiwanese to "refrain from rash and thoughtless acts" and "treason," and to "voluntarily cancel their illegal organizations." He concluded by reminding Taiwanese of "the debt they owe to the entire nation which has undergone so many sacrifices and bitter struggles for the last 50 years in order to recover Taiwan."[29]

[28] Ibid., 144, 148.
[29] Quoted in Kerr, *Formosa Betrayed*, 307–309.

Troops and armed police landed at Keelung and Kaohsiung on March 8–10. Random shootings, bayoneting, rapes, and robberies of any civilians unfortunate enough to be caught on the streets began immediately, and looting of homes and buildings soon followed. Indiscriminate violence was particularly heavy in Keelung, Taipei, Kaohsiung, and Chiayi. Troops seized control of key facilities such as radio stations, utilities, and transportation hubs. By March 13 they had reestablished government authority in the cities, although fighting in the central highlands continued until March 21.

There is some evidence suggesting that both Chiang Kai-shek and Chen Yi sought to preclude excessive violence by ROC troops. Chiang instructed Chen to "strongly restrain your forces, preventing them from taking revenge." Chen commanded his troops to avoid looting or unjustified shootings, warning that violators would be summarily executed. Years afterward, however, one of Chen Yi's former bodyguards testified that Chiang sent Chen a telegram with the terse order, "Kill them all; keep it secret." In any case, some ROC commanders involved in the crackdown ordered massacres, and the lack of discipline among ROC troops led to unrestrained cruelty.[30]

With Taiwan's major cities recaptured, the KMT leadership set out on a campaign to locate and liquidate political enemies throughout the island and thus preclude any future uprisings. The government described this campaign as "exterminating traitors" and, since many of those wanted by the authorities had fled the cities into the countryside, "cleaning out the villages."[31] Particularly at risk were politicians, journalists, and other prominent citizens who had publicly expressed misgivings about the ROC government, and even those Taiwanese, in some cases young students, who had volunteered to serve as police or other public servants after the mainland Chinese fled their posts. Many of these Taiwanese were hunted down and killed, as were many family members, innocent bystanders, and people who had at some time offended a mainland official. Soldiers executed some Taiwanese men immediately after dragging them from their homes. Some of those who had shown leadership during the crisis died in organized public executions, forced to wear humiliating placards, their bodies left lying in the street as a grisly warning to the

---

[30] Ch'in Hsiao-I, ed., *Tsung-t'ung Chiang-kung ta-shih ch'ang-pien ch'u-kao* (Taipei: Koumintang Central Committee Archives, 1978), vol. 6, pt. 2, 403; *K'an-luan shih-ch'i chung-yao wen-chien fan-an chi-p'ien* (Taipei, 1955), no. 36, Document 38, 134; *Tai-wan hsing-sheng-pao*, Mar. 16, 1947, 3; Lai, Myers, and Wei, *Tragic Beginning*, pp. 149, 161; Julian Baum, "Past Time: Government Makes Amends for 1947 Massacre," *Far Eastern Economic Review*, Mar. 23, 1995, 22.

[31] Li Hsiao-feng, *Taoyu hsin t'aichi: tsung chungchan tao 2–28* (Taipei: Tzuli Wanpao Wenhua Ch'upanshe, 1993), 180–185.

community. Some of the dead had been tortured or mutilated. Chinese soldiers typically looted the homes of their victims. The wife of one victim, thirty-three-year-old Chiu Huo-tu, recalled, "After we took the bloody bodies of my husband and my brother-in-law home, we found that our possessions were ransacked. We did not have anything for the bodies to wear for the burial. The Chinese soldiers took everything."[32]

Taiwanese killed and arrested included members of the Provincial Consultative Assembly and the Taipei City Council. In the case of Taiwanese nationalist agitator Wang T'ien-teng, police doused him with gasoline and burned him to death. At the same time, much of the killing appears to have been random, tolerated or encouraged by army officers as a means of terrorizing the population. During this purge and another in 1949–51, the KMT crushed most of the potential leadership of future Taiwanese nationalist movements; most of those activists not killed were co-opted by the party or forced to flee the island.

Contending interpretations of the incident, each of which had serious if differing political implications, would influence Taiwan's domestic affairs for decades to come. An immediate question was who or what was responsible. Pai Chung-hsi, ROC defense minister, visited the island in late March to investigate. In his report, he blamed the turmoil on several factors, including the influence of the Japanese, who had allegedly taught Taiwanese to hate the Chinese and prepared them to fight against the Chinese Empire; hard economic times; the small number of Taiwanese in important positions; and the presence of a few corrupt mainland administrators. A public version of his report also gave a prominent role to Communist agitators. In an internal memorandum for government use, however, Pai ascribed much less influence to the Communists.[33]

Another report for the central government by Yang Liang-kung, chief of the Supervisory Yuan for Fujian and Taiwan provinces, attributed the incident to several prevailing conditions and to the activities of a number of groups. The conditions included lingering anti-China sentiment fostered by the Japanese colonial government, economic hardships, some poor policies made by Chen Yi's administration, and inadequate ROC military forces on the island to maintain public security. The groups Yang singled out for blame included opportunistic politicians, troublemaking students, Communists, irresponsible journalists, and a limited number of corrupt or inept officials.[34]

[32] "228 Massacre: Taiwan's Tragedy Remembered," University of Saskatchewan Taiwanese Students' Association, online at http://duke.usask.ca/~ss_tsa/228/victims.html, p. 5, accessed Sept. 18, 2001.

[33] Kerr, *Formosa Betrayed*, 315; Lai, Myers, and Wei, *Tragic Beginning*, 5.

[34] Chiang Yung-ching, Li Yun-han, and Hsu Shih-shen, *Yang Liang-kung Hsiensheng Nienpu* (Taipei: Lianching Chupan shihyeh kungssu, 1988), 393–402.

While these reports identified several contributing factors, including poor leadership by Chinese officials, the public KMT line in the months that followed tended to emphasize the roles of Communists, the Japanese legacy, and unpatriotic Taiwanese elites in causing the upheaval, as in Chiang's March 10 statement. Such an interpretation helped establish a new political climate in which advocates of Taiwanese self-government and critics of the ruling regime were in grave danger of being officially denounced as traitors or criminals and punished accordingly.

In fact the role of Communists in either causing or leading the uprising was insignificant, contrary to the claims of both the KMT and the Chinese Communist Party (the latter claimed Taiwanese rioters were inspired by Mao and the successes of the communist revolution). Taiwanese students had organized a Taiwan Communist Party (TCP) in Shanghai in 1928. For several reasons, however, Taiwan's Communist movement was never large or influential. First, the island's steady economic progress under Japanese rule precluded a large groundswell favoring socioeconomic revolution. Second, the Japanese security forces were effective in rooting out TCP members and activities and fought it to the brink of extinction by war's end. Finally, surviving TCP members were divided among factions that disagreed about whether their party should place itself under the leadership of the Chinese Communist Party, the Japanese Communist Party, or neither. The only notable Communist participation in the incident was the ascension of Hsieh Hsueh-hung, a Taiwan Communist Party member, to the leadership of the committee that briefly claimed control of Taichung.

With an obvious interest in countering claims it had carried out a "massacre," the government initially reported that only a few hundred were killed, including about a hundred soldiers. Other, more recent estimates of the number of Taiwanese killed during the recapture of the cities and the purge that followed range from several thousand to ten thousand, although some claim as many as twenty thousand.[35] Thousands of Taiwanese also went to prison. About three thousand Taiwanese dissidents fled the island. Many of these worked from bases overseas to discredit the KMT and promote independence for Taiwan.

Through the combination of death, imprisonment, and intimidation, leadership of the movement for Taiwanese autonomy was greatly weakened. The nature of governance in Taiwan was no longer subject to debate between Mainlander officials and the advocates of enlarged autonomy for

[35] The well-researched book on the incident by Lai et al. concludes that up to eight thousand Taiwanese were killed. Lai, Myers, and Wei, *Tragic Beginning*, 155–164. A March 1995 report commissioned by the ROC government estimated that security forces killed between 18,000 and 28,000.

and empowerment of Taiwanese. Rather, the KMT imposed its agenda and suppressed organized opposition. In a sense, the February 28 incident marked the end of the home rule movement that had developed under the Japanese occupation. Symbolically, Lin Hsien-t'ang left Taiwan soon afterward to reside in Japan, where he died in 1955.

Censorship and punishment of journalists critical of the government began after March 17. An editorial in the *Ch'uanmin Jihpao* explained the ground rules of political dissent for the post–February 28 era. "Critiquing" government policy with a view toward correcting errors and serving the public interest was acceptable; "opposing" the state's national agenda, associated with Communist-inspired subversion, was not acceptable. The difficulty of knowing beforehand whether the authorities would interpret politically oriented discourse as "critique" or "opposition" gave pause to potential critics and activists.[36] In particular, the Taipei government sought to suppress public discussion of the February 28 incident. The opposition, however, kept the issue alive until, more than forty years later, political liberalization would force the government into acknowledgment and investigation.

Chen Yi, as well, departed the island. On March 22, the KMT Central Executive Committee censured him and called for his dismissal as governor-general. He tendered his resignation on March 28. Chiang, an ally and past beneficiary, waited until March 31 to accept it. Before Chen Yi left Taiwan about a month later, the government announced all Taiwanese school children were to make a cash donation, five yen for primary schoolers and ten yen for middle school students, as a token of "thanksgiving" to the KMT. Demonstrating that Chen Yi still enjoyed Chiang's favor, the generalissimo brought him back to Nanjing as special advisor to the government, and soon thereafter named him governor of their native Zhejiang Province—in effect a promotion, since Zhejiang was much larger than Taiwan. Ironically, Chen Yi was soon thereafter to be executed on Chiang's orders. As the KMT lost ground to the CCP forces, Chen Yi appeared to be positioning himself to make a separate peace with the Communists that would allow him to retain a high official position in Zhejiang. After he instructed a regional military commander in January 1949 to cease making defensive preparations, Chiang had Chen Yi arrested and imprisoned in Taiwan. A firing squad shot him in Taipei in June 1950. By that time Chiang and the remnants of the ROC central government had taken up permanent residence on Taiwan, and Chiang sought to gain po-

---

[36] "'Fan-tui cheng-fu' yu 'p'i-p'ing cheng-chih,'" *Ch'uanmin Jih-pao*, Aug. 5, 1948, 1; Phillips, "Between Assimilation," 298. Phillips translates *p'i-p'ing* as "comment on," while I have rendered it as "critique."

litical mileage from Chen Yi's execution by announcing it was based on the former governor general's crimes against the Taiwanese people. News of Chen Yi's death sparked celebrations on the island.

A Disastrous Reunion

ROC leadership everywhere in China, not just Taiwan, had serious shortcomings. The weaknesses of KMT-style rule were especially keenly felt in Taiwan because the separation from China during the Japanese occupation had allowed Taiwan to grow apart from the mainland economically, politically, and socially. Taiwanese and Mainlanders alike were bitterly disappointed by the problems that stemmed from Taiwan's return to China. Each side had expectations of the other that, while understandable, were difficult if not impossible to fulfill. For the Taiwanese, Japanese rule had set high standards in some aspects of government and created demands, long unrequited, for greater opportunities. The new ROC government did not satisfy the Taiwanese in either of these respects. Rather, from the viewpoint of Taiwanese, the KMT had treated their island as a defeated enemy territory rather than a victim of Japanese imperialism—not only in the establishment of a military government, but also in the multifaceted policy of stripping the island of its wealth and resources, and in the systematic privileging of well-connected Mainlanders while Taiwanese suffered economic and political handicaps, as during the Japanese occupation. In keeping with one of the recurring themes of Taiwan's history, anger toward the authorities sparked a violent rebellion that in turn invoked retaliation with overwhelming force and an escalation of violence.

The events of the first two years of Mainlander rule wreaked severe damage to relations between Taiwanese and the ROC government that persisted until the decade of the 1990s. If anything mitigated the disaster of the February 28 incident, it was that the KMT learned lessons for improving its governance on Taiwan thereafter, including the need for greater Taiwanese representation in government and reduced restrictions on free enterprise.

✳

Martial Law and Kuomintang Domination

Despite the recent uprising and months of energetically removing Taiwan's wealth and resources to the mainland, by late 1948 it was apparent that the ROC regime would have to evacuate to Taiwan and make the island its new base. This involved a reversal of policy from stripping down Taiwan to building it up, officially implemented beginning with a government order on October 27, 1948, that halted the transfer of food and other supplies from Taiwan to the mainland. In the months that followed, Mainlanders affiliated with the KMT regime made frantic efforts to move assets and property to Taiwan, including the national treasury—gold, silver, and foreign currency reserves—and the large collection of Chinese artwork that now fills Taiwan's National Palace Museum. (From the KMT's point of view, this was safeguarding China's heritage from falling into the hands of Communist barbarians; the CCP called it embezzlement.) Indeed, the large amounts of currency brought in by Mainlander refugees worsened inflation on the island. Between 1.5 and 2 million Mainlanders fled to Taiwan at the end of the Chinese Civil War. The largest group of evacuees was ROC soldiers, numbering about 600,000. These, too, increased the strain on Taiwan's economy. One Taiwanese writer complained, "With young and old, women and invalids, excluded, every two able-bodied Formosans have to house and feed one Chinese soldier."[1] The KMT hoped to reconcile with and win the support of the Taiwanese through improved governance based on lessons learned on both Taiwan and the mainland. Many influential KMT leaders wanted to raise living

[1] Joshua Liao, *Formosa Speaks* (Hong Kong: Formosan League for Reemancipation, 1950), ii.

standards for ordinary Taiwanese and were not opposed to limited and gradual political liberalization. At the same time, however, the exigencies of the Communist threat stiffened and prolonged the KMT's accustomed authoritarianism. The goals of consolidating the party's authority on Taiwan and enlisting the islanders' cooperation in the defeat of the Communist government on the mainland led to bluntly repressive policies such as the "white terror" and the permanent imposition of martial law.

The interests of the state and of the ruling party overlapped almost completely. There was little distinction between the KMT and the government, as most high-ranking ROC officials were KMT members, and government policies privileged the KMT. The KMT maintained its power by locking Taiwanese out of the national government's parliamentary institutions, by cultivating its influence over local politics, and by using its powerful security apparatus to neutralize dissent. But to carry out its agenda or even to assure its continued survival, the KMT needed considerable support from the majority (about four-fifths) Taiwanese population. The party realized it had to win this support by addressing local political and economic demands and could not merely rely on brute police force or on the appeal to save the mainland from communism.

Aborted Reconciliation

The administration of Chen Yi's replacement as governor-general, Wei Tao-ming, made efforts to reconcile Taiwanese and the Mainlander-run state in the wake of the February 28 crackdown. A former mayor of Nanjing, Wei had been China's ambassador to the United States during World War II and had a favorable reputation among many U.S. officials. His office replaced all but one of Chen Yi's commissioners. Seven of Wei's fifteen commissioners were Taiwanese, although three of these were Half Mountain People[2] who had served in Chen's administration in Zhejiang, and another three were widely considered Japanese collaborators. Each also had a powerful Mainlander as vice commissioner. Wei restructured the Trade and Monopoly bureaus, facilitating private enterprise, and allowed Taiwanese to hold more high positions in state-owned industries. Wei also announced he would discontinue martial law, halt the campaign to hunt

---

[2] Taiwanese colloquially referred to the mainland as "the mountains" and Taiwan as "the sea." The Half Mountain People (*Ban Shan Ren*) were native Taiwanese who had gone to the mainland and obtained positions in the KMT or the ROC government. Those who returned to Taiwan after the war were well placed to mediate between the Mainlander authorities and the local population, but fellow Taiwanese often suspected the loyalty of the Half Mountain People to their native land had been compromised.

down rebels in the countryside, and reduce restrictions over the press. Concessions such as these were appropriate in Taiwan's domestic context, but the larger milieu of the worsening Chinese Civil War was unfavorable to an effective reconciliation. The military and public security forces did not subscribe to Wei's softer approach to state-society relations. They continued to monitor and arrest Taiwanese with proindependence, pro-UN-intervention, or "Communist" views. The government worried about Communist agents infiltrating the island among the thousands of refugees arriving on the island daily by December 1948. Public order and compliance with authority on Taiwan became even more important with the realization the island would be the KMT's last bastion against the Communist forces. General Chen Cheng, a close ally of Chiang, replaced Wei as governor-general on December 29, 1948. Police searches, arrests, and executions were heavy through 1949. Chiang's eldest son, General Chiang Ching-kuo, came to Taiwan with the official title of chairman of the Taiwan Provincial KMT Headquarters, but his principal function was to oversee internal security. Before taking a post as assistant chief of security in Jiangxi Province in 1938, the younger Chiang had spent twelve years in the USSR attending a Russian university and marrying a Russian woman. In Taiwan, he began operating what would grow into a numerically huge and pervasive network of agents and informants. Chen Cheng's government tightened the supervision of ports of entry into Taiwan in February and began an investigation of family registries on the island in May. Chen declared martial law on May 20, 1949, on the grounds that Taiwan was under imminent threat of attack from CCP forces. Martial law would remain in force for thirty-eight years.

The Exiled Kuomintang's Agenda

The KMT's vision, with Sun Yat-sen's key doctrines as touchstones, began with the unification of China. The CCP's conquest of the mainland meant that a second Northern Expedition was necessary. Even into the 1960s, by which time it was clear ROC recapture of China was unfeasible, Chiang continued to repeat the mantra that "to us recovery of the mainland is a sacred mission and to end Communist aggression in Asia is to remove the danger of a nuclear war. It is our duty to launch a punitive expedition against the rebels, to deliver our compatriots from under tyranny, and to recover the mainland."[3]

There was a strong spiritual, quasi-religious character to the KMT's self-

[3] *The China Post* (Taipei), Oct. 11, 1963.

image. Like the Communists, KMT members felt the weight of China's long history and the conviction that Chinese civilization was the finest the world had produced. Their total defeat by the Communists would amount to more than one regime losing the throne to another; they would be historical "sinners" who had squandered a birthright of incalculable worth. The KMT leadership therefore saw theirs as an immensely consequential project, one that overshadowed local political issues such as Taiwanese self-rule.

To reinforce its agenda, the KMT government served its people a heavy diet of propaganda. In the cities, posters and billboards exhorted the population to work toward the reunification of China. Announcements during radio and television broadcasts frequently reminded listeners and viewers to beware the Communist menace. In the cinemas, the national anthem preceded every film, bringing the audience to its feet. The government paraded heavy weaponry and well-drilled troops every National Day (October 10), underscoring the commitment to reconquer the mainland. Ironically, such features made Taiwan look and feel more like its purported enemy, the Communist dictatorship.

The KMT's fixation on recovering China had contradictory consequences for Taiwan. On one hand, the ROC government required of Taiwan's people dedication and sacrifice toward the objective of returning the KMT to power on the mainland. This point was not negotiable, even if many Taiwanese cared less than Mainlanders whether or not Chiang Kai-shek ruled China. On the other hand, the KMT believed that successfully "implementing the Three Principles of the People in Taiwan," or creating a prosperous and contented society that could serve as a model of effective KMT rule, would raise its prestige and weaken support for the CCP on the mainland. Thus, doing well by the Taiwanese would help the KMT win back China.

The early postwar KMT contained a germ of democracy. Sun Yat-sen's doctrine held that democracy was an eventual goal. The KMT under Chiang Kai-shek retained this goal, although by "democracy," the party meant anticommunism, fighting corruption, educating the mass public, and protecting the freedoms of religion and academic discussion.[4] To realize this objective, however, China first needed to establish the preconditions for successful democratization. Paradoxically, a period of dictatorship under the KMT was necessary to build up these preconditions. The postwar KMT leadership held to this approach in Taiwan, turning away the argument of Taiwanese elites that Taiwan was ready for thoroughgo-

[4] Steven J. Hood, *The Koumintang and the Democratization of Taiwan* (Boulder, Colo.: Westview Press, 1997), 29.

ing political liberalization. Rather, Taiwan first needed to pass through a stage of economic, political, and social development. According to KMT doctrine, one prerequisite of democracy was a degree of material prosperity. The citizens of a democratizing state also needed an understanding of and respect for democratic institutions. The people would acquire these by practicing electoral politics at the lower levels of government before gaining empowerment over politics at the national level. Finally, the KMT aimed to inculcate a patriotic civic culture. Chiang often spoke in particular of the need to inspire his people to dedication and self-sacrifice in the pursuit of national goals.

There is a strong element of Confucian elitism that rubs uncomfortably against the KMT's philosophy of ultimate democratization, at least as the concept of democracy is generally understood in the West. During the period of KMT "tutelage" over society, KMT cadres, intellectually and morally superior men, would ennoble the attitudes of the masses by instruction and example. Society would learn from the party rather than the reverse. No serious political opposition would be allowed, as this could only distract the people's vision from the path the KMT had already determined was best. Indeed, the KMT during these early postwar decades saw itself as the only political party capable of saving China and of offering any real hope of eventual democratization.[5] In this, KMT thinking ran parallel with that of the archrival CCP, which had a similar messianic view of itself. The general policy that emerged from this mix of liberal and paternalistic principles was this: committed to eventual democracy for China, the KMT implemented limited democratization in Taiwan, but enforced the limits harshly with martial law and a fearsome public security apparatus.

After his party's banishment to Taiwan, Chiang Kai-shek evidenced an awareness that poor policies and leadership by the KMT had led to defeat on the mainland and that changes were needed. He founded an institute for training party cadres in October 1949 and told its first graduating class, "The reason I founded this Academy was to make it possible for everyone to review our past mistakes and to have a solid understanding of our past defeats."[6] Within three years, the institute had trained about thirteen thousand cadres.[7] In early 1950, many KMT officials considered corrupt, incompetent, or disloyal, including such influential figures as Sun Fo, H. H. Kung, and T. V. Soong, resigned or were forced out of the

[5] Hood, *Koumintang*, 7.

[6] *Zongtong Jiang gong dashi changbian chugao* (Taipei: [n.p.], 1978), vol. 7, part 2, 393.

[7] Linda Chao and Ramon H. Myers, "A New Kind of Party: The Kuomintang of 1949–1952," in *Proceedings of Centennial Symposium on Sun Yat-sen's Founding of the Kuomintang for Revolution*, vol. 4 (Taipei: Chin-t'ai Chung-kuo ch'u-pan-she, 1995), 32.

party. Under Chiang's orders, the KMT Central Advisory Council retired older party leaders to elevate younger members who exhibited more flexible thinking. In July, Chiang established a sixteen-member Central Reform Committee made up of relatively young KMT cadres to make recommendations on reconstructing the party. The committee stressed the need for higher standards of formal education, a commitment to serving the public, and an understanding of the party's goals and principles among party cadres, as well as the party's need to establish a good relationship with Taiwanese elites and intellectuals. These years of reform and reorganization saw growth in discipline, efficiency, and morale within the KMT, resulting in a dramatic increase in membership. Starting with about 100,000 members in 1950, the KMT grew to nearly 1 million strong by the end of the 1960s. Even more significantly, by 1952 over half of the KMT's members were Taiwanese.

These reforms had not included "democratizing" the party. Members were expected to follow the orders handed down from the party headquarters. Yet the KMT regime was never totalitarian. Notwithstanding its close monitoring of the population for certain attitudes and behavior considered dangerous, the authorities did not attempt to control the economic decisions of households or the social life of individuals, nor did they systematically suppress informal political criticism. In general, the state tolerated limited political dissent within the following ground rules: (1) the 1947 ROC constitution would be the basis of KMT power and legitimacy in Taiwan, and the government had the right to adjust the provisions of the constitution to fit the unusual circumstances of Taiwan's standoff with the CCP-dominated mainland; (2) the KMT would be predominant in a one-party system, with token opposition provided by the two other state-approved parties, but the government would not allow the organization of a strong opposition party; (3) the government would promote limited democratization, beginning with elections for local provincial officials and later expanding to open elections for the offices of some national representatives; and (4) in public political discourse, promotion of Communist ideology and serious attempts to discredit the central government were not permitted.[8]

The ROC Political System on Taiwan

The ROC capital officially moved to Taipei on December 7, 1949. The dominant figure in Taiwan's new political system, every bit as much a

---

[8] Ibid., 46.

"paramount leader" in his own (admittedly much smaller) sphere as was Mao on the mainland, was Chiang Kai-shek. The first National Assembly organized after the promulgation of the Republic of China constitution in 1947 had elected Chiang president in March 1948. Li Tsung-jen, a capable former general who was not a protégé of Chiang, was named vice president. With his defeat at the hands of the Communists sealed, Chiang "retired" from the presidency of the ROC on January 21, 1949, leaving Li to preside over the fall of Shanghai, Nanjing, Chungking, and the other remaining major Chinese cities to Mao Zedong's forces. Chiang retained his positions as head of the KMT and commander-in-chief of the armed forces. Li was unable to replace government officials with appointees of his own choosing. Chiang continued to conduct international diplomacy without consulting Li. Relocating to Taiwan, Chiang began ordering the evacuation to the island of military units loyal to him. Aware of Chiang's political maneuvers, Li warned him, "Without an election by the National Assembly you have no legal ground to become again the President of China."[9] To many American officials, Li represented a potential noncommunist alternative to the unpalatable Chiang, to whom the Truman administration had discontinued heavy funding. Li sought American help, asking U.S. ambassador to China John Leighton Stuart to get Chiang invited to visit the United States to weaken Chiang's continued control of the ROC government. Li was visiting the United States and scheduled to meet with Truman in Washington in March 1950 when Chiang announced that he had accepted a request from the Executive Yuan to take back the presidency. Whether or not it had legal grounds, Chiang's move left Li shorn of authority. After returning to the presidency, Chiang purged nearly one hundred civilian and military leaders, executing his vice minister of defense among others.

Chiang held the three most powerful positions on Taiwan: ROC head of state, commander of the ROC military, and chairman of the ruling party. He also held immense prestige among the mainlander community on Taiwan. He had been a colleague of Sun Yat-sen, hero of the Northern Expedition that nominally unified China in 1928, and leader of all mainland China. Chiang had been welcomed by President Roosevelt to sit with the other leaders of the victorious great powers. After losing mainland China to the Communists, Chiang could have retired into a comfortable foreign exile, but instead chose to make a stand on Taiwan, vowing to defeat the CCP and return triumphantly to China. The party reinforced Chiang's prestige by promoting a personality cult. Soon larger-than-life statues and

---

[9] *The Chinese World* (San Francisco), March 7, 1950; Fred W. Riggs, *Formosa Under Chinese Nationalist Rule* (New York: Octagon Books, 1972), 35.

images of Chiang crowded the island, and the media spoke of his leadership and ultra-heroism in grandiose terms reminiscent of the regime-supporting propaganda of Stalin, Mao, and North Korea's Kim Il Sung.

A veteran of the mainland KMT's intricate factional politics, Chiang did not hesitate to oust competent officials who might challenge his authority. As part of his effort to revive U.S. aid to Taiwan, Chiang had named as head of the ROC armed forces General Sun Li-jen, who was a graduate of the Virginia Military Institute and whom many influential Americans held in high esteem. Sun's fame and reputation for intelligence and integrity made him a potential rival to Chiang. Sun was interested in recruiting and training young Taiwanese men for military service, a policy that suggested a lack of enthusiasm for Chiang's view that retaking the mainland should be the primary objective of the ROC's armed forces. Sun had also argued that the KMT should be liberalized. In 1955, a former subordinate of Sun's confessed to being a Communist agent. Accused of "negligence," Sun was forced to resign and spent thirty-three years under house arrest. Another potential rival was Chen Cheng. Praised for his leadership of the land reform program while premier, Chen also lacked a strong commitment to returning to the mainland and had many American supporters—all danger signs from Chiang's standpoint. Chiang might have felt compelled to move against Chen as well had not Chen died of cancer in 1965.

The ROC constitution limited the president to a maximum of two six-year terms. To allow Chiang to remain in office after he reached the end of his second term in 1960, the KMT Central Standing Committee asked the National Assembly to exempt Chiang from the two-term limit. The exemption passed and the way was clear for Chiang to remain president for life, but at the cost of offending younger and more liberal KMT members.

The ROC government's 1947 constitution outlined a democratic republic and guaranteed a broad range of political rights for ROC citizens. The KMT had proclaimed that the period of one-party dictatorship was completed and that China was prepared to move on to constitutional government, the third and final phase of Sun Yat-sen's long-term political blueprint. The KMT had invited all political parties to participate in the 1948 elections for the new National Assembly. The Democratic Socialist Party and the China Youth Party, really factions within the KMT umbrella rather than distinct parties, participated. The CCP and the Democratic League did not, and thus lost official sanction. The Chinese Civil War precluded full implementation of this constitution. In May 1948, the National Assembly enacted the "Temporary Provisions Effective During the Period of Communist Rebellion," which suspended the constitution and transferred to the president the rights and powers normally reserved to other branches of government. The provisions also forbade the formation of new political parties; thereafter, only the KMT, the Democratic Socialist Party and the China Youth Party were legal. The KMT said its goal was a democratic republic consistent with Sun Yat-sen's Three Principles of the People, and that civil liberties would be restored after the emergency situation created by the Communist threat had passed. The Temporary Provisions originally had a two-year time limit, underscoring the KMT's positions that the war would soon be won and democracy realized throughout China. When the time limit was reached, the Temporary Provisions were extended indefinitely, pending the defeat of the Communists.

The constitution provided for direct elections to determine membership of the three-thousand-seat National Assembly (empowered to appoint and dismiss the president and vice president, propose laws, and amend the constitution) and the Legislative Yuan (the chief law-making body). The Legislative Yuan in turn appointed members of the Executive Yuan (the cabinet, headed by the premier), charged with overseeing government ministries and commissions. Provincial and city governments named members of the Control Yuan, which censures government officials found to behave illegally or unethically. The National Assembly, Legislative Yuan, and Control Yuan comprised the parliament. In practice, Chiang's position as KMT leader combined with the party's dominance of official positions gave Chiang powers that overwhelmed the institutional balances between the respective strength of the president and the parliament. Members of the latter became "rubber stamps of the executive."[10]

Taiwan also had its own provincial government, with a governor, provincial assembly, and a hierarchy of local government offices. The duplication of ROC and Taiwan provincial government bodies generated complaints of redundancy and inefficiency, captured in the aphorisms "too many Buddhas crammed into one small temple" and "if you throw a stone, it will hit an official."

The KMT ensured its own continued dominance of politics at the national level partly by freezing Taiwanese out of national political offices, with the exception of a few serving in cabinet positions during the 1950s and 1960s. The parliamentary institutions posed an awkward political problem. The last all-China elections for the ROC's National Assembly, Legislative Yuan, and Control Yuan were held in late 1947. The constitution stipulated elections for the Legislative Yuan every three years, and for the National Assembly and Control Yuan every six years. After the CCP

---

[10] Jaushieh Joseph Wu, *Taiwan's Democratization: Forces Behind the New Momentum* (Hong Kong: Oxford University Press, 1995), 27.

gained control of the mainland, it was obviously impossible for the ROC to hold any further elections with the participation of any provinces of China other than Taiwan. To sustain its claim to be the government of all of China, however, the ROC needed to maintain elected representatives from all of China. In 1954, therefore, the Council of Grand Justices ruled that the one thousand representatives from the mainland elected in 1947 who had reached Taiwan could occupy their seats until the next ROC election on the mainland—that is, for life. As sitting members died, the government appointed in their place candidates who had finished second or third in the 1947–48 elections. Taiwanese complained that not only was this a transparent effort to maintain the Mainlander hold on political power, but filling seats with the *losers* of elections was fundamentally undemocratic.[11] Pressure for new parliamentary elections increased as the passage of time wore down more of the original members. The government allowed the first supplementary elections in 1969, adding eleven new members to the Legislative Yuan and eight to the National Assembly.

At the lower levels of government, however, the regime was less reluctant to implement elections. These local elections, mostly open and competitive, provided the strongest support for the KMT's claim of legitimate rule over Taiwan. With its control of electoral regulations and a vast surveillance and police network, the KMT could have systematically managed the results of each of these elections, but it refrained from doing so. Blatant and consistent rigging of the electoral process to ensure the success of KMT-backed candidates would have damaged rather than enhanced the government's legitimacy, which was the point of the exercise. Nevertheless, the KMT enjoyed considerable advantages. Since opposition parties were banned, anti-KMT candidates had to run as independents. The KMT had vast wealth to draw from during electoral campaigns. The government controlled most of Taiwan's mass media, which gave KMT candidates extensive and positive coverage. The KMT virtually owned large blocs of voters, such as the military. The farmers' associations proved useful for mobilizing voters in rural areas. And the party was adept at using its wealth and connections to manipulate local politics. Overall, these advantages combined with occasional cheating and dirty tricks allowed KMT candidates to win most elected positions.

The government set up a Provisional Provincial Assembly in 1951. Members were elected by county and municipal assemblies. In 1959 the name of this body was changed to the Provincial Assembly and its members were elected by direct popular vote. Most of the winning candidates were backed by the KMT, but the assembly included a few independent

---

[11] Ibid., 30.

members who pushed for reforms that could potentially weaken the KMT's hold on the national political agenda. The KMT accepted this risk as the price of enhanced legitimacy.

Allowing Taiwanese to compete for local positions posed comparatively little threat to the KMT's national agenda. These contests focused attention on local rather than national controversies. Furthermore, local elections provided the KMT with a mechanism for neutralizing or co-opting some of its opposition. Joining the KMT and running for elected office with the party's blessing offered Taiwanese with political ambitions an attractive alternative to challenging the system in the streets or in the pages of the underground press. Since it controlled the government, the KMT could buy the cooperation of local politicians by granting lucrative favors, such as issuing licenses for various businesses. Local elections also generated petty factionalism that worked to the KMT's advantage. The KMT nurtured competing factions in a given area and then pitted them against each other in a contest to win the KMT support and funding that would boost their own candidates. The ruling party would reap the political rewards as each faction strove to demonstrate the greatest loyalty to the KMT.

The KMT sometimes provided voters with transportation, meals, entertainment, or gifts. With no comparable treasury, independents could not hope to match the KMT's largesse. Critics also alleged that the government manipulated election results through registration procedures and by intimidating voters at polling places. On occasion the party relied on its control of the state apparatus to engineer the outcomes it wanted. For example, in the 1956 election for Taoyuan district magistrate, popular opposition candidate Hsu Hsin-Chih was poised to defeat the KMT candidate. The day before the election, Hsu was abruptly summoned to report for military service and was thereby forced to withdraw from the race.[12] At the same time, however, KMT candidates frequently lost elections to opponents who were both popular and vociferously critical of the KMT. Kuo Kuo-chi, who had been imprisoned after the February 28 incident and was a vigorous career opponent of the KMT, won a seat in the Legislative Yuan in 1969. During the campaign for the 1969 supplementary elections to central government organs, the government not only tolerated severe criticism from opposition politician Huang Hsin-chieh, but even assigned him heavy police protection, fearing the KMT might be blamed if enraged audiences attacked Huang. In sum, the government allowed non-KMT candidates with widely varying philosophies to stand for elections (although they had to do so as independents), and these candidates generally had a fighting chance to win. The regime's approach facilitated the

[12] *Tzuyu Chungkuo,* no. 17 (April 1, 1957), 221.

KMT's dominance over the important political issues and thus protected the core KMT agenda while demonstrating that the government would permit a measure of pluralism.

The ban on opposition parties was a major impediment to mounting an effective challenge to the KMT, and non-KMT politicians and intellectuals badgered the government to repeal the restriction. After the elections of 1957, in which KMT candidates dominated the races for mayors and county magistrates and won forty-four of sixty-six Provincial Assembly seats, the famous liberal writer Hu Shih led a group of prominent people who sent a petition to the government in 1958 asking for the right to form a new political party. After five months, the government refused the request. The petitioners persisted, suffering harassment from public security officers, until they were temporarily silenced by a government-planted story that they were linked with a Communist agent. By 1960, pressure from intellectuals, including several mainland Chinese, had resumed. They called for greater civil liberties, an end to government subsidization of the KMT, decreased military spending, and a discontinuation of threats to attack the mainland. Publicly, the KMT said it welcomed the participation of non-KMT anticommunists in the political process, suggesting an acceptance of the principle of a loyal opposition. In a press conference, Premier Chen Cheng gave qualified assent to the formation of a legitimate opposition party. The KMT could accept such a party if it was not "a party of warlords, hoodlums or rascals," he said.[13] It was easy, nonetheless, for the KMT to snuff out repeated efforts to form a new party on the grounds that the organizers were troublemakers or closet Communists. Indeed, following Chen's remarks came a concerted effort to undercut the attempt of a group of both Mainlanders and Taiwanese from establishing what they named the China Democratic Party (CDP). This included negative media reports about the new party, revelations from the public security apparatus that the CDP had Communist connections, government obstruction of party activities, and finally an outright ban on the party (because, the government reported, it was linked with organized crime) and the imprisonment of its four founding members.

One of the four was journalist Lei Chen, an elderly Mainlander who had formerly been a high official in Chiang Kai-shek's government. Editor of the Hu Shih-founded magazine *Tzuyu Chungkuo* (*Free China*), Lei Chen called for a Western-style pluralistic political system with protection of individual liberties and for a market-oriented economic system, arguing that its authoritarianism was one of the reasons the KMT lost the mainland. Police arrested Lei Chen on the accusation that he belonged to a

---

[13] Hood, *Koumintang*, 44.

Communist-inspired conspiracy, a charge ostensibly unrelated to his role in the CDP. Chiang Kai-shek weighed in, asserting that Lei's writings were seditious and had attacked his authority. When Lei Chen's wife sought defense counsel for her husband, several lawyers refused the case, saying they were sympathetic to Lei Chen's plight but feared government retribution against them or their families. The government's case against Lei Chen, who was tried in a military court, rested primarily on the confession of his China Democratic Party codefendant Liu Tzu-ying. Liu admitted to having been a subversive agent and said he had tried to recruit Lei seven years earlier. Lei Chen did not join with Liu, but rather rebuked him for his plans. But since Lei Chen had not turned in a known Communist agent, prosecutors argued, it followed that Lei Chen's critical writings were intended help the Communists overthrow the ROC government. Lei Chen was sentenced to ten years in prison, and Liu to twelve. The case further strained relations between the more liberal and more conservative elements of the KMT and also between the party and independent politicians, who argued that the KMT had not lived up to its pledge to tolerate criticism from non-KMT politicians who were not Communists, a description that had clearly fit Lei Chen.

Several prominent citizens unsuccessfully petitioned the government for Lei Chen's release. Among them was Taiwanese politician Su Tung-chi. A year after Lei Chen was arrested, the authorities picked up more than a hundred Taiwanese activists, including Su, who was popular in southern Taiwan but, unlike Lei Chen, unknown abroad. In the wee hours of September 19, 1961, police raided Su's house and arrested him and his wife. Su was charged with plotting a rebellion and executed about a year later. Su's wife was interrogated for two days despite her illness and protests that her six children were alone at home. After complaining publicly about her treatment by security personnel, she was sentenced to life imprisonment.

State Control over Society under Martial Law

The government's publicly stated rationale for declaring and maintaining martial law was summarized in many public statements such as this one by Chiang Ching-kuo:

[W]e hope that the Taiwanese people can maintain their security, peace, happiness, and prosperity. We also hope to preserve effective political functions for safeguarding our democracy and freedom. But . . . in world history there has not been a single free, democratic state like the ROC that has for so long confronted an expanding communist totalitarianism. Because of this fact, the ROC relies on law and implements martial law to preserve our nation's security and to prevent the communists from exercising all sorts of subversive activities.[14]

In other words, the KMT was committed in principle to a fully democratic system on Taiwan, but this had to wait until the Communist threat passed because liberalization would create vulnerabilities the enemy could exploit. Freedom had to be traded for security. This same argument in slightly different forms has been common among the authoritarian governments (both Communist and noncommunist) of developing countries from the end of the era of Western imperialism/colonialism through the present day.

Under martial law, the Taiwan Garrison Command was responsible for arresting and punishing individuals who threatened ROC security and public order. Civilians were subject to arrest by military personnel and trial by military courts. By one estimate, military courts tried the cases of more than ten thousand civilians during the martial law period.[15] Public security laws targeted Communists, advocates of violent uprising, and critics of the Chiang family or of key KMT doctrines such as Taiwan's status as a province of China or the commitment to recapture the mainland. In practice, as we have seen, the state's broad powers of arrest and indefinite detention without trial could also be used against advocates of political reforms such as legalizing opposition parties or opening more powerful positions to Taiwanese. These powers also allowed police sweeps against persona non grata in general. As an example, during two months of 1963 police arrested more than nine hundred people and summarily incarcerated them on a small offshore island. A newspaper report described the detainees as "thieves, Liu-mang [members of Taiwanese youth gangs], professional gamblers, and others."[16] More interested in combating what they saw as unpatriotism than in stimulating constructive political debate, the public security organs employed their powers bluntly. One critic argued,

> The KMT's censorship policy was everywhere in society and for no explicable reason the KMT prohibited every kind of behavior: it forbade any revision of the constitution before recovering the mainland; it forbade any new

---

[14] *Chiang Ching-guo Xiansheng zhuanji bianji weiyuanhui, Chiang Ching-guo Xiansheng quanji* (Taipei: Government Information Office, 1991), vol. 15, 63.

[15] Hung-mao Tien, *The Great Transition: Political and Social Change in the Republic of China* (Stanford, Calif.: Hoover Institution Press, 1989), 111.

[16] *Lianhebao*, Oct. 21, 1963.

party from forming; it forbade the registration of any new newspaper; it forbade strikes, demonstrations, and criticisms of national policy; it forbade the election of a provincial governor and the mayors of Taipei and Kaohsiung cities; it forbade the reading of works published by mainland China authors; it forbade the expression of views by political rallies; it forbade students to have long hair and to help politicians in elections. Most of these kinds of activities do not violate the constitution. They are merely the subjective views held by those in power and run counter to society's contemporary trends and the natural inclinations of our people.[17]

In keeping with its professed interest in working toward democracy, the KMT's orientation toward dissent showed signs of gradual evolution in the direction of greater tolerance. Security regulations were modified in the early 1950s to make a few concessions, such as allowing a defendant's family member to be present during a trial, permitting defense lawyers in military courts, and requiring police warrants before the arrest of civilians. The Legislative Yuan passed a Law of Compensation for Wrongful Detentions and Convictions.

Despite these concessions to society, however, the state continued to imprison and execute large numbers of Taiwan's people for essentially political offenses. Taiwanese nationalism, stimulated by the disillusionment of the late 1940s, provided the single greatest target for internal security forces. While the ROC had its own plan for expanded self-government in Taiwan, the state's objective was to strengthen rather than weaken Taiwan's links to China and to the central government. The KMT viewed activism for Taiwanese self-government outside party auspices as a treasonous effort to create an independent Taiwanese state.

The darkest facet of Taiwan's martial law was a campaign of large-scale, politically motivated arrests of intellectuals and others during the 1950s that became known as the "White Terror." Part-time or amateur political activists were frequently collared, charged with a serious crime such as plotting the overthrow of the government, and sentenced to death or life imprisonment. Estimates of the number of victims of the White Terror run as high as ninety thousand arrested and about half that number executed.[18] The numbers of arrests and executions from the 1960s through the mid-1980s may have been lower, but a similar pattern continued. This was not solely an anti-Taiwanese campaign; thousands of Mainlander refugees were killed as well.

[17] Chen Yanghao, "Jin! Jin! Jin!" *Nuanliu Zazhi*, no. 19 (Jan. 20, 1984), 5.

[18] Hung-mao Tien, "Taiwan in Transition: Prospects for Socio-political Change," *China Quarterly* 64 (December 1975): 629.

An early and prominent critic of the abuses of the martial law regime was Wu Kuo-chen, named Taiwan's governor-general in December 1949 when Chen Cheng left that position to become ROC premier (head of the Executive Yuan). The appointment of Wu, who was educated in the United States and relatively liberal, was apparently intended to favorably impress an American government disillusioned with Chiang's regime. Wu worked toward political and economic reforms, but Chen Cheng, Chiang Ching-kuo, and other more conservative officials frequently frustrated his efforts. Openly critical of the Chiangs' authoritarianism, Wu survived at least two assassination attempts and then resigned in 1953 while in the United States. After Wu and his wife settled in Illinois, Chiang held their young son hostage in Taipei for over a year to deter Wu from criticizing the regime from abroad. Wu later made extensive criticisms of the Chiang regime, including the following:

> The present methods adopted by the Kuomintang government are entirely devoted to the purpose of perpetuating its power. It is directly contrary to the fundamental principles of modern democratic government. . . . .During my more than three years' administration . . . hardly a day passed without some bitter struggle on my part with the secret police. They interfered with free elections. The made numberless illegal arrests. They tortured and they blackmailed. . . . Formosa has become virtually a police state. The liberties of the people are almost totally suppressed.[19]

Chiang Ching-kuo's office had a struggle of its own in its effort to assert control over the various security forces of different government agencies that were accustomed to operating independently and even competing with each other in the discovery and apprehension of alleged offenders. The two major security organizations engaged in this rivalry were the Bureau of Central Investigation and Statistics and the Bureau of Military Investigation and Statistics. The various security agencies were unified under the National Security Bureau after the establishment of the National Security Council in 1967. Feared and secretive, the National Security Bureau was typically headed by a former general. The government's huge force of some 50,000 full-time and 500,000 part-time informants helped contribute to a chilling political climate.

The armed forces themselves were closely watched as well. The Ministry of Defense established a Political Affairs Department in 1950, also under Chiang Ching-kuo, to supervise a commissar system among military personnel. This system placed political officers in the ranks from the

[19] Quoted in George H. Kerr, *Formosa Betrayed* (Boston: Houghton Mifflin, 1965), 480–482.

office of top military commander, General Sun Li-jen, down to the platoon level. These commissars both organized indoctrination activities and watched for suspicious behavior that might betray "Communist" sympathy.

In 1952, the younger Chiang created a counterpart of his military commissar system for the universities. The Chinese Anticommunist National Salvation Youth Corps (commonly known in Chinese by its shortened form Chiukuo Tuan) trained students to report suspicious activities while indoctrinating them in KMT values. Professors and students alike were subject to arrest for dissent. In a famous case, National Taiwan University (NTU) professor and chairman of the Political Science Department Peng Ming-min and two of his students, Hsieh Tsung-min and Wei Ting-ch'ao, were arrested in September 1964 for distributing literature criticizing the ideas of the KMT recapturing mainland China and of Taiwan being considered part of China. Their trial, by a military court, was not held until April 1965 and lasted only one day. The authorities sentenced Peng and Wei to eight-year prison terms while Hsieh got ten years. With Peng's conviction, his sister, a professor at another college in Taipei, also lost her job even though she was not accused of any illegal activities. Under U.S. pressure, Taipei released Peng to exile overseas in 1970. In other cases the state's retribution was more subtle. After NTU professor Yin Hai-kuang published essays in *Tzuyu Chungkuo* advocating liberalization, in 1966 the state-sponsored university kept him in its employ but forced him to give up teaching.

Each university's Disciplinary Office had the power to grant or refuse requests for assemblies on campus and to preview all written material and speeches. Military training took place on university campuses, creating another means of pressure and control. At the same time the Ministry of Education sponsored social activities such as dances in an attempt to channel the interests of students away from political activism. The government also spied on students studying overseas and some were punished on their return to Taiwan for antigovernment statements made while they were abroad.

Under martial law, the military command and national defense agencies had the power to ban any publication or speech judged detrimental to public or national security. Not all discussion unfavorable to the government was silenced, but repeated criticism, and particularly attacks on KMT sacred cows, would put journalists at great risk of arrest and their publications of being shut down. One of many journalists who ran afoul of the state was Kuo Yi-tung (his pen name was Bo Yang), who was arrested in March 1968 over a newspaper cartoon of Chiang Kai-shek he produced that offended the authorities. He was tried before a military court. During his trial the government accused him of being a Communist agent. The evidence for this charge was that Kuo's girlfriend had attempted to learn from a military officer how many bicycles were in his regiment, and that Kuo had advised one of his friends to remain in mainland China after it fell to the Communists rather than flee to Taiwan. Kuo drew an eighteen-year sentence, of which he served nine years before being released. He said the court never informed him what crime he had committed or what law he had violated.[20]

After the White Terror, such punishment of critics of the state was selective. Mark Mancall terms the arrangement "submerged totalitarianism": every dissident and opposition politician or activist knew what kind of powers the state possessed to detect and punish its domestic enemies, and that the authorities could be ruthless in employing those powers. By permitting some dissent to go unpunished, the regime could claim to audiences both at home and abroad that it tolerated criticism. Excessive criticism was deterred, however, by the possibility of punishment and by guidelines that were intentionally vague. Many potential critics of the government thus censored themselves.[21]

Repression and the White Terror prompted many Taiwanese political activists and intellectuals to flee the island and continue their activities from havens overseas. Taiwanese Communist Hsieh Hsueh-hung escaped to Japan and helped organize the Taiwan Democratic Autonomy League. Hsieh's group later relocated to China, where she was eventually purged like so many other casualties of the PRC's vicious factional politics. Liao Bun-gei, who held a doctorate degree in engineering from Ohio University, had sent a petition to the United Nations after the February 28 incident calling for UN trusteeship over Taiwan while its residents decided through a referendum whether the island would be independent or join the Republic of China. Unlike Hsieh, Liao was anticommunist as well as anti-KMT. After arriving in Japan in 1950, Liao and his supporters founded the Taiwan Democratic Independence Party. MacArthur's occupation government arrested Liao at Chiang Kai-shek's request. Released after the occupation, Liao became the provisional president of a "Republic of Taiwan" in exile. Liao's group was small and weakened by infighting. Liao reconciled with the KMT and returned to Taiwan in 1965. There were several other pro-Taiwanese organizations based in Japan, most notably the Taiwan Youth Association, a group of Taiwanese students disaffected

---

[20] "Taiwan Regime, in Drive on Dissidents, Jails Novelists and Other Intellectuals and Long-Haired Youths," *New York Times*, July 3, 1969, 3; Chao and Meyers, "A New Kind of Party," 5.

[21] Mark Mancall, ed., *Formosa Today* (New York: Praeger, 1964), 37–38.

with Liao's party. They founded the political magazine *Taiwan Seinen* (*Young Formosan Monthly*) in 1960, which published through the end of the twentieth century. Taipei continually pressured the Japanese government to crack down on these groups. But postwar Japan had expanded civil liberties, and the Japanese harbored a parallel resentment of the ROC for allowing Okinawans in Taiwan to organize Okinawan independence activities.

Taiwanese-Mainlander Relations

Strained relations between Taiwanese and Mainlanders marked a fault line that ran through both politics and society. While increasing numbers of Taiwanese were filling political offices, Taiwanese complained that Mainlanders still unfairly dominated the island's affairs. Even after Wu Kuo-chen named seventeen Taiwanese among his twenty-three provincial commissioners, for example, there were frequent complaints that many of the Taiwanese appointees were incompetent or former collaborators and that the government intentionally assigned Taiwanese to oversee unpopular and controversial tasks.[22] Two decades after the Japanese surrender, the government pointed out that the number of Taiwanese in provincial government positions had doubled. The Taiwanese population, however, had also doubled during the same period, negating the apparent gain in the relative political power of the Taiwanese community.

Beyond the ideological issue of safeguarding the civilization of greater China, maintaining their disproportionate power was for Mainlanders a means of political self-defense. To a large degree, the Mainlander community owed their status and livelihoods to the survival of the KMT regime. Few Mainlanders owned businesses or land in Taiwan. Many relied on employment within the bureaucracy or in government-owned firms. Relinquishing their political and economic privileges might leave them at the mercy of a hostile majority. The ethnic divide is one of the domestic political factors that explains why the Chiang regime hung on so long to the notion that Taiwan was a staging area for the ROC's reconquest of the mainland.

The PRC's hostility and almost limitless pool of manpower presented the ROC with a compelling need for a large number of soldiers. Integrating Taiwanese into the armed forces, however, proved politically nettlesome. The KMT government feared the notion of arming the Taiwanese, especially after seeing them capture control of the island in March 1947. A

[22] Riggs, *Formosa*, 48–49.

less sensitive objection to recruiting Taiwanese was that they were more expensive than Mainlanders. Taiwanese were accustomed to a higher standard of living, including bathing daily in hot water, than the typical Mainlander soldier. Taiwanese men also had relatives on the island to support, while the impossibility of remitting funds back to China eased this responsibility for Mainlanders. As for Taiwanese attitudes, many were amenable to military service, but generally on the condition that their mission would be to defend their home island from attack rather than to fight Chiang's war on the mainland. Despite these obstacles, the military started drafting young Taiwanese men in August 1951. They soon comprised the majority of enlisted men and noncommissioned officers. The officer corps remained predominantly (about 90 percent) Mainlander between 1950 and 1965.[23] The KMT derived a political advantage from military necessity: as part of their training, recruits received indoctrination in party values and goals. Because military service has reinforced the KMT's strength and prestige, Taiwanese as a group have been more critical than Mainlanders of the ROC's huge, expensive military establishment and the requirement that all young men fulfill a stint in the armed forces. As a political training ground and apparent proof that the government planned to recapture China, Taiwan's oversized Cold War military protected the regime as much as the island.

Language became a battleground for Taiwanese-Mainlander political tensions. The KMT regime had an obvious interest in stamping out the use of the Japanese language in Taiwan, which Mainlanders viewed as a holdover of Japan's systematic program to de-Sinicized the Taiwanese. An official ban on Japanese provided younger generations of Taiwanese educated under the Japanese occupation with an ironic means of expressing their Taiwanese nationalism. One Taiwanese recalled that during his service in the ROC military, "We Formosans used Japanese loudly on purpose. It was not by accident that we wrote letters in Japanese. We knew our letters were censored but we wrote them in the prohibited language intentionally. It was not from our love of Japan that we used Japanese, but the use of it certainly had a nuisance value as our tiny means of retaliation against the Nationalist regime."[24] The government made Mandarin the official language on Taiwan, as it had been on the mainland under ROC rule (a policy the CCP continued). Mandarin predominated in the civil service, over the airwaves, and in the schools, all of which were under some de-

---

[23] Chian Liang-jen, "Taiwanjen Ti Erh Ke Shang-chiang," *Hsin Hsinwen* 39 (Dec. 7, 1987): 9.

[24] *Formosan Quarterly* 1, no. 3 (January 1963): 30; Meisner, "The Development of Formosan Nationalism," in *Formosa Today*, 158.

gree of government control. This was consistent with the KMT's view of Taiwan as an integral part of China and the temporary depository of Chinese civilization. From the point of view of the Taiwanese, however, this marginalization of local dialects (principally "Taiwanhua" or Minnanyu, which is similar to Fujianese) was forcible alien acculturation scarcely different from the assimilation the Japanese had attempted.

In education, as well, Taiwanese perceived cultural imperialism. Use of non-Mandarin dialects on school grounds was punishable by fines. Portraits of Chiang Kai-shek and Sun Yat-sen hung in every classroom. The curriculum was Chinacentric, with little attention paid to Taiwan. In the late 1940s the government tried to mollify public opinion by announcing it was reserving 70 percent of the admissions into Taiwan's higher education system for Taiwanese. Taiwanese critics complained, nonetheless, that college entrance tests were systematically biased to the advantage of Mainlanders and against Taiwanese because of questions requiring in-depth knowledge of mainland Chinese history and literature and the Three Principles of the People.

There was little social mixing between Mainlanders and Taiwanese. Intermarriage between the two groups was initially uncommon outside of what the Chinese consider low-status classes (many ROC soldiers, for example, married local women). In business, the staff of a given company was usually drawn predominantly from one group or the other, creating a division between "Mainlander" and "Taiwanese" firms.

Economic Recovery

After the end of Chen Yi's administration Taiwan's economy had continued to decline, with recovery made more difficult by the exodus of many capable Mainlanders, who were frightened off by the February 28 incident, and the deterioration of the KMT's position on the mainland. Supporting the unnaturally large KMT administration, built for governing all of China, and a comparably bloated ROC army, was a huge burden on the productive side of Taiwan's economy. The island suffered increasing unemployment and hyperinflation, with prices rising perhaps ten-thousandfold between 1945 and 1950. To combat inflation, the government reformed Taiwan's currency in June 1949, introducing the New Taiwan dollar at an exchange rate of one per forty thousand old Taiwan dollars. The government reduced the amount of currency in circulation by raising interest rates the following year to a temporary compounded annual rate of 125 percent. Inflation fell from 3,000 percent in 1949 to 300 percent in 1950 and to 8.8 percent from 1952 onward.[25] From 1955 through 1960, the New Taiwan dollar was gradually devalued to forty New Taiwan dollars per one U.S. dollar.

Stabilizing the wartime economic turmoil was not enough. The KMT realized economic development would bolster its legitimacy with the Taiwanese. Beginning in the late 1950s, KMT discourse placed increasing emphasis on promoting economic growth in Taiwan along with militarily defeating the Communists. Prosperity on Taiwan would improve the KMT's standing in the eyes of both its Taiwan audience and observers on the mainland. The regime succeeded admirably, bringing Taiwan into the ranks of the newly industrializing countries that would force China and other Asian Marxist states to reassess their aversion to engagement with the international economy.

Taiwan's "economic miracle" was built primarily on two policy pillars. First, the government reduced the barriers impeding education and entrepreneurship, unleashing the economic potential of Taiwan as a whole and opening up opportunities of upward socioeconomic mobility for individual families.[26] The Taipei government greatly expanded facilities and opportunities for education between 1952 and 1960. According to government statistics, the number of primary schools increased from 1,248 to 1,982, secondary schools from 148 to 299, and colleges from 4 to 15. Enrollment rates increased accordingly. In 1965, the ROC government increased the number of years of compulsory education from six to nine. The state also subsidized primary education. These measures would expand the economy's pools of technical and organizational expertise and skilled labor.

From 1950 onward, the state took steps to stimulate private enterprise. Certain state-owned industries were transferred to private ownership. In the case of textiles, the government encouraged the growth of private industry by helping firms obtain funding and raw material. The government increased wages for some state-owned firms and introduced a program providing accident insurance to industrial workers. Further, deeper privatization faced resistance from conservatives. In 1958, 80 percent of Taiwan's industry was government-owned. Consistent with the Sunist notion of the need for heavy state influence during the critical early stage of national development, this also assured Mainlander domination of the

---

[25] Shirley W.Y. Kuo, Gustav Ranis, and John C.H. Fei, *The Taiwan Success Story: Rapid Growth with Improved Distribution in the Republic of China, 1952–1979* (Boulder, Colo.: Westview Press, 1981), 65.

[26] Chao and Myers, "A New Kind of Party," 42–44.

economy and allowed the KMT to provide jobs to its supporters. Privatization, however, would see economic power devolve back into the hands of Taiwanese. They planned to stay on the island and would resist the KMT's objective of orienting the economy toward supporting the reconquest of China. As economic power leads to political power, privatization might also help Taiwanese to more quickly mount a challenge to KMT dominance over the island's politics. In the late 1950s the reform faction argued that enough basic infrastructure was in place for Taiwan's economy to take the next step, which would require liberalizing controls over trade and investment. Chiang sided with the reformers against the conservatives beginning in 1958, and in 1959 he accepted an offer from the U.S. government: Taiwan would qualify for substantial additional economic aid if it implemented reforms that would demonstrate its commitment to free-market capitalism. The privatization that followed indeed worked to empower Taiwanese politically. A direct result was the beginning of the Taiwanization of the KMT, as wealthy Taiwanese businessmen and the KMT power structure realized they needed each other and large numbers of Taiwanese began joining the party.

The second pillar of Taiwan's economic takeoff was the government's administrative guidance. In the early postwar years, Taiwan imported extensively while exporting little more than rice and sugar, resulting in a large trade deficit and a lack of foreign currency reserves. In the 1950s the government implemented an import substitution strategy that favored labor-intensive light manufacturing such as textiles. Beginning later in the decade, the government used tax breaks to encourage international investment on the island and to nurture certain targeted domestic industries in which Taiwan was judged to enjoy a comparative advantage. The government especially promoted labor-intensive industries such as chemicals, textiles, paper, rubber products, and plastics, which required little high technology or start-up capital but employed large numbers of unskilled laborers and helped even out the distribution of income among the islanders.[27] In the early 1960s, the state shifted to an export-led development strategy, a decision partly spurred by the promise of increased U.S. aid. In preparation, Taiwan's government enacted further economic reforms, including increasing the supply of electricity, reducing controls over foreign currency exchange, and establishing a stock market and an investment banking system. Additional tax incentives also helped make Taiwan's export processing zones, beginning with Kaohsiung harbor in

<hr>

[27] Peter Chen-main Wang, "A Bastion Created, A Regime Reformed, An Economy Reengineered, 1949–1970," in Murray A. Rubinstein, ed., *Taiwan: A New History* (New York: M.E. Sharpe, 1999), 332.

1966, successful in attracting foreign investment, providing jobs, and furthering the ROC's industrial development.

Foreign assistance was also a significant factor in Taiwan's postwar economic development. Japanese-built infrastructure had already brought Taiwan to the threshold of industrialization. Many ROC economic planners got advanced training overseas. Taiwan officials received abundant advice from U.S. experts. Although KMT officials often resented meddling in ROC internal matters by Americans who did not support all the party's goals, Taiwan could not afford to reject the aid the United States offered. Some of Taiwan's most successful economic policies were based on sound foreign advice tailored to local conditions by a younger generation of Western-educated Chinese. The Joint Commission on Rural Reconstruction (JCRR), founded in 1948 and composed of two Americans and three Chinese, recruited a staff of mostly U.S.-trained experts that helped shape Taiwan's land reform program in 1949–1953, among other successes. United States advisers consistently urged Taiwan's leaders toward privatization and openness to foreign investment. Some U.S. aid was tied to progress in economic reforms. On occasion U.S. officials pressured the ROC government not to proceed with plans for huge, costly public works projects. American advice and coercion not only clinched victory for Chen and other pro-reform ROC officials in internal policy debates, it provided these officials a measure of protection, allowing them to blame American demands for adjustments that proved painful in Taiwan.[28]

The $100 million in nonmilitary aid Taiwan got annually from the United States provided about 40 percent of the ROC's capital formation and gave an important boost to the building of infrastructure and the training of technical specialists.[29] Over 80 percent of U.S. economic aid to Taiwan was in the form of grants the ROC was not required to repay. American aid during this period accounted for more than one-third of Taiwan's total investment and 74 percent of all investment in agriculture.[30] Washington closed this pipeline in 1965. Congress had grown increasingly hostile toward foreign aid. To help preserve its foreign aid program, the U.S. government decided to characterize Taiwan as a model U.S. aid recipient. As part of this strategy, U.S. economic aid to Taiwan ceased in 1965. Taipei protested in vain that this was too soon to cut off American assistance.

Taiwan's postwar land reform program is widely considered one of the

[28] Nancy Bernkopf Tucker, *Taiwan, Hong Kong, and the United States, 1945–1992* (New York: Twayne, 1994), 59.
[29] Wang, "A Bastion Created," 328.
[30] Neil H. Jacoby, *U.S. Aid to Taiwan* (New York: Praeger, 1966), 38, 53.

KMT's most successful policies in both economic and political terms. This brought an important socioeconomic boost to a large segment of the island's population without the bloodshed that often accompanies large-scale land redistribution. Chen Cheng appears to have been chiefly motivated by the desire to prevent social and political unrest, believing that land reform would undercut potential support for communism. This was another area in which Chen and other KMT leaders implemented in post–Civil War Taiwan lessons learned from mistakes made on the mainland. Chen recognized that the old land ownership system, in which "the life of ease and happiness enjoyed by the landlord was built entirely on the miseries of the tenant. . . . provided the Communist agitators with an opportunity to infiltrate the villages." This, he said, was "one of the main reasons the Chinese mainland fell to the Communists."[31]

Taiwan's was one of the most ambitious land redistribution programs in history. The preparatory work alone required more than two thousand inspectors, who attempted to ascertain the size, quality, and ownership (the latter often unclear, as we have seen) of over 2 million plots of land.[32]

The task was eased by the comparative lack of opposition by politically powerful elites, which for some other countries has been a major obstacle. Indeed, serious land reform and other economic restructuring programs by the ROC in mainland China were impossible to carry out because of resistance from the wealthy classes, upon whose support Chiang's government depended. Taiwan, however, was different. At the time Taiwan became the seat of the ROC government, few high-ranking KMT officials had large land holdings on the island. Besides lacking a sense of permanent attachment to Taiwan, Mainlanders tended to prefer investing their money in industrial enterprises with more promise of quick returns rather than buying land. Hence a small number of Taiwanese landlords owned most of the island's farmland. These wealthy Taiwanese lacked the influence to forestall a land reform program favored by a Mainlander-dominated government that had little reason to protect the interests of local landlords. Arousing the deep resentment of the landlords, it turned out, was not politically cost-free for the KMT. Since most Taiwanese intellectuals were the products of landlord families, land reform would fan articulate opposition to the regime even as it benefited large numbers of working-class Taiwanese.

The government instituted the land reform program in three phases: re-

[31] Ching-yuan Lin, "Agriculture and Rural-Urban Migration: The 1949–53 Land Reform," in James C. Hsiung et al., eds., *The Taiwan Experience 1950–1980* (New York: Praeger, 1981), 140; Ch'en Ch'eng, *Land Reform in Taiwan* (Taipei: China Publishing, 1961), 47–48.
[32] W. G. Goddard, *Formosa: A Study in Chinese History* (West Lansing: Michigan State University Press, 1966), 193.

duction of rent (1949), sale of public land (1951), and transfer of land own-ership to tenant farmers (1953). Since the departure of the Japanese, who enforced rent control, tenant farmers on Taiwan had typically paid their landlords 50 percent of their crop yield as rent. The Rent Reduction Act of 1949 reduced rent to a maximum of 37.5 percent. The rationale underlying this figure was that 25 percent should first be deducted from the total an-nual yield of the main crops to compensate the tenants for their labor and investments in the farm, and the remaining 75 percent was to be split evenly between the tenants and the landlord. In 1951, the government of-fered about one-fifth of the island's arable land for sale to tenant farmers. These were properties the ROC had confiscated from Japanese officials, corporations, and military men after the war. To ensure that this land was distributed among a large number of Taiwanese farmers rather than bought up by a few rich families, the government limited individual pur-chasers to one plot of a size judged necessary to maintain a family of six (the actual acreage varied by area, depending on the quality of the soil). The price was set at two and a half times the value of the normal annual yield of the main crop (it was a Chinese custom to charge a fixed amount of rent from year to year, regardless of the actual size of a given year's har-vest). This was well below the market price for land. Buyers were allowed to pay for their land in produce rather than cash over ten years with no in-terest on the debt. More than 150,000 tenant farm families bought land under this program.[33]

The 1953 Land to the Tiller Act permitted landlords to retain a limited amount of land for their own tillage,[34] but they had to sell their holdings beyond that limit to the state. Landlords received 70 percent of their com-pensation in the form of land bonds and 30 percent in shares of stock in four government industries: Taiwan Cement, Taiwan Pulp and Paper, Tai-wan Agriculture and Forestry, and Taiwan Industry and Mining. The state then resold this land to the former tenants who had farmed it at a price of 2.5 times the land's annual crop value. The new owners were eligible for loans to be repaid over ten years and for grants to assist with moderniza-tion and irrigation.

More than 2 million Taiwanese gained property rights under the land reform program, and the income of farmers nearly doubled. From 1949 to 1953, the percentage of agricultural land in Taiwan cultivated by the own-ers of the land rose from 51 percent to 79 percent. The higher rate of land

---

[33] John F. Copper, *Taiwan: Nation-State or Province?* (Boulder, Colo.: Westview Press, 1996), 131.

[34] The law limited a single landlord to ownership of three *chia* of rice field and six *chia* of farmland producing crops other than rice. A *chia* is equal to about 9,700 square feet.

ownership among farmers also increased productivity, as farmers worked harder on their own land than rented land. Overall agricultural production rose by more than 50 percent between 1952 and 1963.[35]

A more far-reaching effect of the KMT's land reform program was the leveling of Taiwanese society. As elsewhere, the landlord class had traditionally enjoyed entrenched, semifeudal privileges in Taiwan. Forced to give up their land, most landlords sold off the stock they received for compensation. Later, both land prices and the value of these stock shares appreciated, creating wealth among Taiwanese outside the traditional landed elite class and greatly reducing disparities of income throughout society.[36] The disparity between the rich and the poor shrunk steadily until by the 1980s Taiwan's rate of income inequality was one of the lowest in the world, besting both the United States and Japan. At the urging of the JCRR, Chen allowed elections for representatives to the farmers' associations (which persisted from the Japan colonial era). This gave ordinary people in Taiwan additional experience in grass-roots democracy and would hasten the growth of pressures on the KMT to liberalize the political system as a whole.

Critics argue that the success of the land reform program was mitigated by other government policies that exploited Taiwan's farmers. An example was the fertilizer exchange policy. The government provided farmers with chemical fertilizer, the supply of which was controlled by a government monopoly. Farmers paid for it in rice at the rate of one ton of fertilizer for one ton of rice. This was a poor deal for farmers; in 1949 a ton of fertilizer had a market value of $70 versus $170 for a ton of rice, and through the 1950s the value of rice relative to fertilizer grew even higher. Sugarcane farmers similarly had a sizeable proportion of their potential profits skimmed off. Inheriting the island's Japanese sugar processing industry, the government-owned Taiwan Sugar Corporation took much of the farmers' crop as processing fees and forced them to sell still more at artificially low prices. This generated handsome profits for the state sugar industry, but left the farmers with only about 20 percent of their crop to sell at the market price.

In the white-collar economy, stemming from their control of the first postwar administration, the minority Mainlanders were overrepresented in prestigious business positions. Taiwanese were the predominant owners of agricultural land and controlled many small and medium-sized

[35] F. A. Lumley, *The Republic of China Under Chiang Kai-Shek: Taiwan Today* (London: Barrie & Jenkins, 1976), 69; S. Long, *Taiwan: China's Last Frontier* (Basingstoke, U.K.: Macmillan, 1991), 79; Goddard, 194.

[36] John H. C. Fei, Gustav Ranis, and Shirley W. Y. Kuo, *Growth with Equity: The Taiwan Case* (Washington, D.C.: International Bank for Reconstruction and Development, 1979), 38.

businesses. In larger enterprises and state-owned industries and utilities, however, government control led to preferential hiring and promotion of Mainlanders and discrimination against Taiwanese. Wealthy Taiwanese entrepreneurs who sought to establish new firms complained that they were disadvantaged because they had comparatively weak personal connections with the Mainland-dominated bureaucracy, important in negotiating a path through government regulations. As during Chen Yi's tenure, this pattern carried over into education as well. Aside from the field of medicine, Mainlanders continued to dominate the ranks of university professors and principals of elementary and middle schools.

Taiwan was not yet a wealthy country. In many rural areas during the 1960s, families were eating more sweet potatoes than rice (an indication of poverty in a culture that considers sweet potatoes fodder for animals). Taiwan's feet, nevertheless, stood firmly on the path to prosperity. During the decades of the 1950s and 1960s, Taiwan's primarily agricultural economy developed into a semi-industrialized economy, domestic consumption demand greatly increased, and unemployment faded as a serious problem. Through the 1950s, Taiwan's annual gross national product (GNP) grew at a rate greater than 8 percent. In the 1960s the growth rate rose to nearly 10 percent, while inflation was kept below 5 percent. Paralleling Taiwan's economic performance, the literacy rate increased, and the key indicators of public health and welfare rose as well.

Taxation to support Taiwan's large armed forces cancelled out some of the benefit of the country's overall economic growth. Military spending consumed 10 to 12 percent of Taiwan's gross domestic product during this period.

Summary and Conclusions

Like any group of politicians, the most fundamental objective of KMT leaders was to maintain their own power and status. Preserving KMT rule in Taiwan against both internal threats (e.g. Taiwanese nationalism) and external threats (the PRC) was therefore the party's minimum goal. Secondarily, the KMT sought to bring about prosperity and stability on Taiwan and to promote local support for KMT rule and the ROC identity. The ultimate goals were to restore KMT rule on the mainland and eventually to preside over the realization of Sun Yat-sen's vision throughout all of China. Accordingly, the KMT that was exiled on Taiwan aimed for a mixture of strong central rule and limited liberalization with the promise of more in the future. The commitment to eventual full democracy was consistent with the party's basic doctrine and also served to enhance the

ROC's legitimacy by distinguishing it from its unworthy counterpart on the mainland.

The Taiwan-based KMT had greatly cleaned up its act compared to Chiang's regime on the mainland. With the reform of the party, governance was more efficiently organized and administered, and the leadership promoted economic development and land reform programs that raised the standard of living for the majority of Taiwan's population. Part of this improvement resulted from the leadership learning the lessons of past mistakes, and part from Taiwan's less challenging circumstances (e.g., smaller size compared to the mainland, less susceptibility to Communist insurgency, and little land ownership among the party elites).

Despite the harsh treatment of some political offenders, the combination of modest political reforms and respectable management of Taiwan's improving economy began to gain the KMT some legitimacy in the eyes of many Taiwanese. Over the long term, however, this commitment to democratization left the party vulnerable to increasingly strong criticism from opposition politicians that the persistence of martial law and its suppressive effects were proof that the KMT was fundamentally authoritarian and unable to relinquish real power to the people.

1. A boulevard in modern Taipei.

2. Taiwan aborigines in traditional dress.

3. Chiang Kai-shek, president of the Republic of
China on Taiwan from 1950 to 1975.

4. Chiang Ching-kuo, president of the Republic of China from 1975 to 1988.

5. Loudspeaker truck during the December 2001 election campaign. Photo: Shu Ming-sung.

6. Chiang Kai-shek Memorial, Taipei. Photo: Shu Ming-sung.

7. National Concert Hall, Taipei, with the Hsinkuang Sanyue building in the background. Photo: Shu Ming-sung.

8. Retirees socialize at the Lungshan Temple, Taipei. Photo: Shu Ming-sung.

9. Interior view of
Lungshan Temple, Taipei.
Photo: Denny Roy.

10. A typical Taipei side street, filled with parked motor scooters. Photo: Denny Roy.

11. Presidential Palace, Taipei. Photo: Denny Roy.

12. The February 28 Peace Memorial Monument, Taipei. Photo: Denny Roy.

13 and 14. Riot police block a planned opposition rally in the dying days of martial law, May 1987. Photos: Denny Roy.

15. Lee Teng-hui, first island-born president
(1988–2000) of the Republic of China.
Photo: Chung Ju-yu.

16. Chen Shui-ban, elected president of the ROC in
2000. Photo: Chung Ju-yu.

Taiwan in the Cold War

The Cold War created a new international political context that gave the continuing Chinese Civil War an enlarged, global significance. Most significantly for Taiwan, the United States government's policy changed from abandoning the ROC to defending it after the Korean War caused Washington to reinterpret Taiwan as part of the Cold War battleground. This gave the KMT access to America's vast resources, but also brought the challenges of persuading the United States to support Taipei's agenda and avoiding a dependence that would give Washington excessive control over Taiwan's destiny. The KMT also knew American officials were prone to push for economic and political liberalization, which the top party leadership tended to view as naive and arrogant. Chiang's attitude toward the United States had always been ambivalent. He was suspicious, if not hostile, toward ROC political figures he considered too friendly with the United States, as was evident in the purges of Sun Li-jen and later former foreign minister and ambassador to the United States Yeh Kung-ch'ao (George Yeh). Consequently, despite close U.S.-ROC cooperation during the Cold War, the relationship also generated continual friction and disagreements—much like Chiang's relationship with the Americans before the Cold War.

Wartime and Postwar U.S.-ROC Relations

Chiang and the U.S. government were alliance partners during the Pacific War. The two states' deep common interest in defeating Japan sustained the relationship despite disagreements over the conduct of the war. The ROC clearly benefited from American support. The Allies accepted

China into the club of major powers. Chiang was named Supreme Commander of Allied forces in the China theater. He attended the wartime summit meetings at Cairo and Tehran, and China occupied one of the permanent seats in the new United Nations Security Council. The United States relinquished its privilege of extraterritoriality[1] in China and repealed the Chinese Exclusion Act, which had all but banned Chinese immigration into the United States. Wartime propaganda in the United States portrayed China as a protodemocratic and proto-Christian country putting up a gallant fight against a powerful and cruel fascist invader. Chiang's American-educated wife Sung Mei-ling won congressional and public favor in an eloquent appeal for support delivered before the U.S. Senate and House of Representatives. Pro-ROC sentiment grew within American society as a whole, which paid Taipei dividends after the war.

Yet Chiang hardly got everything he wanted from the Americans. Differing agendas strained ROC-U.S. relations. Chiang's government resented the Allies' "Europe first" strategy and the awarding of former Japanese interests in Manchuria to the USSR in return for the Soviets' late entry into the Pacific War. Chiang was fighting three enemies at once in China: the Japanese, the Chinese Communists, and rival military strongmen who were nominally part of his KMT coalition. He wanted to leave the fight against Japan to the United States and preserve his forces for a final campaign to eliminate the Chinese Communists. Republic of China leaders frequently expressed the hope that the United States would send 1 million ground troops to fight the Japanese troops in China. The American government, on the other hand, expected Chiang to contribute to the defeat of Japan by destroying as much as possible of the large Japanese army campaigning in China. Washington was therefore disappointed at Chiang's reluctance to send his forces into battle against the Japanese. United States officials who worked closely with Chiang, such as his U.S. deputy commanders General Joseph W. "Vinegar Joe" Stilwell and General Albert C. Wedemeyer, became disillusioned with the KMT regime. Chiang's military decision-making was highly political, taking into account regional and personal loyalties. This led him on occasion to retain commanders who were corrupt or incompetent, or to position troops or individual officers with a view toward preventing generals he distrusted from gaining too much political power, or to withhold his best-trained and most loyal troops from combat. To American observers focused on defeating the Japanese and lacking appreciation for the complex context of political in-

---

[1] Extraterritoriality allowed foreigners accused of committing crimes in China to be judged and sentenced by their own officials according to their own laws. Westerners had enjoyed this privilege since the nineteenth century.

trigue within which Chiang operated, the generalissimo's decisions often appeared irrational, and his army's performance dysfunctional.[2]

After the war these patterns continued. Washington and Nanking were allies against a common enemy, but some of their goals differed, and each government frequently failed to meet the other's expectations. Of immediate concern in this regard was the failure of attempts by Ambassador Patrick J. Hurley and General George C. Marshall to mediate a nonviolent settlement between the Kuomintang and Communist forces. Both sides were eager to position themselves for what they believed would ultimately be a military showdown. Both parties were also disappointed by U.S. involvement. Past American support for the Chiang regime made it impossible for the CCP to believe that the United States was a neutral arbiter. At the same time, the KMT believed that to some degree the United States had betrayed the Republic of China. In the KMT's view, Washington had forced the KMT to make concessions to the Communists while attempting to arbitrate a reconciliation. The United States failed to provide the ROC as much support as the CCP got from the Soviet Union. Then the United States cut off military aid altogether when the ROC needed it most. KMT leaders held that American policies were an important reason the CCP conquered the mainland. Washington did not fully support the ROC in international diplomatic circles either. Chiang hoped to rally the Asian states under threat of Communist takeover into a NATO-like alliance. He elicited statements in support of the idea from South Korean president Syngman Rhee and Philippine president Elpidio Quirino in 1949 before Secretary of State Dean Acheson publicly killed the planned alliance, saying it would antagonize India.

Many Americans agreed that the United States had let the ROC down. Supporting the ROC against the PRC was a popular position in the United States, where Chiang still enjoyed the benefits of a favorable image built up by wartime propaganda. Not a few Americans preferred to believe his defeat by Mao's forces resulted from a Communist conspiracy, a theory promoted by political opportunists such as Senator Joseph McCarthy. With revulsion toward communism already deeply ingrained in the United States, the PRC quickly earned a negative image through its mistreatment of Westerners in China[3]. The American perception that Mao's

[2] See Edward L. Dreyer, *China at War, 1901–1949* (New York: Addison Wesley Longman, 1995), especially chaps. 6 and 7.

[3] For example, the Chinese put the U.S. consul in Mukden, Angus Ward, and his staff under detention for a month and took over the U.S. embassy in Beijing. The CCP also departed from an international legal custom by announcing in 1947 it was not obligated to honor the financial and diplomatic agreements entered into by the previous KMT government.

China was an aggressive, irresponsible state in league with Moscow hardened after China entered the Korean War. Many influential individuals and lobbying groups such as the Committee of One Million urged continued support for "free China" and opposed normal relations with Beijing. Politicians were under pressure to demonstrate they could effectively stand up to the Communist challenge, as the defeat of Democratic Party candidates in the 1950 congressional election and in the 1952 presidential election demonstrated.

Taiwan Abandoned, Then Embraced

Ironically, before the end of the Pacific War, the CPP officially urged Taiwan to seek independence (from Japan). Mao himself is on record as saying in 1936 that he did not consider Taiwan one of China's "lost territories," but rather that he supported Taiwanese independence.[4] This may seem remarkable today, but points up the fact that only recently in historical terms have Chinese considered Taiwan a part of China. Nevertheless, with the establishment of the People's Republic, the CCP committed itself to winning control of the island. This created a problem for American military planners, for whom Taiwan had compelling strategic significance. If the island fell under the CCP's control, Soviet air and submarine bases on Taiwan would pose a serious threat to the sea lanes between America and Northeast Asia and between Japan and Southeast Asia. General Douglas MacArthur, one of a large number of senior American officials who favored a stronger U.S. commitment to the ROC, reprised an earlier Japanese characterization of Taiwan as "an unsinkable aircraft carrier and submarine tender" from which Soviet-aligned forces could block operations out of the Philippines and Okinawa. Conversely, under a pro-U.S. government Taiwan would be an important asset to either a containment strategy, as part of an island chain fencing in the Communist camp, or a "rollback" strategy, as a site for bases and a springboard in a campaign to win back Asian territory under Communist rule.

Despite the value of keeping a friendly government in Taiwan, U.S. president Harry Truman and Secretary of State Acheson concluded that continued military assistance to Chiang's regime would waste American money and erode American prestige. They accepted the conclusions of Wedemeyer's one-month fact-finding visit to China in August 1947. Wedemeyer reported publicly that corruption and incompetence had

---

[4] "Is Taiwan Really Part of China?" *The Economist*, Mar. 16, 1996, 40.

gravely weakened Chiang's government. Instead of relying on outside assistance, he said, China's leadership needed to make immediate political and economic reforms. "Military force in itself will not eliminate communism," he concluded.[5] Similarly, the Truman administration's 1,054-page China White Paper released in August 1949 argued that the Kuomintang lost the civil war on the mainland due to inefficient and inept governance despite what should have been ample U.S. economic and military aid.

The KMT leadership naturally condemned this interpretation of their defeat and began a long-term campaign to combat it both at home and abroad. In the early 1950s Taipei circulated documents, which later proved inaccurate, suggesting that U.S. "China hands" John Service and Owen Lattimore had pro-CCP sympathies. Ambassador to the United States Wellington Koo and other ROC officials secretly paid American journalists who wrote disparaging reports about U.S. China experts considered unfriendly to the Chiang government.[6] Taipei openly criticized U.S. China scholar and Harvard professor John King Fairbank, who in his writings and in testimony to the U.S. Congress argued that mainland Chinese accepted communism because of its similarities with traditional Chinese culture. Kuomintang members criticized scholars and politicians in Taiwan who associated with Fairbank or accepted money from the Ford Foundation, allegedly under Fairbank's control.

By 1949 Washington was clearly distancing itself from the KMT, and in January 1950 Truman would announce that "the U.S. government will not provide military aid or advice to Chinese forces on Formosa." From Washington's perspective, the ideal scenario was a separated Taiwan under a U.S.-aligned, noncommunist ruler other than Chiang, brought about by a means that did not irretrievably antagonize China. Ultimately, the Truman administration hoped to improve relations with China and split Beijing away from the Soviet Union. Thus, behind closed doors Acheson told his colleagues, "We must carefully conceal our wish to separate the island from mainland control."[7]

Truman's advisers recommended the U.S. government encourage political reform on Taiwan (to inoculate it against Communist subversion) and cultivate a relationship with "potential native Formosan leaders with a view at some future date to being able to make use of a Formosan autonomous movement should it appear to be in the U.S. national interest to

[5] U.S. Department of State, *United States Relations with China, With Special Reference to the Period 1944–1949* (Washington, D.C.: U.S. Government Printing Office, 1949), 763–764.

[6] Bruce Cumings, "Eulogy for John S. Service," *Bulletin of Concerned Asian Scholars* 32, no. 3 (July–Sept. 2000): 43–46.

[7] Bruce Cumings, *Parallax Visions* (Durham, N.C.: Duke University Press, 1999), 154, citing the Harry Truman presidential archive.

do so."[8] As large numbers of KMT and ROC military personnel relocated to Taiwan throughout 1949, U.S. officials realized this nonmilitary strategy was unlikely to succeed. Direct U.S. military intervention to save Taiwan was also ruled out, as the U.S. Joint Chiefs of Staff advised Truman that Taiwan's strategic importance was not great enough to justify such a drastic step. Significantly, the Joint Chiefs added that they might recommend intervention to save Taiwan if a larger war broke out in Asia. Absent such a conflict, and with Chiang remaining in power, the Truman administration was prepared to abandon Taiwan.

This policy position was highly controversial, and many U.S. officials and private citizens lobbied against it, believing that Taiwan's strategic and political significance and Chiang's anticommunist commitment justified further U.S. support for the ROC. The Truman administration acquiesced in the attempt by several influential Americans, motivated by a mix of commercial and ideological interests, to arrange unofficial shipments of heavy weapons to Taiwan. Since the administration wanted Taiwan but not Chiang, U.S. State department officials Dean Rusk and Paul Nitze discussed the possibility of a U.S.-supported coup d'etat to replace Chiang with a leader Washington perceived as more competent and respectable. This, they postulated, might restore the political consensus within the United States in favor of resuming the flow of military aid to Taiwan. Frequently mentioned candidates to succeed Chiang were liberal political thinker Hu Shih and General Sun Li-jen, who had a U.S. education and many friends among the American elite. Rusk reportedly met Hu Shih at the Plaza Hotel in New York on June 23, 1950, and asked if Hu was interested in leading a new government. Although critical of Chiang, Hu declined, saying he had no political power base. Another aspect of these plans was the notion of placing Taiwan under a UN trusteeship. If Taiwan's (new) leader requested UN involvement in a reassessment of the island's international status, the U.S. Navy would shield Taiwan from attempts by China to interfere. Reopening the question of whether Taiwan was part of China was anathema to the KMT as much as the CCP, of course. But from the American standpoint this was desirable because it would deny Beijing control of the island, and Taipei could be forced into submission if told UN trusteeship was the only alternative to conquest by Mao.

The February 1950 treaty between China and the USSR, following Mao's statement the previous year that China would "lean to one side" toward the Soviet camp, increased pressure on Truman to resume aid to

[8] The passage is drawn from National Security Council memorandum 37/2, approved by Truman, Feb. 4, 1949.

the ROC. One of the strongest arguments for withholding aid was that if the United States accommodated China, Beijing would break from the Soviets and reconcile with the U.S. bloc. Now the Sino-Soviet relationship was getting stronger despite the cessation of U.S. military assistance to Taiwan.

Nevertheless, with no sign of a dramatic change in the U.S. position, Taiwan expected to be overrun by a Communist invasion in the summer or fall of 1950. The ROC military suffered from poor morale, limited numbers, and the loss of its former bases of armaments production on the mainland. Knowing that future aid from an increasingly skeptical American government was hanging in the balance, the ROC military had made extensive preparations to defend resource-rich Hainan Island, but the Communist People's Liberation Army (PLA) had conquered it swiftly in April 1950. Only the large natural moat of the Taiwan Strait prevented CCP forces from finishing off the KMT soon after the last major ROC-held cities on the mainland fell in 1949. For the young PLA, a successful amphibious invasion across the strait was a difficult but not an impossible proposition, especially given the leadership's willingness to suffer high casualties in pursuit of a political victory of such magnitude. The Chinese had reportedly mobilized 150,000 assault troops and collected in Fujian ports a large number of motorized junks for transporting these troops by mid-1950.[9] These junks were difficult to sink with naval gunfire; the shells tended to pass cleanly through their wood hulls leaving holes that could be plugged. They were fitted with 40 mm guns that would allow them to put up a stiff defense against both aircraft and destroyers. The Sino-Soviet alliance that coalesced in early 1950 increased the likelihood the PLA would conquer Taiwan. Stalin refused to get directly involved in the invasion, but agreed to help beef up Chinese naval and air capabilities in preparation for the assault.[10] United States and British intelligence analysts predicted the invasion would take place sometime in the summer of 1950; the U.S. government ordered its nonessential personnel in Taiwan to evacuate on May 26. During the year prior to the expected PLA assault, Chiang brought in as advisers several Japanese military men notorious from the fascist era, including General Okamura Yasuji, who had been imprisoned for war crimes committed in China, and former Taiwan governor-general Hasegawa. With the ROC seemingly facing imminent extinc-

[9] Ta Jen Liu, *U.S.-China Relations, 1784–1992* (Lanham, Md.: University Press of America, 1997), 205.

[10] Chen Jian, *China's Road to the Korean War: The Making of the Sino-American Confrontation* (New York: Columbia University Press, 1994), 97–98; Sergei N. Gancharov, Xue Litai, and John W. Lewis, *Uncertain Partners: Stalin, Mao and the Korean War* (Stanford, Calif.: Stanford University Press, 1993), 69, 99–100.

tion, Chiang reportedly hoped to raise an army of 300,000 Japanese mercenaries to help him reconquer China.[11]

But external forces would once again decisively influence the course of Taiwan's history. Just as the Japanese invasion of China probably saved the CCP from destruction by the KMT, the outbreak of the Korean War on June 25, 1950, probably spared Chiang's ROC from conquest by the CCP. For Taiwan, the most important consequence of the war arose from Truman's announcement on June 27 that in connection with U.S. intervention to rescue the South Korean government, "I have ordered the Seventh Fleet to prevent any attack upon Formosa." The interposition of the U.S. Navy would make an assault on Taiwan by the PLA impossible. Truman indicated, however, his support for the KMT regime was limited. He added that as a "corollary" he was "calling upon" Taipei to cease attacks against the mainland, and that the "future status of Formosa" was not yet settled—sharp jolts to two core KMT principles. The status of Taiwan had seemed a settled issue. The Cairo Declaration, as we saw, stated that Taiwan "shall be restored to the Republic of China." After the war, having recognized the ROC as one of the major Allied powers, the U.S. government declined to push for independence or UN trusteeship for Taiwan, adhering to the position that Taiwan was part of the ROC even after the abuses of the Chen Yi administration came to light. It was the Chiang government's defeat by numerically smaller Communist forces despite substantial U.S. aid, rather than questions about the justice or competence of its rule on Taiwan, that degraded the KMT's status in the worldview of American officials. International politics, not Chinese or Taiwan politics, moved Washington to reopen the question of Taiwan's status. In short, the United States was now following a "two Chinas" policy to justify denying Taiwan to the CCP.

A successful anti-Chiang coup might have had the same effect, but the fighting in Korea caused an overnight reversal of U.S. policy toward Taiwan: from abandoning the island to CCP takeover to guaranteeing Taiwan's protection through U.S. military deployment. The outbreak of the Korean War in June convinced key U.S. policymakers, including Truman and Acheson, that the contest with the Sino-Soviet bloc had entered a new, more intense phase. In Truman's words, "The attack upon Korea makes it plain beyond all doubt that Communism has passed beyond the use of subversion to conquer independent nations and will now use armed forces and war. . . . In these circumstances, the occupation of Formosa by Communist Forces would be a direct threat to the security of the Pacific

---

[11] Bruce Cumings, *The Origins of the Korean War*, vol. 2, *The Roaring of the Cataract, 1947–1950* (Princeton, N.J.: Princeton University Press, 1990), 524.

Area and to the United States." Strong assumptions about deterring communism had never been far below the surface of American strategic thinking. All that was missing was the triggering event that, in the minds of American strategists, demonstrated the Communist bloc was pursuing its goals through military aggression. Harking back to recent experience with Nazi Germany, American leaders emphasized the importance of responding to aggressive moves by their adversary with resolve rather than concessions. A firm response would intimidate the enemy, while showing weakness would encourage further attacks on other parts of the noncommunist frontier. Within this context, as the Joint Chiefs had said, the United States perceived a much greater interest in denying the CCP a victory on Taiwan.

Truman so quickly decided on using the Seventh Fleet to enforce a neutralization of Taiwan because his advisors had already discussed this contingency, although they had linked it with Chiang's removal by a coup d'etat. Since the war preempted the coup, the United States was now stuck protecting Chiang.[12]

After the Korean War, Taipei and Washington shared the objectives of protecting Taiwan and Penghu from being overrun by China, spying on and harassing the PRC government, and preserving the ROC's international diplomatic status while minimizing that of Beijing. Beyond this common ground, however, Taiwan and the United States disagreed on grand strategy against the PRC. The ROC wanted to overthrow the CCP government. The KMT insisted the CCP was unpopular on the mainland and remained in control only by exercising its police powers to crush dissent and organized resistance. Chiang consistently argued that once ROC forces landed on the mainland, the Chinese people, now disillusioned with communism, would be emboldened to rise up against the CCP. Thousands of anticommunist guerrillas already in China would also join the fight. Chiang recalled that the campaign that eventually unified China began with the establishment of the Whampoa Military Academy and its first class of five hundred cadets, poorly fed and confined to a five-kilometer-square island in the Pearl River, with unfriendly armies on all sides. Chiang had conquered China once before starting with five hundred men on a tiny islet. Now he had "a sizable base of operations. The population of and area of Taiwan . . . are thousands of times greater than those of Whampoa."[13]

The source of instability in Asia was the CCP regime in China, the KMT

---

[12] Ibid., 524–543.

[13] Keiji Furuya, *Chiang Kai-shek: His Life and Times* (New York: St. John's University Press, 1981), 933, 914.

told U.S. officials. The leadership in Beijing would continue to torment the region, forcing costly countermeasures by the United States, until the Communists lost control of China. Taipei reiterated this argument with each new crisis: CCP support for Communist parties abroad, the Korean War, the Vietnam conflict. Chiang Kai-shek tirelessly asserted it was better for the United States to deal with China (by supporting an ROC invasion) immediately rather than waiting until China got stronger and fomented more political and military tensions.

United States officials did not believe the KMT's plan to reconquer China was realistic. An attempted ROC invasion of the mainland was far more likely to result in the surrender of Taiwan to the PRC, through the waste of men and resources who might otherwise strengthen the main island's defenses, than in the restoration of KMT rule in China. Washington, of course, was not sympathetic to the KMT's sense of sacred responsibility to nation and history. Resigned to the survival of the CCP regime, the United States wanted to weaken it and induce it to break away from the Soviet camp and seek accommodation with the democratic-capitalist world. The United States therefore favored small-scale ROC military activities on the mainland that would harass the CCP regime and make it appear incapable of policing its own territory, but opposed operations that might lead to a major war involving the United States or would divert too much ROC strength away from the defense of Taiwan.

As a result of these differing positions, the U.S. government supported many low-intensity ROC military activities against the PRC, but refused repeated requests for U.S. assent to a large-scale invasion. Washington nevertheless believed it had to profess support in principle for the KMT's goal of reconquering the mainland. Otherwise, Taiwan might suffer a collapse in morale and the KMT might strike a bargain with Beijing.[14]

Chiang repeatedly requested U.S. support for an ROC military campaign to retake control of China, but in each case Washington refused. In May 1953 Chiang proposed an attack on the mainland with sixty ROC divisions (a force that would take another three years to raise) if Korean War peace talks failed. He argued that China would be vulnerable for a few years because the PLA had suffered large casualties in Korea and the CCP's economic development plans were at an early stage. Chiang also agreed to place his troops under the command of an American general if the United States military participated. The Korean War truce in July halted U.S. consideration of Chiang's proposal. When he renewed the idea in 1954, the Joint Chiefs rejected it. The U.S. military high command was

---

[14] John W. Garver, *The Sino-American Alliance: Nationalist China and American Cold War Strategy in Asia* (Armonk, N.Y.: M.E. Sharpe, 1997), 88.

generally more pessimistic than Chiang about the capabilities of the ROC forces and worried that squandering too many soldiers and resources in an attempt to retake China might leave Taiwan too weak to repulse a Chinese invasion. In 1956 Chiang again petitioned the U.S. government to allow him to invade the mainland, arguing in a May letter to Eisenhower that China was undergoing "extreme social and economic difficulties" and that its people would "rise in revolt" after ROC forces landed on the coast. Chiang asked only for U.S. logistical support, not direct involvement by U.S. troops in combat, and assured Eisenhower that the Soviets would not intervene as long as Soviet territory was not attacked.[15] Eisenhower responded that Chiang's plan should await clear signs of CCP collapse. Chiang argued that the opportunity had arrived after China suffered a series of natural and manmade disasters starting with Mao's Great Leap Forward in 1958. The Great Leap mobilized the entire Chinese population in an attempt to create rapid industrialization. The results, however, were severe damage to China's economy and large-scale starvation. Parts of China suffered floods and droughts in 1962, while much of the PLA was tied down by military tensions on the borders with India and the Soviet Union. Chiang told his people on January 1, 1962, "Have no fear of being alone in rising against the Communists. Have no fear of lack or shortage of supplies or help. Both will be forthcoming once you take action."[16] The ROC government made apparent preparations for war. These included implementing a war tax to raise an additional $60 million, extending the period of compulsory military service, and training cadres who would establish KMT administrations in occupied areas of mainland China. This alarmed both China and the United States. The PRC stationed additional troops on the coastal region opposite Taiwan and several U.S. officials warned Taipei that the Kennedy administration would not support an ROC invasion of China. The Soviet Union weighed in as well, with Premier Nikita Khrushchev declaring in July 1962, "Anyone who dares to attack the People's Republic of China will meet a crushing rebuff from the great Chinese people and the people of the Soviet Union and the whole socialist camp."[17] Lacking crucial U.S. support, KMT invasion fervor died down in 1963, and ROC military action against the mainland was limited to a few commando raids. The ROC saw yet another window of opportu-

---

[15] Chiang Kai-shek letter to President Eisenhower, Apr. 16, 1956, *Foreign Relations of the United States, 1955–57*, vol. 2 (Washington, D.C.: U.S. Government Printing Office, 1986), 343–348.

[16] Hungdah Chiu, "The Question of Taiwan in Sino-American Relations," in Chiu, ed., *China and the Question of Taiwan: Documents and Analysis* (New York: Praeger, 1973), 173.

[17] Harold C. Hinton, *Communist China in World Politics* (Boston: Houghton Mifflin, 1966), 272.

nity during the Cultural Revolution. Although Beijing continued to reaffirm its determination to "liberate" Taiwan, this outward bravado belied China's serious internal political turmoil. In January 1967, Taipei's ambassador to the United States, Chow Shu-kai, said publicly that 1967 might be year the ROC recovered the mainland. Again, however, U.S. officials quickly discouraged any plans to attack the mainland. Chiang's October 10 National Day speech showed the effects of U.S. pressure: he said the campaign to recapture China should be 70 percent political and only 30 percent military.[18]

A related and similarly subterranean issue of dispute was Taiwan's ultimate political destiny. A "two Chinas" outcome, with Taiwan permanently separated from the control of the government in Beijing, seemed to serve American interests well. This would facilitate tying Taiwan into the U.S. defense structure in the western Pacific. Americans also expected that once Beijing acquiesced to the "loss" of Taiwan and the KMT to the loss of the mainland, tensions between the PRC and the ROC would subside. Chiang understood and vigorously opposed these U.S. efforts to solidify the two-China status quo.

Despite these divergent strategies, the two governments quickly took concrete steps after the outbreak of the Korean War that would culminate in a military alliance. By the end of 1951, a U.S. embassy had replaced the American Consulate General in Taipei, Congress had passed a bill providing $300 million in aid to Taiwan, and a U.S. general headed a Military Assistance Group on the island. The election of Republican Dwight D. Eisenhower as U.S. president hastened this process. While Truman had tried to distance the United States from Chiang's government, Eisenhower welcomed Chiang as an ally.[19] Eisenhower announced in his first State of the Union message in February 1953 a "deneutralization" of the Taiwan Strait: while continuing to guard against a PRC invasion of Taiwan, the United States would no longer restrain ROC attacks against the mainland. Eisenhower said he saw no "logic or sense in a condition that required the United States Navy to assume defensive responsibilities on behalf of the Chinese Communists, thus permitting those communists, with greater impunity, to kill our soldiers and those of our United Nations allies in Korea." Chiang welcomed Eisenhower's move as "not only judicious but also militarily sound."[20] Britain, India, and some Southeast Asian states, however, criticized the change as an invitation to a wider conflict.

[18] *Free China Review* 17, no. 11 (November 1967): 88.

[19] Garver, *Sino-American Alliance*, 291.

[20] The China Handbook Editorial Board, *China Handbook 1953–1954* (Taipei: China Publishing, 1953), 152–153.

Chinese Civil War combat smoldered on through the 1950s and 1960s. While mutual hostility remained deep, fighting was limited to peripheral areas (the mainland's coastal region, a few areas near China's borders, and the Taiwan Strait) and small in scale. The obstacles of geography and American intervention prevented a resolution of the stalemate. Republic of China aircraft bombed targets on the Chinese coast, and ROC commandos and other infiltrators, sometimes delivered or supplied by U.S. Air Force aircraft or U.S. Navy vessels, repeatedly landed on the mainland. In numbers ranging from a handful to eighty, their objectives were to destroy infrastructure, kill PLA troops or CCP cadres, take prisoners, and seize useful documents. Commando activity in China was especially heavy in 1962–1965. In a single incident in July 1964, the ROC forces lost 150 men and four transport vessels. At sea, the ROC conducted low-intensity naval warfare against China in the 1950s and early 1960s, which had U.S. approval after the Korean War. Republic of China ships laid mines near the Chinese coast and fought in several small naval battles, in which vessels from both sides were sunk. In June 1949 the ROC declared a "closure" of Chinese ports under the CCP's control (as opposed to a "blockade," which would have implied the PRC was an enemy state rather than a group of rebels). This led to the interception of foreign vessels. Many of these ships were British, and a few were from Soviet-bloc countries. With its railroad network still underdeveloped, China was highly dependent on the sea lanes along its coast to move coal south and foodstuffs north via junks and barges. The ROC recruited pirates from the Jiangsu and Zhejiang coasts, near the principal port of Shanghai, and benefited from reports by coastal spies on the movements of Chinese ships. Republic of China naval activities also curtailed PRC fishing, causing considerable hardship to some Chinese communities. When the PLA Navy devoted more resources to combating ROC maritime interdiction operations, ROC crews employed trickery such as disguising their vessels as fishing boats or flying the PRC flag before suddenly firing on approaching PLA Navy ships. This ROC naval campaign significantly slowed Chinese economic development during the PRC's early years. But in addition to destroying Chinese resources, ROC vessels carried out a strange campaign of capturing and indoctrinating Chinese fishermen. During fishing season, a ROC fleet consisting of two landing ship tanks (LSTs) and several warships rounded up groups of Chinese fishing boats, sometimes after driving away PLA Navy escort ships. The ROC sailors then moved the Chinese crews into the spacious LSTs. There the fishermen watched movies, heard anticommunist propaganda, enjoyed a banquet, and received gifts. Afterward they returned to their boats and went back to fishing. The crews of 370 Chinese fishing boats underwent this process.[21]

Two Taiwan Strait Crises Test the New Alliance

Menacing PLA moves toward the offshore islands beginning in September 1954 gave impetus to serious negotiations about a U.S.-ROC defense treaty. The ROC government hoped a formal alliance would lock in an American defense commitment, make it more difficult for Washington to concede Taiwan to the PRC or support an independent Taiwan, and gain prestige for the KMT leadership.[22] Eisenhower's administration determined that U.S. interests required retaining Taiwan as part of the structure designed to protect noncommunist states on the western rim of the Pacific. In particular, a treaty would help deter Beijing from attacking Taiwan and provide a stronger international legal justification for basing U.S. forces on the island.[23]

Chiang got the treaty he wanted, but only after agreeing to substantial constraints. The U.S. government was wary of sanctioning the ROC's vision of conquering the mainland and of being dragged into a war with the PRC. Foreign Minister Yeh proposed the treaty should apply "to all the territories which are now, or which may hereafter be, under the control of the ROC." This wording committed the United States to help defend a hypothetical ROC beachhead on the mainland as well as any of the thirty smaller ROC-held islands beyond Taiwan and the Penghu group. The U.S. government wanted the text of the treaty to specify that the agreement applied only to the main islands. Article 6 of the December 1954 treaty in its final form limits applicable ROC territory to "Taiwan and the Pescadores." As a compromise, the text adds that the treaty also applies to "other territories as may be determined by mutual agreement."

Foreshadowing a PRC position that would become prominent in the 1990s, Taipei insisted it had a sovereign right to use force against rebels within its territory. The U.S. government, however, insisted that the ROC must gain Washington's consent before carrying out military operations against China. Sympathetic to the KMT's need to uphold its legitimacy at home, the United States supported resolution of this issue through an unpublicized agreement not written into the treaty. In an exchange of diplomatic notes, Dulles and Yeh agreed that the "use of force will be a matter

---

[21] Garver, *Sino-American Alliance*, 116–119, 108.

[22] Shao Yu-ming, *Chung-mei kuanhsi yanchiu wenji* (Taipei: Chuanji Wenhsueh Chubanshe, 1980), 111–116.

[23] Garver, *Sino-American Alliance*, 54.

of joint agreement."[24] Yeh asserted in a public statement Taipei's position that the treaty "did not signify in any way that the ROC did not have the right to recover the Mainland," but subsequent statements by U.S. officials made clear that the United States did not intend through the treaty to encourage offensive ROC military action against the mainland and the treaty did not apply to the smaller islands. As for the treaty's duration, the U.S. proposed ten years and the ROC pressed for a longer commitment. The two sides agreed to make the treaty's lifespan "indefinite," but subject to cancellation by either side with one year's notice.

Two crises over the smaller ROC-held islands in the Taiwan Strait strained the U.S.-ROC relationship at one of its weak points. Heavy fighting in 1952–53 had forced the ROC to abandon some of the smaller offshore islands to ensure it could sufficiently defend the larger islands. The principal ROC-held offshore islands were Jinmen (also known in the West as Quemoy), just off the Chinese port of Xiamen, and Matzu, near Fuzhou. Jinmen had withstood an amphibious assault by three PLA divisions in October 1949. The U.S. government felt these islands, only a stone's throw from the Chinese coast, were indefensible without heavy U.S. assistance, and not worth risking a major war. Washington urged Chiang to abandon them and concentrate on defending the main island. Chiang, however, insisted on retaining these islands. Bases on China's doorstep would be necessary to support any ROC military campaign on the mainland. The islands thus had great symbolic political value: retaining them was evidence the KMT was serious about retaking the mainland, while conceding them would have cast doubt on the possibility of reconquering China. Chiang argued that holding Jinmen and Matzu was necessary to avoid demoralizing anticommunist elements on the mainland. He knew it was also necessary to avoid weakening the legitimacy of KMT rule in Taiwan. Defense of the offshore islands was a particularly difficult issue for the United States because Chiang insisted he would occupy and defend them even without American help. If Washington left Taiwan to fight this battle alone, ROC forces could suffer a devastating defeat that might, in the words of Eisenhower's secretary of state, John Foster Dulles, prove a "severe political and psychological blow" to the KMT. This might lead, the Americans believed, to the Finlandization of Taiwan. Indeed, Chiang had a record of trying to influence his allies by threatening to cooperate with the opposing side.[25]

[24] Ibid., 58.
[25] *Foreign Relations of the United States, 1952–54*, vol. 14 (Washington, D.C.: U.S. Government Printing Office, 1985), 244–245; John W. Garver, *Chinese-Soviet Relations, 1937–1945: The Diplomacy of Chinese Nationalism* (New York: Oxford University Press, 1988); Garver, *Sino-American Alliance*, 126.

In August 1954, the PRC government renewed its criticism of the American intervention in Taiwan that had begun with the Korean War, threatened to "liberate" Taiwan, and moved some 100,000 PLA troops toward the Fujian coast. Heavy PLA artillery bombardment of Jinmen began September 3, sparking retaliatory bombing raids by ROC aircraft on mainland gun batteries and shipping. Washington considered but decided against sending U.S. aircraft to strike the Chinese coast. The PLA also threatened the ROC-occupied Dachen island group lying between Keelung and Shanghai. Despite a show of force by nearby U.S. warships, PLA troops captured Yi Kiang Shan, only eight miles from the Dachens, on January 20, 1955. Its entire garrison of 720 ROC troops died in defense of the island.

Chiang wanted a public commitment of assistance from the U.S. government in defending the remaining ROC-held islands. Dulles assured Yeh this was forthcoming. At Eisenhower's request, Congress passed the Formosa Resolution by a near-unanimous vote on January 24. The resolution authorized the president to employ the U.S. military to defend the offshore islands if this was necessary to protect Taiwan and the Penghu group. Eisenhower thus had congressional backing to fight for the offshore islands provided he made the case that a PLA attack on the islands posed a serious danger to Taiwan. But despite Dulles's claims, Eisenhower did not commit the United States to defend the offshore islands, presenting an angry Chiang with another American sellout. Furthermore, the White House pressured Chiang into evacuating the eleven thousand troops and twenty thousand civilians from the Dachen islands in February, abandoning them to PRC control. The ROC later abandoned Nanchi Island as well, leaving Jinmen and Matzu as the only sizable ROC-held islands beyond Taiwan and the Penghu group. Chiang had lost more territory and gained only an ambiguous American commitment to defend Jinmen and Matzu.

The crisis wound down in March 1955 as the PRC ceased shelling Jinmen and Matzu amidst U.S. threats of escalation. Dulles subtly suggested that the United States might employ nuclear weapons, and after a visit to Taiwan he said that under some circumstances U.S. warships and aircraft might help the ROC defend the offshore islands. This first crisis in the strait, however, worsened the dispute between the U.S. and ROC governments about the strategic role of the offshore islands. Washington urged Chiang to deploy only small garrisons of a few thousand troops on Jinmen and Matzu. Chiang did the opposite, packing the islands with about 100,000 troops and one-third of the ROC ground forces' combat equipment by 1956. This may have been an effort to compel the United States to intervene in a China-Taiwan war. With so much of Taiwan's defense capability committed to the offshore islands, a PRC attack on them would have clearly met the condition established in the Formosa Resolution, reducing the U.S. president's leeway to stay out of the fight.[26]

In April 1955, a PRC delegation led by Premier Zhou Enlai attended the landmark conference of Asian and African countries held in Bandung, Indonesia. The PRC leadership used the conference to unveil a shift in tactics: Beijing would attempt to influence U.S. Asia policy through negotiation rather than confrontation. Zhou made remarkably conciliatory statements about the United States, including an offer to open discussions with Washington on "the question of relaxing tension in the Taiwan area." As part of its peace offensive, Beijing organized a strange campaign of personal appeals in 1955. Republic of China leaders received "letters" published in newspapers or broadcast by radio from relatives, friends, and former colleagues on the mainland urging them to work toward unification.

In a July 1955 report to the National People's Congress, Zhou explained that China could discuss Taiwan with the United States without compromising Chinese sovereignty. "Liberation of Taiwan" was a strictly domestic issue, he said, not subject to Chinese negotiation with any other government. Tension over Taiwan, however, was an international issue, caused by U.S. "occupation" of Chinese territory and "interference" in Chinese internal affairs, and was an appropriate matter for negotiations with Washington. "These two questions cannot be mixed up," Zhou said. The PRC was prepared to fight if necessary to reclaim Taiwan, but was willing to negotiate with the ROC government, provided the latter accept the premise that the relationship was one "between the central government and local authorities." Finally, Zhou indicated Beijing was sensitive to and strongly against "ideas or plots of the so-called two Chinas."[27] An ROC spokesman called Zhou's position on Taiwan an "insulting gesture" because it was the mainland, not Taiwan, that needed liberation.

Sino-U.S. peace talks at the ambassadorial level began in August 1955. Taipei was unhappy with these talks, as it generally opposed high-level negotiations between the United States and China. Even if the two giants did not bargain away the ROC, which was possible, such meetings gave the CCP leadership additional prestige that would solidify its position on the mainland and make its overthrow more difficult. Beijing, however, became disappointed with the talks. A major reason was Dulles's insistence

---

[26] Tang Tsou, "The Quemoy Imbroglio: Chiang Kai-shek and the United States," *Western Political Quarterly* 12 (1959): 1088; Garver, *Sino-American Alliance* 134–135.

[27] Chinese People's Institute of Foreign Affairs, *Oppose U.S. Occupation of Taiwan and "Two Chinas" Plot* (Beijing: Foreign Languages Press, 1958), 35–36.

that Beijing openly renounce the use of force against Taiwan. The Chinese insisted on their sovereign right to use force within their own territory and understood that such a concession would weaken their claim to ownership of Taiwan. Although these talks continued through 1971, they had soured badly by 1958, and the PRC resumed aggressive military posturing toward Taiwan. Taipei reacted by declaring a state of emergency that summer.

A second Taiwan Strait crisis began with intense artillery bombardment of Jinmen on August 23, 1958. The island reportedly absorbed forty-two thousand shells during a two-hour period that morning. A blockade settled in as shelling targeted Jinmen's airstrip and beach, and Chinese patrol boats attacked ROC ships bringing supplies. In skirmishes that followed, the ROC air force claimed it shot down thirty-one PLA MiG aircraft and sunk sixteen patrol boats, against the loss of only one ROC F-86 fighter. Chiang wanted to launch air attacks against mainland artillery batteries. Washington ruled this out, but moved quickly to assist in the defense of Jinmen. The Eisenhower administration now accepted a mini-domino theory that acquiescing to the fall of Jinmen would seriously compromise Taiwan's security, especially since so many ROC troops were now based on Jinmen. The United States dispatched a shipment of modern weapons to Taiwan, including jet fighters and antiaircraft missiles. Howitzers capable of firing atomic shells shipped to Jinmen implied another threat to use nuclear weapons against China. Nuclear-capable Matador missiles had already been deployed to Taiwan beginning in 1957. A large U.S. Navy task force, including six aircraft carriers, steamed into the area. To break the PLA blockade, Jinmen had to be resupplied by amphibious landing because a ROC ship sunk by the shelling was blocking the island's harbor. The United States supplied additional landing vessels and training in amphibious operations. Eisenhower said on August 27 the offshore islands were more closely linked to the defense of the main islands than had been the case in 1955, a warning to Beijing about the likelihood of U.S. intervention. On September 7, U.S. Navy warships escorted a convoy of ROC supply vessels to within three miles (the recognized limit of Chinese territorial waters) of Jinmen to break the blockade. The Chinese refrained from firing at the convoy. With no sign that U.S. support for Taiwan was weakening, Beijing announced on October 25 a bizarre "even-day cease fire": PLA guns would shell Jinmen only on odd-numbered days. By the time the crisis passed in November, according to the ROC government, over half a million artillery rounds had struck Jinmen and about three thousand resident civilians and one thousand soldiers had been killed or wounded. Mao seems to have feared that continued Chinese pressure on the offshore islands might have resulted in Washington forcing Chiang to abandon them. As Jinmen and Matsu were a symbolic and geographic link between Taiwan and the mainland, this would be a setback for the CCP and the KMT's common goal of avoiding the permanent division of China.[28]

Like the first, this second crisis renewed the discontent within the ROC-U.S. relationship. Chiang was again angry that Washington would not allow stronger and more direct military action against the PRC and preferred to perpetuate a divided China, while U.S. officials were more bitter than ever about the ROC's insistence on retaining the offshore islands and saw Chiang trying to maneuver the United States into a major war with China. The U.S. defense secretary again raised the idea of encouraging a coup d'etat in Taipei.[29]

At the same time, the second Taiwan Strait crisis accelerated the split between China and the Soviet Union. Although the Soviet leadership gave verbal public support to the CCP during the crisis, Moscow was emphasizing peaceful coexistence with the United States and did not welcome Chinese military action against Taiwan. Like the Americans, the Soviets feared being drawn into a major war over an issue that to them was of only peripheral interest. Soon afterward, in talks with Mao in October 1959, Khrushchev suggested China should accept Taiwan's independence. This in turn helped persuade Mao that the Soviet Union cared more about stable relations with the United States than supporting China's quest to incorporate Taiwan.[30]

Taiwan remained the principal reason why U.S.-China relations stagnated during the 1960s despite the increasingly clear falling out between China and the Soviet Union. The PRC sought to steer nearly all negotiations with the United States toward the goal of reducing American support for a noncommunist Taiwan. Zhou said publicly in 1960, "So long as the United States continues to occupy Taiwan, there can be no basic improvement in the relations between the United States and China."[31]

U.S.-ROC Cooperation in Conflicts on the Asian Mainland

In attempts to weaken the PRC government and counter its influence, Taiwan and the United States saw opportunities for cooperation in several

[28] Nancy Bernkopf Tucker, *Taiwan, Hong Kong, and the United States, 1945–1992* (New York: Twayne, 1994), 43.

[29] Gordon H. Chang, "To the Nuclear Brink: Eisenhower, Dulles and the Quemoy-Matsu Crisis," *International Security* 12, no. 4 (spring 1988): 198.

[30] Garver, *Sino-American Alliance* 141–142.

[31] Chiu, "The Question of Taiwan," 172.

politico-military operations on the Asian mainland. In some cases Washington, with its global agenda and fear of a war with China (the very outcome Taipei wanted), acted to restrain the ROC's more ambitious aims. On other occasions ROC personnel were welcome proxies for achieving U.S. goals.

Washington and Taipei disagreed over the participation of ROC troops in Korea. Contention over Taiwan's role in the war was the immediate cause of MacArthur's dismissal as UN forces commander. Days after hostilities began, Taipei offered to contribute thirty-three thousand troops to fight under the UN banner. MacArthur supported the idea, but Washington declined Chiang's offer in deference to the wishes of Britain and India. More broadly, Truman and Acheson saw the Korean War as a temporary setback to U.S.-China relations and expected to return to their prewar policy of accommodating China and dissociating the U.S. government from Chiang's regime. Accordingly, to minimize PRC antagonism, they sought to limit the war as much as possible and to emphasize that U.S. military protection of the ROC was a short-term expedient. MacArthur, in contrast, viewed the ROC as a valuable anticommunist asset and favored a U.S.-ROC military alliance. These views bonded MacArthur with the KMT leadership, which saw him as a friend and influential advocate. After PLA "volunteers" entered the war, MacArthur recommended allowing ROC troops to attack the Chinese mainland, which would force the PLA to redeploy some of its forces from Korea and relieve pressure on the UN armies. Washington rejected the idea, fearing a larger war that might ultimately draw in China's alliance partner the USSR. MacArthur made several statements and gestures indicating his support for a U.S.-ROC military alliance and expansion of the war into mainland China. This was in diametrical opposition to the policy of the Truman administration, which warned MacArthur to cease undermining the purposes of his commander-in-chief. MacArthur persisted. Truman relieved the general of his UN command in April 1951 after a Republican congressman publicly read a letter from MacArthur that again recommended allowing ROC troops to attack the mainland.

Despite the exclusion of ROC troops from combat in Korea, Taipei scored a political victory at the end of the conflict. To clear the way for a Korean War armistice in July 1953, Beijing dropped its demand that Chinese and North Korean prisoners of war be repatriated to their homelands, rather than being allowed to choose to defect to South Korea or Taiwan. Understanding the potential for a political victory, the ROC organized the delivery of welcome letters and fourteen thousand gifts to encourage defections. Taipei also sent advisers to the camps to tutor Chinese prisoners in correctly responding to interview questions so as to ensure they would not be sent back to China.[32] More than fourteen thousand of a total of twenty thousand Chinese POWs (mostly peasant recruits from Sichuan Province, and many former KMT soldiers) went to Taiwan, arriving in January 1953. Taipei accentuated its public relations coup over the mainland by proclaiming January 23 "World Freedom Day."

Small-scale, covert ROC activities on the mainland were acceptable to the United States. To assist ROC spies and commandos, several hundred CIA employees on Taiwan provided training in guerrilla warfare and political agitation techniques. The CIA-owned aviation company Civil Air Transport (CAT, later known as Air America) was headquartered at Sungshan Airport in Taipei and also had repair facilities in Kaohsiung and Tainan. In early 1951 CAT aircraft transported, in separate missions, a total of 212 ROC agents who parachuted into China (most of whom were quickly captured).[33]

Republic of China cooperation was valuable to U.S. efforts to gain information about the Chinese government and military. The ROC shared with the United States some information gained from ROC spies on the mainland or from the interrogation of PRC officials captured in commando raids. American equipment set up on ROC territory monitored PRC communications. Pilots from Taiwan flew spy missions over the mainland in U.S.-supplied reconnaissance aircraft. The ROC forwarded the information from these missions to U.S. analysts, which avoided the risk of American personnel being shot down over Chinese territory. Initially the U.S. government resisted giving Taiwan the most advanced American aircraft for fear these might end up in PRC and later Soviet possession and their innovative technologies scrutinized. In response to this decision, ROC officials complained about the risks that ROC pilots with substandard equipment took against improving PRC air defenses. Eventually the United States decided to give Taiwan the highly capable U-2 spy plane. Beijing offered a $250,000 reward to any ROC pilot who defected to China with a U-2, but none did.[34] The PRC claims it shot down five ROC U-2s between 1963 and 1967.[35]

The ROC and the United States also cooperated in abetting anti-PRC activity in Tibet. Tibetan guerrillas received training in Taiwan and the United States beginning in the late 1950s.[36] The ROC supported the Ti-

[32] Tucker, *Taiwan, Hong Kong,* 34.

[33] Garver, *Sino-American Alliance* 100, 101.

[34] Ibid., 191–195.

[35] Kenneth W. Allen, "PLA Air Operations and Modernization," in Susan M. Puska, ed., *The People's Liberation Army After Next* (Carlisle, Pa.: Strategic Studies Institute, U.S. Army War College, 2000), 191.

[36] Garver, *Sino-American Alliance* 172.

betan resistance in the hope armed opposition to the CCP would spread into the Muslim region of Xinjiang and then into central China. Civil Air Transport aircraft operating from bases in Taiwan ferried personnel and supplies into Tibet. While it helped Tibetans resist PRC rule, Taipei did not support Tibetan independence. Like the CCP, the KMT considered Tibet part of China. After 1962, the ROC government focused its policy on encouraging Tibetans to overthrow the Communist government but to remain citizens of a new, benevolent Chinese state. Republic of China propaganda reflected this emphasis. More important, the ROC government sought to exploit an ethnic division among Tibetans. Amdo Tibetans were more culturally similar to Chinese than Khampa Tibetans, and less supportive of independence from China. Taipei courted the Amdo faction and encouraged them to take over leadership of the Tibetan resistance movement. This contributed to bloodshed between the two groups and expulsion in 1963 of the Amdoans from the Tibetan resistance's base in Mustang, Nepal, near the Chinese border. Taipei's policy thus had the counterproductive effects of both undercutting the influence of the preferred faction and strengthening the CCP's control of Tibet.[37]

Pro-KMT irregular soldiers based in Burma initially enjoyed U.S. support, but later became an irritant to U.S.-ROC relations. After the Chinese Civil War, about 12,000 KMT soldiers found refuge across the border in Burma, where they were beyond the reach of the shaky, postindependence Burmese government. These soldiers, the largest group of whom was commanded by General Li Mi, continued to fight the CCP as guerrillas. Growing to as many as 18,500 troops by recruiting local bandit gangs, they made repeated forays into China's Yunnan Province, killing CCP cadres and clashing with PLA forces. Both Taipei and Washington supported them. Taipei paid Li Mi a salary, gave him the title governor of Yunnan, and dispatched technical advisers to assist his forces. Beginning in 1951, the CIA arranged for the delivery of arms and other equipment to Li Mi's soldiers via CAT flights. Knowing the United States was involved, the Burmese government appealed to the U.S. government to remove these troops from Burmese territory. Washington responded that it had no influence over KMT remnants in Burma. After Burma appealed to the United Nations for help in 1953, the new Eisenhower administration began pressuring Taipei to withdraw these soldiers to Taiwan. The U.S. government had concluded that the KMT guerrilla campaign would not significantly affect the CCP regime or its policies and that KMT activities were making it harder for the Burmese central government to defeat their own Communist insurgency. From the ROC government's point of view,

[37] Michel Peissel, *Mustang, The Forbidden Kingdom* (New York: E. P. Dutton, 1967), 38–39.

Washington's request was surprising and irksome because KMT military harassment was clearly consistent with American interests and had enjoyed strong U.S. support until this abrupt reversal. Following Washington's lead, Taipei claimed it did not control the guerrillas, and that they would resist relocating to Taiwan because most of them had developed strong ties in the region of eastern Burma and southwestern Yunnan. ROC officials stalled for months, prompting Eisenhower to send a letter to Chiang in September asking him to use his influence to resolve this issue, and then to raise the matter again during a meeting with visiting Chiang Ching-kuo. Both Chiangs maintained Taipei was doing the best it could. After evacuations were again delayed by allegations that Burmese aircraft were still bombing KMT troops attempting to withdraw, the first group of Li Mi's soldiers arrived in Thailand in November 1953 for transport by air to Taiwan. Both Burmese and American observers noted these men were comparatively old and unfit, and that they did not bring their unit's newer weapons. This raised the suspicion the KMT Chinese intended to put on a show of withdrawing while leaving their most capable forces behind to continue the campaign. After the U.S. government applied additional pressure and agreed to pay $250,000 to help compensate uprooted guerrillas, more KMT soldiers left Burma for Taiwan in 1954. Nearly 6,000 had evacuated by the end of that year. Li Mi declared that his army had disbanded, and the ROC government told the UN it would acquiesce to whatever action the Burmese government took against any remaining KMT fighters. In fact, there were several thousand left, and Taipei continued to supply and command them, even flying about 1,200 well-equipped reinforcement troops into northern Burma in 1961. Kuomintang soldiers suffered heavy losses as infrastructure improvements and tighter political organization in Yunnan enabled the PLA to counterattack more effectively. Rangoon also allowed the PLA to attack KMT enclaves on Burmese territory. Incursions into Yunnan by KMT guerrillas dropped off by the late 1960s. Having settled in prime opium-producing land within the Golden Triangle, the expatriate Chinese harnessed the local narcotics industry as a means of funding their guerrilla war. The drug trafficking continued to thrive after the fighting died out, and these KMT loyalist communities now help supply the world with opium and its derivatives.[38]

As in Korea, Taipei failed to gain U.S. assent to send troops to Vietnam. Chiang's government argued, not surprisingly, that the best way for the United States to relieve Communist pressure on South Vietnam was to invade North Vietnam and to allow the ROC to launch a campaign to recapture China. Otherwise North Vietnam and China would continue to serve

[38] Garver, *Sino-American Alliance*, 148–164.

as sanctuaries and suppliers for the insurgents. During a visit to Washington in 1965, then–defense minister Chiang Ching-kuo urged President Lyndon Johnson, Defense Secretary Robert McNamara, and Secretary of State Dean Rusk to "root out the root of aggression—destroy the Chinese Communist regime." It was important to act as soon as possible, Chiang added, because China had developed an atomic bomb and was working on a hydrogen bomb.[39] Washington, however, was cautious about provoking China, fearing a repeat of the Korean War scenario, in which China sent in large numbers of ground troops to rescue an ally under U.S.-led pressure. Some U.S. officials worried that even the involvement of ROC troops in the fighting in South Vietnam, with no pretense of crossing into the North, would invite greater PRC involvement in the conflict. Thus the United States refused South Vietnamese President Ngo Dinh Diem's request for ROC combat troops. Taiwan did, however, send advisers to South Vietnam. These were principally of two types. The first were agricultural specialists who organized farmers' associations (based on those in Taiwan) and instructed Vietnamese agricultural researchers in modern techniques designed to increase and diversify food production. Another group of some thirty ROC advisers provided training in the conduct of political warfare against Communist insurgents. Both groups were effective, even if this success escaped notice amidst the overwhelming problems that ultimately doomed the South Vietnamese government. American aircraft involved in the war effort in Indochina flew from Taiwan's Ching Chuan Kang air base. A U.S. KC-135 tanker squadron was based in Taiwan. The U.S. military also maintained maintenance and repair facilities in Taiwan for both naval ships and army vehicles, allowing the American government to take advantage of Taiwan's proximity to the war zone and much lower labor costs. The United States had nuclear weapons on Taiwan until 1974.[40] Finally, Taiwan was a frequent host of U.S. military personnel on recreational leave.

International Political Setbacks

The post-World War II peace treaty between Japan and its former adversaries raised two difficult issues involving the PRC-ROC rivalry for Taiwan. First, in delineating the new status of former Japanese posses-

---

[39] *Chiang Buchang fang Mei Jiyao*, Oct. 15, 1965, Political Warfare Office, Ministry of National Defense, Taipei, 58–62; Garver, *Sino-American Alliance*, 213.

[40] This is based on a Henry Kissinger memo declassified in 1999. China News, May 15, 1999, online at http://www.taipei.org/gionews/chinanew/cn-05-15-99, accessed Aug. 17, 2000.

sions, would the treaty state that Japan passed ownership of Taiwan to "China"? Both the ROC and PRC governments favored this. The United States government opposed it, however, because it made the conflict over Taiwan a domestic Chinese issue and was therefore inconsistent with U.S. intervention to defend Taiwan from the PLA. Washington's view prevailed, and in Article 2 of the treaty Japan renounces its claim to Taiwan and the Penghu Islands but does not specify the new owner. Second, which government would represent "China" at the peace conference? Britain, which had broken from Washington and recognized the PRC in January 1950, and other European and Commonwealth countries maintained that officials from Beijing should attend the conference in San Francisco in September 1951, and that the treaty should specify that Japan was returning Taiwan to "China." Opposing this, the U.S. worked out a compromise with Britain: neither the PRC nor the ROC would be represented at the conference, attended by fifty-two other countries. The ROC would have the opportunity to establish a separate treaty with Japan afterward. The United States would pressure Japan to sign with Taipei rather than Beijing, but only on the condition that this ROC-Japan peace treaty encompassed Taiwan and the Pescadores, not the mainland. Thus in both of these documents Washington worked to weaken the KMT's claim of jurisdiction over the mainland and to deepen Taiwan's separation from China. Peace treaty negotiations between ROC foreign minister George K. C. Yeh and Japanese delegate Isao Kawada in the spring of 1952 were lengthy and difficult even though Chiang called for a conciliatory approach and did not ask the Japanese for reparations. The Legislative Yuan debated the proposed treaty vigorously before ratifying it in July 1952.

This was hardly the end of the difficulties in Taiwan-Japan relations caused by the rivalry between Taipei and Beijing. Tokyo remained torn between the need to get along with the PRC and the affinity of many Japanese for Taiwan based on ties of history and ideology, not to mention pressure from Washington to follow the U.S. lead on relations with the PRC. The KMT government, aware that many Taiwanese spoke nostalgically about Japanese colonial rule, remained suspicious that Japan preferred a divided China. In 1952 Japanese prime minister Yoshida Shigeru told the Diet he favored official relations with both Taiwan and China, drawing immediate criticism from Washington that forced him to backtrack. In 1963 PRC diplomat Zhou Hungjing went to the Soviet embassy in Tokyo and asked for political asylum. He expressed interest in several options, including defecting to Taiwan. Ultimately Japanese immigration authorities decided to send him back to China. Taipei, already unhappy about growing PRC-Japan trade, strongly criticized the decision, recalled its diplomats from Tokyo, and announced a boycott of Japanese products.

Yoshida, now acting as envoy, had to travel to Taipei bearing a letter of explanation for Chiang to defuse the minicrisis. Yoshida made the concession of pledging that Japan's Export-Import Bank would not follow through with plans to assist the PRC's industrial development.

A diplomatic breakthrough for the PRC began in 1970. With Beijing's gains, the ROC suffered proportional losses. Global sentiment toward China began to soften. One reason was a widespread desire to welcome China back into the international community after the PRC's (partly self-imposed) isolation. Another reason was China's greater flexibility compared to the ROC. Beginning with Canada in 1970, Beijing established normal relations with several other governments after they agreed to "take note" of the PRC's claim to Taiwan, but without requiring them to sever relations with the ROC. In contrast, Taipei followed the pattern set with France in 1964. France recognized Beijing without specifying that it intended to break diplomatic relations with Taipei. It was the ROC, rather, that severed relations with France in reaction to normalized Sino-French relations. A third reason for the PRC's diplomatic ascension was the improvement in relations between China and the United States. By itself a momentous change in Taiwan's world, this thaw affected many of the ROC's other bilateral relationships as well.

The Sino-American rapprochement resulted mainly from both countries seeking support against their common adversary the USSR. No matter how strongly Taiwan opposed it, this was an event stemming from global forces over which Taipei had little control. While Nixon wanted to improve U.S. relations with China, he also felt it was important not to abandon Taiwan. Thus his administration repeatedly signaled its continuing support to Taipei even as it pursued rapprochement with Beijing, a contradictory policy that deepened the ROC's sense of betrayal. Washington discontinued regular patrols by the Seventh Fleet in the Taiwan Strait and announced it could accept PRC membership in the United Nations provided this did not infringe on the ROC's status in the UN. A U.S. State Department spokesman said in April 1971, "In our view, sovereignty over Taiwan and the Pescadores is an unsettled question." Taipei interpreted this as further evidence America was reinterpreting its relationship with the PRC to the detriment of the ROC. Seeing the trend, Chiang Kai-shek told a U.S. journalist that month, "In dealing with friends we should be loyal and faithful. In all of our relations with friendly nations, we have been strictly adhering to these principles of loyalty and faithfulness. Of course, we expect our friends to do the same."[41] To soften these blows to ROC morale, officials of the Nixon administration assured Taipei on some

[41] Liu, *U.S.-China Relations*, 294–295.

fifty occasions that the U.S.-ROC relationship would not be downgraded.[42] During Chiang Ching-kuo's visit to Washington in April 1970, Nixon famously told him, "I will never sell you down the river." In a more concrete gesture of support, the United States for the first time sold two submarines to the ROC in 1971.

Despite its suspicions, Taipei was shocked and alarmed by the initially secret visit to Beijing in July 1971 of U.S. national security advisor Henry Kissinger. The U.S. government informed Shen of the visit only twenty minutes before Nixon announced it on television. Not only was the U.S. clearly moving toward normal relations with Beijing, but also Washington was acting unilaterally without consulting Taipei on a matter of life-and-death importance to the ROC. Nixon's historic visit to China in 1972 and the resultant Shanghai Communiqué struck the ROC as a sellout. Even before Nixon announced his plan to visit Beijing, protestors in Taiwan broke windows in the U.S. consulate and set off bombs in the Bank of America's Taipei branch and the library of the U.S. Information Service office in Tainan. The latter incident severely injured several Chinese patrons.

The United States had made compromises that clearly weakened the diplomatic standing of the ROC despite its being an alliance partner with which America had formal diplomatic relations. Nevertheless, Washington had refused to fully accommodate Beijing on the Taiwan issue, even at the risk of smothering the spark of rapprochement. The February 1972 Shanghai Communiqué presents separate, carefully worded PRC and U.S. positions on Taiwan. Beijing's position asserts that the PRC is the sole government representing China, Taiwan is part of China, "the liberation of Taiwan is China's internal affair in which no other country has the right to interfere; and all U.S. forces and military installations must be withdrawn from Taiwan." In the American statement on Taiwan, "the United States acknowledges that all Chinese on either side of the Taiwan Strait maintain there is but one China and Taiwan is a part of China. The United States Government does not challenge that position. It reaffirms its interest in a peaceful settlement of the Taiwan question by the Chinese themselves." This amounts to a rather weak acceptance of the "one China" principle, without specifying which of the two contending governments represents the "China" of which Taiwan is a part. Still, this was enough to indicate the United States had officially dropped the two Chinas position dating from Truman's statement on June 27, 1950. The American premise that the Taiwan question must be resolved peacefully created a future basis for U.S. military intervention to protect Taiwan from threatened PRC

[42] Tucker, *Taiwan, Hong Kong*, 128.

military action: if Beijing resorts to military coercion, Washington will not respect China's claim that Taiwan is an internal matter.

From Taipei's standpoint, the U.S. commitment in the communiqué to "progressively reduce its forces and military installations on Taiwan as the tension in the area diminishes" was a clear defeat, confirming that America's future involvement with the ROC would decline. The days of the Mutual Defense Treaty, in particular, were numbered. Kissinger had also promised the Chinese there would be further negotiations on limiting American arms sales to Taiwan. The U.S. government thereafter implemented a guideline that the arms America provided to Taiwan would be defensive rather than offensive in character and would not create a military imbalance in the strait. Frustrated that large powers were determining Taiwan's fate, the ROC Ministry of Foreign Affairs reacted by declaring "null and void any agreement, published or secret, involving the rights and interests of the government and people of the Republic of China."

Signals of a Sino-American rapprochement opened a floodgate of diplomatic recognition of Beijing during the first half of the decade. In 1968, the ROC had diplomatic relations with 64 countries, the PRC with 45. By mid-1975, however, the number of countries recognizing Taipei had dropped to 26, while the PRC had normalized relations with 112 states. Japan recognized Beijing in September 1972, simultaneously breaking all official ties with the ROC. This necessitated further adjustments that angered Taipei. Tokyo granted Beijing the right to take possession of the buildings and property on the site of the former ROC embassy to Japan, eliciting a strong protest from the ROC Ministry of Foreign Affairs. Under pressure from Beijing, Tokyo announced in 1974 a plan to downgrade the privileges of China Airlines' operations in Japan: the ROC flag could no longer be used, the airline's name would be changed, and its aircraft could not use airports servicing PRC airliners. Taipei called the changes insulting and forbade air traffic between Taiwan and Japan. Funeral diplomacy occasioned by the deaths of Chiang Kai-shek and former Japanese prime minister Sato Eisaku enabled the restoration of air links in 1975, albeit with compromises. Initially flights were scheduled so that China Airlines and PRC aircraft would not be on the ground at the same time. After the opening of Narita Airport in 1978, China Airlines confined its operations to Tokyo's Haneda Airport. Flights to Taiwan by the national carrier Japan Airlines operated under the name "Japan Asia Airlines."

Another two-China controversy involved a dormitory in Kyoto the ROC government purchased in 1952 to house Chinese students. A Japanese court ruled in 1977 that with Tokyo's diplomatic recognition of Beijing, ownership of the dormitory had passed automatically to the PRC government. Taipei appealed. In 1987, with the Japanese pro-Taiwan lobby bringing its influence to bear, the court gave ownership of the dormitory back to Taipei. Beijing criticized not only the decision, but the fact that the Japanese government allowed consideration of a case filed on behalf of the ROC, from which Tokyo had officially withdrawn its recognition.

Despite a few such small victories, by 1979 the PRC had decisively won the diplomatic campaign, enjoying relations with 117 governments, including the world's major states, while only twenty-four states of relatively little consequence recognized the ROC.

Another major diplomatic blow influenced by the improvement in Sino-U.S. relations was the ROC's ouster from the United Nations in October 1971. In this episode, as well, Taipei felt let down by the Americans, although the ROC's own mishandling of the campaign to influence the UN vote also played a part.

Sparring between the ROC and the Soviet bloc states began in the UN as early as 1949, when the General Assembly responded to an ROC complaint by passing a resolution that criticized the Soviet Union. The Soviets, according to the resolution, violated the UN Charter by assisting the Communist insurrection and "obstruct[ing] the efforts of the National Government of China in re-establishing Chinese National authority" in Manchuria. (Soviet troops entered Manchuria in the last days of the Pacific War and turned over captured Japanese armaments to CCP soldiers, impeding the efforts of KMT forces to reestablish Chiang's control over northeast China.) In January 1950, the Soviet representative to the Security Council, Jacob A. Malik, demanded that KMT representative Tsiang Tingfu yield the China seat to a PRC delegate. After the council rejected his demand, Malik walked out in protest, saying the USSR would boycott the council until the ROC was expelled. It was the absence of a Soviet representative that allowed the United States to get the Security Council to condemn North Korea as an aggressor and to authorize UN military intervention to defend South Korea.

Beginning in 1950, challenges raised by socialist governments led to annual General Assembly votes on the question of whether the ROC or the PRC should represent China in the UN. The low point for China was 1952 (near the end of the Korean War), when only 12 percent of the assembly voted for seating the PRC. The argument for seating the PRC rather than the ROC in the UN was based on the facts that the CCP had effective control of the territory of mainland China, and thus of the vast majority of territory comprising China; and the people in areas under CCP control generally followed the regime's orders ("habitual obedience" in legal terminology). The CCP therefore merited recognition as the state holding the right to represent the Chinese people in the UN, which espoused the principle of universality and had not excluded other Communist states from membership. Otherwise the hundreds of millions of Chinese on the mainland, a substantial percentage of humanity, would have no voice in the UN. On the other hand, the Republic of China and its supporters argued that Taipei was the proper representative of the Chinese nation because the majority of mainland Chinese did not consent to the CCP as their legitimate rulers. The Communists were essentially un-Chinese: a small, unpopular minority, organized around an alien ideology that was inconsistent with traditional Chinese thought and values. The regime stayed in power only through harsh repression. Furthermore, the PRC had been condemned by the UN as an aggressor state and was therefore unworthy of membership. The PRC lacked the other UN members' commitment to values such as cooperation and preserving peace. Beijing would bring its agenda of revolution and confrontation, subjecting the UN to "incessant quarrel and endless recrimination, engendering bitterness, hatred, and wars."[43]

Through the 1950s, the United States successfully rallied a majority of member states in support of a moratorium against considering the PRC for admission to the UN. Beijing, however, made gradual progress at Taiwan's expense in the annual votes among UN members on which government should occupy the China seat. Decolonization caused General Assembly membership to swell with the admission of new Third World states, many of which were sympathetic to Beijing. In 1961 the United States bought more time by successfully proposing that the matter of the PRC replacing the ROC be considered an "important question," requiring a two-thirds vote of the General Assembly to pass. In 1970 an annual Albanian resolution to expel the ROC to admit the PRC received over half the vote for the first time. Beijing capitalized on increasing international support by announcing in August 1971 it would not accept a UN seat unless the ROC was expelled. This was calculated to sway governments that felt strongly the PRC should be in the UN, but had no particular desire to throw out the ROC.

With the tide turning, the U.S. government suggested to Taipei a change of strategy: they would work toward dual representation, with both the ROC and the PRC holding seats in the General Assembly, instead of fighting against the admission of the PRC. Taipei strongly opposed letting Beijing into the UN, but the Americans argued this was the ROC's only chance to avoid ouster. Chiang agreed on the condition the United States would use its influence to ensure Taipei kept the China seat in the Security

---

[43] Chinese Institute for International Affairs, *China and the United Nations* (New York: Carnegie Endowment for International Peace, 1959), 258.

Council. Prior to the key vote, however, the United States conceded it would accept giving the ROC's Security Council seat to Beijing if UN members would vote to allow Taipei to remain in the General Assembly. Furthermore, U.S. president Richard Nixon had already announced his plans to visit Beijing. In October, shortly before the UN vote on the China question, Kissinger visited China a second time. With these signs of improvement in U.S.-China diplomatic relations, many U.S. allies saw no further need to oppose China's entry into the UN.

Angry that Washington had reneged, the ROC government ceased coordinating its UN strategy with the Americans. Republic of China representatives worsened their own predicament by their own inflexibility, insisting that the UN must choose between the ROC and the PRC. The Albanian resolution calling for the "restoration of the lawful rights of the People's Republic of China in the United Nations," including the expulsion of the ROC to allow the PRC to occupy the China seat, passed by a General Assembly vote of 76 to 35 on October 25, 1971. Minutes before the vote, ROC delegate Liu Chieh announced his government was withdrawing from the UN, allowing Taipei the small dignity of being able to claim it that chose to leave. Republic of China foreign minister Chow Shu-kai complained that UN members were betraying a "loyal member of the Organization" in favor of a regime that "is oppressive at home and aggressive abroad" and "will surely transform the United Nations into a Maoist front and battlefield for international subversion."[44]

With the loss of its seat in the UN, the ROC also lost its membership in UN-affiliated intergovernmental organizations. A week prior to leaving the UN, anticipating expulsion from the International Monetary Fund, the ROC exercised its membership privilege to withdraw the maximum available amount of $59.9 million before Beijing got the chance to do so. (Because Beijing was not immediately able to meet the obligations of membership, Taipei would remain in the IMF and the World Bank until 1980.)

Taiwan's people had few outlets for redressing the dissatisfaction they felt over their treatment by the United States. Occasionally U.S. government personnel working in Taiwan were roughed up under circumstances that suggested the complicity of local authorities. One such incident arose in connection with a sensational crime case. An American soldier based in Taiwan, U.S. Army sergeant Robert Reynolds, shot and killed Liu Tze-jan, a thirty-year-old Chinese man, outside Reynolds's quarters in May 1957. Reynolds said the victim had been peering through the window at Reynolds's disrobed wife, and that he feared the man was planning an attack. A court-martial acquitted Reynolds, sparking a wave of anti-Ameri-

---

[44] *Ministry of Foreign Affairs Weekly* (Taipei), no. 1071, Nov. 2, 1971, 1–4.

can protests. Americans in the streets were harassed, Liu's widow went on a hunger strike and led a demonstration, and an angry crowd occupied and set fire to the U.S. embassy. Based on reports that the destruction went on for some seven hours despite Taiwan's reputation for tight police control, Americans suspected the ROC government condoned the violence. There were at least two possible motives. Taiwan's people resented the wealth and privileges, including immunity from the local legal system, that the American community enjoyed in Taiwan, and this was an opportunity for them to blow off steam. At a higher level, the KMT might have used the incident to remind Washington not to take Taiwan's support for granted.[45] Chiang nonetheless promptly relayed his "profound regret" to Eisenhower and Dulles, explaining that the destruction of U.S. property was a reaction to the Reynolds case specifically, not an expression of a deeper and more general antipathy toward America. The ROC government fired three high-ranking officers in the public security forces over the incident and promised to pay compensation to the U.S. government.

Another manifestation of Taipei's dissatisfaction was flirtation with Moscow. Soviet-ROC hostility had decreased during the 1960s with the deterioration of Sino-Soviet relations. Soviet support for China's goal of reincorporating Taiwan faded. Taiwan in ROC hands forced the PRC to maintain a substantial military capability on the Chinese southeast coast, limiting the military resources available to deploy at the Sino-Soviet border. The Soviet press and Soviet diplomats gave indications of accepting the idea that the ROC on Taiwan was a state rather than a province of China. In 1969, the year fighting broke out on part of the Sino-Soviet border, Beijing accused the USSR of "counterrevolutionary collusion with the Chiang Kai-shek bandit gang."[46] On the ROC side, the press criticized Moscow less harshly and favorably distinguished Soviet communism from Chinese communism. Chiang Ching-kuo's Russian wife, hitherto hidden from the public, was given a higher profile. Soviet journalist Victor Louis, who also had close unofficial ties to the Soviet leadership, visited Taiwan in 1968 and met with Chiang Ching-kuo. Foreign Minister Chow Shu-kai believed the threat of improved ROC relations with the USSR would induce the United States and China to treat Taiwan with greater consideration. After the ROC's expulsion from the UN, Chow said politics and economics were no longer linked and Taiwan would trade with Communist countries (except the PRC). In early 1972 he told U.S. reporters the ROC would negotiate with Moscow, perhaps through the same kind of "secret talks" that led to the Sino-U.S. breakthrough. Others in the ROC

---

[45] Tucker, *Taiwan, Hong Kong*, 92.
[46] *Beijing Review* 12, no. 11 (March 14, 1969): 13.

leadership, however, thought Chow's blunt play of the Soviet card was immoral and risked alienating U.S. support. This view was a factor in Chow's replacement as foreign minister by Shen Chang-huan in 1972. Republic of China officials continued, nevertheless, to suggest that Taiwan might host Soviet military bases if the United States switched diplomatic relations from Taipei to Beijing. These threats were typically communicated by unofficial, indirect means—such as a statement made to a foreign journalist—and then subsequently denied, but they contributed to Washington's fear that the ROC might seek a separate peace with the Communists if pushed too hard.[47]

These diplomatic setbacks forced the ROC to make compromises. Taiwan accepted the awkward designation of "Chinese Taipei" in 1981 to clear the way for its participation in the Olympic Games and other international activities. Having quit the General Agreement on Tariffs and Trade in 1950, rising global protectionism prompted Taiwan to apply for readmission in 1990. To increase its chances of avoiding fatal PRC opposition, Taipei applied under the title "Customs Territory of Taiwan, Penghu, Quemoy and Matsu." Washington stood up for Taiwan against threatened expulsion by the Asian Development Bank in 1983, but also forced Taiwan to accept the appellation "Taipei, China." Taipei had insisted, as we have seen, that foreign governments have no official relations with Beijing as a condition of normal diplomatic relations with the ROC. Thus in 1984 when Surinam sought to establish relations with the ROC, Taipei required Surinam first break its relations with the PRC. This Surinam refused to do. There were other countries, as well, that wanted relations with the ROC (mainly to gain economic aid) but were not willing to sever relations with Beijing. The weight of these missed opportunities convinced the Legislative Yuan's Foreign Affairs Committee to loosen ROC diplomatic policy. In 1989 Taipei established relations with three states that already recognized the PRC: Belize, Grenada, and Liberia. Most important, Taiwan's loss of diplomatic prestige did not seriously curtail the island's economic opportunities. The island's foreign trade increased nearly tenfold during the 1980s, and the number of foreign visitors doubled.

The United States Switches Recognition

United States officials repeatedly assured Taipei they would not scrap the Mutual Defense Treaty. This, however, was one of three preconditions

---

[47] John F. Copper, "Taiwan's Options," in James C. Hsiung, ed., *The Taiwan Experience, 1950–1980* (New York: Praeger, 1981), 491–492.

Beijing demanded for normalized Sino-U.S. relations. The other two were the withdrawal of U.S. forces from Taiwan and the severance of U.S. diplomatic relations with the ROC. The U.S. government wanted the Chinese to agree to continued American arms sales to Taiwan and to pledge not to use force against the island. Domestic distractions slowed progress on negotiations over these issues. In the United States, the Watergate scandal halted the movement toward normalization because a politically weakened Nixon, and similarly his successor Gerald Ford, could not afford to lose the support of conservative, pro-ROC Republican politicians. The Chinese were preoccupied by events such as the massive Tangshan earthquake and the succession crisis created by Mao's death, both in 1976.

The administration of President Jimmy Carter, more willing than its two predecessors to accept Deng Xiaoping's three Taiwan-related preconditions, placed a high priority on achieving Sino-U.S. normalization. Carter publicly insisted that any deal for the U.S. recognition of the PRC had to include acceptance of continued U.S. military aid to Taiwan and a pledge by the Chinese not to use force in their attempt to reclaim Taiwan.[48] China held firm on both issues. The difficulty of extracting concessions from Beijing slowed Carter's progress toward normalized relations, as he had to guard against the criticism of domestic political opponents that he was abandoning Taiwan.

Taiwan struggled vainly through a variety of channels to forestall Sino-American normalization. Foreign Minister Shen Chang-huan warned the United States that recognizing the PRC was against U.S. interests because it would betray fundamental American ideals and because the United States would lose credibility with its noncommunist allies worldwide.[49] Referring to the underlying strategic rationale, Chiang Ching-kuo cautioned Washington against "letting a wolf in the back door while fighting a tiger at the front door."[50] The ROC's Government Information Office conducted international public relations, inviting influential foreigners to visit Taiwan and churning out literature promoting the ROC's goals. Taiwan's government particularly sought to establish networks with senior staff personnel of members of the U.S. Congress as a means of gaining access to legislators on issues involving Taiwan. The ROC government paid for twelve Americans from Carter's hometown of Plains, Georgia, to tour Taiwan. Taiwan residents sent 200,000 letters appealing to the president not to abandon the island. Republic of China intelligence operatives at-

---

[48] Liu, *U.S.-China Relations*, 329.

[49] Chiu, "The Question of Taiwan," 252–253.

[50] *Perspectives: Selected Statements of President Chiang Ching-kuo, 1978–1983* (Taipei: Government Information Office, 1984), 8.

tempted to engineer a fallout between China and the United States and reportedly considered mailing letter bombs to U.S. academics perceived as pro-China.[51]

The eventual result of the negotiations was that China would not promise not to use force against Taiwan, but would not let continued U.S. arms sales to Taiwan stand in the way of normalization. Satisfied, Carter decided to hold a news conference on December 16, 1978, the day after Congress adjourned for the winter and a few days after Congress passed a resolution that improved Sino-U.S. relations must not result in downgraded U.S.-ROC relations. Carter announced that Washington would recognize Beijing and break official relations with Taipei on January 1, 1979, terminate the Mutual Defense Treaty one year later, and withdraw all U.S. forces from Taiwan within four months (only about a thousand U.S. military personnel remained in Taiwan out of a previous high of ten thousand). Similar to the Shanghai Communiqué, the December 1978 Joint Communiqué marking the establishment of official Sino-U.S. relations contains a weak American affirmation of the one-China principle: "The Government of the United States of America acknowledges the Chinese position that there is but one China and Taiwan is part of China." The official PRC translation renders "acknowledge" as *chengren*, a stronger word that can mean "admit."

The ROC had hoped for three concessions that would soften the blow of U.S.-PRC normalization: a strong statement of the United States' commitment to the security of Taiwan, an accompanying promise by the PRC not to use force against Taiwan, and continued U.S. arms sales. It got only the third. Carter's eagerness to make the announcement, combined with an initial delay in locating the U.S. ambassador in Taipei, Leonard Unger (who was out for the evening attending a social function), led to Unger visiting Chiang Ching-kuo at 2:30 A.M. to give him a few hours' advance notice of Carter's planned announcement—a gesture Taiwan saw as adding insult to injury. In Chiang's public comment, he said that the United States "has broken its assurances" to the ROC and "cannot expect to have the confidence of any free nation in the future." United States recognition of the CCP government was also "tantamount to dashing the hopes of the hundreds of millions of people enslaved on the Chinese mainland for an early restoration of freedom" and "a great setback to human freedom and democratic institutions."[52] Taiwan's stock market fell and the unofficial value of the New Taiwan dollar dropped about 20 percent against the U.S. dollar. Thousands joined anti-U.S. demonstrations in

---

[51] "Foreign Spy Activity Found Rampant in U.S.," *Washington Post*, Aug. 9, 1979, 1A.
[52] Liu, *U.S.-China Relations*, 332–333.

Taiwan's streets, some trampling on peanuts to show disdain for Carter. Chiang placed his armed forces on a heightened state of alert and postponed the elections that had been planned for December 23, prompting opposition politicians to urge the government to "resist the temptation to embrace military rule while showing its determination to promote constitutional government and unify the entire nation in an environment of peace and democracy."[53]

When a delegation led by Undersecretary of State Warren Christopher arrived in Taipei in December, angry protestors attacked their cars with sticks. Again American officials suspected ROC government acquiescence in the demonstrations. Christopher's delegation was unable to satisfy all the ROC government's demands, which included continued government-to-government interaction as well as strong security cooperation and substantial arms sales. It was in Taipei's interest, then and thereafter, to make its contacts with the United States appear as "official" as possible, both to arrest the deterioration of the relationship and to promote friction between Washington and Beijing. Eventually Washington and Taipei established quasi-embassies to conduct consular business. The former U.S. embassy in Taiwan devolved into the American Institute in Taiwan, technically a private corporation run by diplomats and civil servants retired or on leave from government service. Taiwan's counterpart was the Coordination Council for North American Affairs (CCNAA), with a main office in Washington and branches in other major U.S. cities. Washington maintained that the CCNAA was appropriately "unofficial," but in a minor concession, allowed the ROC side to say that the council had an "official nature." Japan made a similar arrangement with Taiwan. The Interchange Association carried out Japan's diplomatic business in Taipei and Kaohsiung, while the East Asia Relations Association operated ROC quasi-consulates in Tokyo, Osaka, and Fukuoka. Retired or temporarily seconded government employees staffed both organizations.

A backlash by the pro-Taiwan faction in the United States was inevitable. A group of politicians led by Senator Barry Goldwater sued Carter and Secretary of State Cyrus Vance in federal court (with the case eventually dismissed by the Supreme Court) for failing to consult with Congress before terminating a treaty. A more significant outcome was the Taiwan Relations Act, which became law in April 1979. The act says threats to Taiwan would be "of grave concern to the United States," and

---

[53] Linda Chao and Ramon H. Myers, "A New Kind of Party: The Kuomintang of 1949–1952," in *Proceedings of Centennial Symposium on Sun Yat-sen's Founding of the Kuomintang for Revolution*, vol. 4 (Taipei: Chin-t'ai Chung-kuo ch'u-pan-she, 1995), 108.

that normal U.S. relations with China are based "upon the expectation that the future of Taiwan will be determined by peaceful means." It codifies continued arms sales, requiring the U.S. government to "make available to Taiwan such defense articles and defense services in such quantity as may be necessary to enable Taiwan to maintain a sufficient self-defense capability."

Taipei and Washington had different ideas about how much was "sufficient." Understandably, Taipei constantly complained that the United States was not transferring enough weaponry for Taiwan to counter the immense military resources of the PRC. The fat years were in the first half of the Cold War. Taiwan received some $2.4 billion in U.S. military aid from 1950 to 1965, the most of any Asian country. Taiwan acquired more than fifteen hundred U.S.-made aircraft, including many advanced warplanes, as well as technical assistance and training in combat skills, weapons systems, and maintenance. In the 1960s the United States supplied Taiwan with F-100, F-104, and F-5 aircraft as well as tanks, artillery, warships, and antiaircraft missiles. Consistent with the Cold War role Washington wanted Taiwan to play, U.S. military support was geared toward bolstering Taiwan's defenses but not its offensive capabilities. The U.S. government did not, for example, provide large numbers of transport aircraft or landing craft suitable for an invasion of the mainland.[54]

United States arms sales to Taiwan after 1975 were comparatively paltry. The incoming Carter administration temporarily froze them altogether while it reassessed U.S. policy. In 1978 Carter's White House blocked the proposed sale to the ROC of an upgraded, all-weather variant of the F-5 fighter (the F-5G) on the grounds that the aircraft's improved navigation system, speed, and range gave it an offensive capability. Taipei and its U.S. friends saw this as excessive accommodation to Beijing, although Carter's White House had announced in 1977 it would not approve the sale overseas of weapons not used by the U.S. military because it opposed designing new weapons systems solely for export. Indeed, Northrop had designed the F-5G for the ROC at the Pentagon's direction. Carter's office also nixed the Harpoon antiship missile and the Standard ship-to-air missile against the recommendations of the Joint Chiefs of Staff to avoid complaints from Beijing. Another one-year moratorium on new U.S.-ROC arms agreements during 1979 followed America's recognition of the PRC. Measured in terms of purchase prices, U.S. arms sales to Taiwan dropped by one-half from 1979 to 1980.

Taiwan welcomed Carter's electoral defeat to the outspokenly anticom-

---

[54] Garver, *Sino-American Alliance*, 66–68.

munist and hawkish Ronald Reagan, who had a record of pro-ROC statements. Overall, however, Reagan proved disappointing. His administration continued the hiatus of new arms sales agreements from the time it took office until the spring of 1982. Taiwan particularly wanted the United States to agree to sell advanced fighter aircraft. Early in 1982 the White House announced it would meet the ROC's need for new fighter aircraft by continuing Taiwan's licensed production of the two-decades-old F-5 rather than providing a newer aircraft such as the F-16. Although the Reagan administration agreed to U.S. defense industries licensing designs and technology to allow the ROC to produce an advanced fighter, the F-16 knockoff "indigenous defense fighter," and modern frigates, it made a major concession to the PRC on the general issue of arms sales to Taiwan in a third Joint Communiqué in August 1982. Departing from the Taiwan Relations Act, which provided for an open-ended U.S. commitment based solely on Taiwan's defensive needs, the U.S. government pledged in the 1982 communiqué "to reduce gradually its sales of arms to Taiwan, leading over a period of time to a final resolution." The U.S. government also promised "that its arms sales to Taiwan will not exceed, either in qualitative or in quantitative terms, the level of those supplied . . . since the establishment of diplomatic relations between the United States and China." Taipei complained bitterly, echoed by some U.S. politicians, that this apparent promise to phase out arms sales to Taiwan stemmed from a desire to improve U.S.-China relations, not from an assessment of Taiwan's defenses. Only three weeks earlier Reagan had said, "We are not going to abandon our long-time friends and allies on Taiwan. And I'm going to carry out the terms of the Taiwan Relations Act."[55]

On at least one occasion Taipei tried to bypass Washington and tap directly into the U.S. arms market. The two submarines the Nixon administration transferred to Taiwan were 1940s models, and to get them the ROC had to promise not to arm them and to use them solely for training purposes. Despite this commitment, in 1974 ROC government agents recruited the assistance of Chinese criminal gangs based in San Francisco in obtaining torpedoes from the black market. The ROC wanted thirty torpedoes and would pay $100,000 apiece for them—a generous price considering the submarines themselves had cost $153,000 each. The U.S. Federal Bureau of Investigation discovered the plan, but the U.S. government let the matter drop to avoid damage to relations with Taipei.[56]

---

[55] Quoted in Harvey J. Feldman, "Development of U.S.-Taiwan Relations 1948–1987," in Harvey J. Feldman, Michael Y.M. Kau, and Ilpyong Kim, eds., *Taiwan in a Time of Transition* (New York: Paragon House, 1988), 159.

[56] David E. Kaplan, *Fires of the Dragon: Politics, Murder, and the Kuomintang* (New York: Atheneum, 1992), 184–191.

China successfully tested a nuclear bomb in 1964. This raised the possibility of the PRC wiping out the ROC's defenses in a single swift attack and then occupying and controlling the island long before the American military could intervene. Chiang lobbied Washington in vain for U.S. attacks on Chinese nuclear weapons installations. Another approach was for Taiwan to deploy its own nuclear weapons to counter China's. This was a serious undertaking that would bring strong opposition from both Beijing and Washington. China went so far as to stipulate the development of nuclear weapons in Taiwan as one of the events that would trigger a PLA attack on the island. The U.S. government opposed nuclear proliferation in general and believed ROC nuclear capability would increase rather than decrease the likelihood of a Sino-Taiwan military conflict. Taiwan's nuclear aspirations would become a recurring irritant in the Taiwan-U.S. relationship.

In 1967, the ROC Ministry of Defense proposed a $140 million program for developing nuclear weapons. The military was interested in a separate program to develop ballistic missiles as well. The nuclear program came under the auspices of the Institute for Nuclear Energy Research (INER) at the Chungshan Institute of Science and Technology, the center of Taiwan's research in advanced weaponry. Part of the program was aboveboard. Taiwan acquired a research reactor from Canada and nuclear technology and material from several other countries (including low-grade plutonium from the United States), ostensibly to aid Taiwan's civilian nuclear energy program. A principal task of the INER, however, was to surreptitiously generate plutonium to fuel nuclear weapons.

By 1974, the CIA believed Taiwan intended to develop nuclear weapons. Soon thereafter, the International Atomic Energy Agency (IAEA), which monitors nuclear energy programs with a view toward preventing them from contributing to the proliferation of nuclear weapons, found evidence of a clandestine ROC effort to produce weapons-grade plutonium, including a hidden port in the bottom of the Canadian reactor's spent fuel pond through which fuel rods containing plutonium could bypass IAEA safeguards. Pressured by Washington, Taipei agreed in September 1976 to discontinue the weapons program. Taiwan shut down the reactor, dismantled its processing facilities, and returned most of the plutonium supplied by the United States. Under President Chiang Ching-kuo, however, work secretly continued until the cover was blown again. Colonel Chang Hsien-yi, whom the CIA reportedly began recruiting in the 1960s while he was a military cadet, had risen to the post of deputy director of nuclear research at the INER. In December

1987, Chang defected to the United States with a cache of incriminating documents and informed the U.S. government Taiwan was still trying to build nuclear weapons. United States satellite photographs of the activities around the research reactor corroborated Chang's report. According to Hau Pei-tsun, who was then the ROC military's chief of general staff, ROC scientists had by then already achieved a controlled nuclear reaction. U.S. president Reagan forced Taiwan's new president, Lee Teng-hui, to promise to halt the program. Yet the idea reemerged in 1995. With Beijing attempting to intimidate Taiwan through nearby tests of PLA ballistic missiles, President Lee Teng-hui publicly said Taiwan should again consider deploying nuclear weapons. Lee's comment drew immediate criticism from several quarters, and a few days later he said Taiwan would not try to develop the bomb.[57] Having laid so much of the groundwork for a nuclear capability, Taiwan remains a "threshold" nuclear state, and opposition to a Taiwan bomb is one of the issues on which the Chinese and U.S. governments consistently agree.

Other U.S.-ROC Tensions

Military strategy was not the only area in which tensions between Taipei and Washington arose. The ROC authorities did not always welcome America's strong cultural influence. During the PRC's Cultural Revolution, Taipei answered with a movement called the Cultural Renaissance, which reaffirmed Sun Yat-sen's Three Principles of the People as the basis of Chinese society. This movement denounced communism but also decried Western liberalism and its undue emphasis on individualism. Police often dragged long-haired Taiwan youth to the station for haircuts. The Kennedy administration sparked an angry reaction from Taipei when it expressed an interest in recognizing the Mongolian People's Republic, which the ROC maintained was rightfully part of China. Two other areas of substantial contention were human rights and economics. Taipei had long been aware of the need to assuage the complaints of some Americans that the KMT regime was excessively illiberal. The past appointments of Wu Kuo-chen and Sun Li-jen, seen in Washington as liberal and progressive, were concessions to American sensitivities. The 1984 murder of Chi-

---

[57] Tim Weiner, "CIA Spy Kept Taiwan from Developing Its Own Nuclear Bomb," *New York Times* News Service, reprint in *China News* (Taipei), Dec. 21, 1997, 1; "Former Top General Reveals Secret Nuclear Weapons Program," *The China Post*, Jan. 6, 2000, internet archives, http://publish.gio.gov.tw/iisnet/20000106/20000106p5.html; David Albright and Corey Gay, "Taiwan: Nuclear Nightmare Averted," *Bulletin of the Atomic Scientists* 54, no. 1 (January/February 1998).

nese-American journalist Henry Liu Yi-liang, however, was a disastrous setback to the KMT's image in the United States. Liu had worked for both the ROC Military Intelligence Agency and the U.S. FBI. Soon after he had finished writing an unfavorable book about Chiang Ching-kuo, Liu (whose pen name was Chiang Nan) was shot to death at his home in Daly City, California. This incident brought to the attention of the U.S. public the ROC government's campaign against dissidents, particularly those residing in America. When the FBI launched an investigation, Taipei had no choice but to cooperate. Chiang himself escaped direct implication, but three high-ranking government officials were convicted and sent to prison for enlisting members of the criminal organization Bamboo Gang to kill Liu. The most prominent of the three was Admiral Wang Hsi-ling, head of the National Intelligence Bureau, who had directed the activities of ROC agents in the United States while he was a military attaché in Washington. Wang and his two associates were promoted while in prison and soon got out on parole. The Taipei-sanctioned assassination of an American citizen on U.S. soil contributed to increased American pressure on Taipei during the 1980s to improve its human rights record. Representative Stephen Solarz and Senator Claiborne Pell led calls from the U.S. House of Representatives and Senate, respectively, for the KMT leadership to discontinue martial law and free political prisoners.

As Chiang Ching-kuo's moves toward political liberalization in the latter part of the decade eased the tensions over human rights, trade issues became a major cause of bilateral friction. Taiwan's thriving underground industry in intellectual and artistic piracy and producing cheap imitations of products with famous brand names cheated many U.S. businesses. More seriously, Taiwan's trade surplus with the United States reached $19 billion in 1987. This was a larger imbalance than the U.S. trade deficit with Japan when measured on a per capita basis (Japan had five times Taiwan's population). Americans noted that Taiwan led the world in foreign currency reserves ($82 billion by 1992), which suggested this was not a struggling country that deserved pity and privileged treatment. Like Japan, Taiwan made a few efforts to encourage buying American products, but this failed to satisfy American critics. The ROC insisted that agricultural trade barriers, for example, were integral to national security, and farmers' groups demonstrated outside the American Institute in Taiwan over U.S. pressure in 1988. American demands for action on the trade imbalance forced the ROC government to make painful adjustments, including revaluating the New Taiwan dollar and reducing tariffs. These policy adjustments brought fast results, reducing the trade imbalance by $9 billion in 1988. While resentful of U.S. pressure, Taipei accepted that the long-term costs of U.S. displeasure would be high enough to outstrip Taiwan's substantial short-term gains. American protectionism was an alarming prospect given Taiwan's heavy dependence on the U.S. market, which absorbed as much as 40 percent of Taiwan's exports. Section 301 of the United States' 1988 Omnibus Trade and Competitiveness Act provided for retaliation against countries that consistently barred U.S. imports. The U.S. government threatened Taiwan with Section 301 sanctions over resistance to importing American tobacco products in 1990, when U.S. tobacco companies pushed aggressively to increase their markets in developing countries. The ROC maintained it wanted to keep out American cigarettes to protect the health of its people, not for economic reasons, and ran an advertising campaign in the United States intended to make this point. The threat of placing Taiwan on the "super 301 list" and carrying out other forms of retaliation receded as the ROC's trade surplus with the United States began to shrink in the early 1990s.

The PRC Shifts Tactics, and Taipei Responds

The decade of the 1970s saw the beginning of serious efforts by Beijing to incorporate Taiwan by diplomatic rather than military means. In an August 1972 meeting with a group of North American overseas Chinese, Zhou Enlai made a start on the exceedingly difficult task of trying to persuade Taiwanese to work toward unification with China. Zhou said that although it was a mistake for some Taiwanese to favor independence, this was understandable given the long separation and KMT propaganda. Taiwanese would have to accept the handover of their private enterprises to government ownership, but Zhou promised this would proceed gradually and without lowering Taiwan's standard of living.[58] (Chiang had tried something similar during the height of the Cultural Revolution in October 1967, calling for anti-Mao elements within the CCP to ally with him in a campaign to overthrow the paramount leader.) At a 1973 Beijing conference commemorating the February 28 incident (interpreted by the CCP, as we have seen, as an anti-KMT insurrection inspired by Mao Zedong's thought), a CCP Central Committee member promised to treat ROC officials who helped bring about reunification "with due respect and forgive them for their past wrongdoings—however serious they were." A former KMT general who had changed sides in exchange for a ministerial position in the Communist government reminded Taiwan that "we are all Chinese" and invited the ROC to "send some people to the mainland,

[58] Yung-hwan Jo, *Taiwan's Future?* (Hong Kong: Union Research institute, 1974), 65–70.

openly or secretly, to have a look and visit relatives or friends."[59] Both the CCP and the KMT shared the assumption that increased economic and social interchange would work to China's advantage, eroding the ROC's resistance to negotiated unification. For the rest of the Cold War and well beyond, the PRC would call for more cross-strait ties than Taipei was willing to allow. In 1975 Beijing released more than five hundred ROC prisoners and offered to repatriate them to Taiwan. Characterized as "war criminals" by Public Security chief Hua Guofeng, most were former KMT generals or officials who had been incarcerated for at least twenty-five years. The ROC government refused to take them back. Taipei did, however, accept the return of agents who had been captured after infiltrating into China during the 1960s. Overall, Taiwan's position on cross-strait relations showed little compromise; as Chiang said, "We shall never deal with the devil."[60] The ban on Chinese imports into Taiwan was eased slightly, allowing for trade in a few select items such as Chinese medicine, but travel between Taiwan and the mainland was forbidden.

Deng Xiaoping's ascension to paramount leadership after Mao's death in 1976 cleared the way for a PRC policy toward Taiwan that, until the crisis of 1995, was mainly conciliatory and rarely involved public threats or military posturing. Xu Xiangqian, the PRC minister of defense, announced in January 1979 that the PLA would stop shelling Jinmen and Matzu as a friendly gesture to Taiwan and in recognition of China's normalization of relations with the United States. At the same time the National People's Congress (NPC) released a "Message to Compatriots on Taiwan." The NPC message promoted a peaceful process of unification beginning with talks by representatives of the two governments and the establishment of trade, transportation, and mail delivery across the strait. In addition to these "three links," the message called for "four exchanges": economic, cultural, scientific, and athletic.

Another important PRC overture followed in September 1981, when NPC Standing Committee chairman and PLA marshal Ye Jianying offered a nine-point proposal "to bring an end to the unfortunate separation of the Chinese nation." Ye's statement offered the CCP leadership's most detailed plan to date. Referring to previous truces during the lead-up to the Northern Expedition and the Japanese invasion, Ye said that the CCP and

[59] Foreign Broadcast Information Service, *Daily Report: People's Republic of China*, Mar. 1, 1973, B5–B9.
[60] Chiang Kai-shek, from a 1973 speech; Ralph N. Clough, "Chiang Ching-kuo's Policies Toward Mainland China and the Outside World," in Shao-Chuan Leng, ed., *Chiang Ching-Kuo's Leadership in the Development of the Republic of China on Taiwan* (Lanham, Md.: University Press of America, 1993), 143.

the KMT should "cooperate for the third time to accomplish the great cause of national reunification." Ye said China would allow an incorporated Taiwan to retain a high degree of autonomy—what became famous in connection with Hong Kong as the "one country, two systems" model, written into the PRC constitution in December 1982. As a Special Administrative Region of China, "Taiwan's current socioeconomic system will remain unchanged, as will its way of life and its economic and cultural relations with foreign countries." Taiwan could also "retain its armed forces," and Beijing would "not interfere with local affairs on Taiwan," Ye said. He added that the Chinese central government would be prepared to offer financial assistance to Taiwan's economy when necessary, an idea that drew snickers on the island. Chiang responded in October: " 'To talk peace with the Chinese Communists is to invite death.' This is an agonizing, blood-stained lesson that we and many other Asian countries have learned."[61] Chiang countered the CCP offer by invoking Sun Yat-sen's patriotic philosophy, arguing that reunification could not be contemplated until the PRC lived up to Sun's Three Principles of the People (nationalism, democracy, and people's livelihood).

Taiwan lost ground relative to the PRC in international public opinion. Beijing appeared more progressive and committed to a peaceful solution, offering what appeared to be substantial concessions, while Taipei stubbornly held to the "three no's" policy: no contact, negotiation, or compromise with the CCP regime. In June 1982 the ROC's relatively liberal premier Sun Y.S. told a group of American scholars that his government was willing to negotiate reunification after further political, economic, and social development made China more compatible with Taiwan. Chiang Ching-kuo nonetheless reiterated the "three no's" policy a month later. In a quiet moderation of ROC policy, however, official use of the slogans "Next year, return to the mainland" and "Counterattack the mainland" ceased. Both the tough stance against official negotiations with Beijing and decreased emphasis on recapturing the mainland helped maintain support for Chiang's government among the Taiwanese community, which opposed wasting Taiwan's resources on a China military campaign and watched suspiciously for signs that the KMT planned to make an accord with the PRC that would compromise Taiwan's independent identity.

There was little movement through the end of the Cold War toward a solution of the difficult issue of politically integrating Taiwan and China.

---

[61] Chiang Ching-kuo during a speech to the KMT Central Standing Committee, quoted in Hung-mao Tien, ed., *Mainland China, Taiwan, and United States Policy* (Cambridge, Mass.: Oelgeschlager, Gunn & Hain, 1983), 243.

In several statements on Taiwan that followed, the Beijing leadership called for negotiations under the party's "Four Cardinal Principles": socialism, leadership by the CCP, dictatorship of the proletariat, and Marx-Lenin-Maoist thought. Taipei, of course, was not willing to endorse the Communist system as a precondition. The insistence on unification under the Three Principles of the People, which became Taipei's standard position, made the reverse and equally unacceptable demand that the mainland must renounce communism.

Even on practical matters and issues of "low politics," the obstacles to cross-strait cooperation were not easily overcome. An airline hijacking in May 1986 illustrated the necessity of a communication channel between the two governments. A pilot from the ROC's China Airlines diverted his aircraft to Guangzhou so he could visit his father. Taipei had no official means of arranging for the return of the aircraft and its crew. The problem was overcome through direct talks between China Airlines and the Civil Aviation Administration of China. Taiwan asserted that since these were two private organizations, the principle of no official contact remained intact.

Economic and social pressures eventually forced Taipei to loosen its restrictions on contact with the PRC. In an ironic reversal of the relationship between Taiwan and China in premodern times, Taiwan business people who traded with or invested in the mainland were theoretically subject to stiff penalties, even execution. In practice ROC authorities found it impossible to enforce these laws. Most ROC-China trade went through Hong Kong and could not be tracked. Fishing boats from China and Taiwan often met in the strait to barter. Beijing encouraged illegal trade and fraternization. In 1981 the Chinese established a "reception center" on Pingtan Island, near Fuzhou and directly across the strait from the northern tip of Taiwan. It welcomed fishermen, traders, and Taiwan residents seeking information about relatives on the mainland. The ROC government did not try to stop its citizens from traveling to Pingtan. Several boats from Taiwan reportedly stopped there annually. By the 1980s, the growing volume of this illegal cross-strait traffic put Taipei in a quandary. The leadership feared unrestricted contact with the mainland would weaken Taiwan's security. Catching all the violators was impossible, and selective enforcement brought complaints that the government's policy was discriminatory. Even some KMT legislators acknowledged that legal restraints forbidding private contacts had become unrealistic. Some challenged the premise that contact with the mainland might make people on Taiwan sympathetic to the CCP's agenda. On the contrary, they argued, such contact might work to Taiwan's advantage, making ROC citizens more appreciative of their government's accomplishments in economic and social development (which would become more clear when contrasted with conditions observed on the mainland) and increasing awareness of Taiwan's successes among mainland Chinese.

In 1987 demonstrations by retired soldiers captured the attention of the public and the government. They asked for the right to visit relatives on the mainland before they died. This group could not be dismissed as Communist agitators, and their desire drew widespread sympathy in a society that prizes filial piety and maintaining close ties with one's ancestral land. In a watershed decision, the government in November 1987 loosened the restrictions on visits to relatives on the mainland. Initially, ROC citizens who were not active duty military personnel or government employees could visit China once a year for no more than three months. Visitors and trade poured across the strait like waters rushing through a breached dam. Within about one year, 200,000 islanders had traveled to China. By the end of 1989, the number was nearing 1 million. Taiwan's socioeconomic progress relative to the mainland made this decision possible. As many in the KMT leadership realized, visiting the mainland was less likely to turn Taiwan's people into Communist agents than to make them more grateful for the KMT's achievements on Taiwan.

Other cracks in the "three no's" policy soon followed. Mail service between Taiwan and the mainland began in 1988, and direct telephone links in 1989. In April 1989, Finance Minister Shirley Kuo attended an Asian Development Bank meeting in Beijing, making her the first ROC official to visit the mainland since the KMT's exile to Taiwan in 1949.

Conclusion

The events of the Cold War and the Chinese Civil War melded together partially but not completely. There was considerable tension between the KMT's need to defend the policy of recapturing the mainland and the U.S. desire to keep its support for Taiwan within the limits defined by overall American Cold War grand strategy. It is not surprising that the United States, a superpower, often forced its will on its small ally. What is remarkable is that Chiang was sometimes able to resist and frustrate Washington's plans. Chiang's career as a political leader on the mainland had prepared him well to contend with a partner within his coalition with one hand while fighting the Communists with the other. He discerned and countered U.S. designs for Taiwan's permanent separation from China even as he explained to the Americans how their support of an ROC invasion of the mainland would serve U.S. interests.

For the assistance it received from the United States, including about

$100 million annually in nonmilitary aid from 1951 to 1964, Taiwan provided America with significant benefits. The island became an important section of the wall containing communism and a proxy military operative against the PRC. "Free China" also drew away support that would otherwise have gone to the PRC and increased the socialist camp's political and diplomatic profile. The ROC controlled the China seats in the UN for two decades. Taipei's cultivation of good relations with African governments, largely through economic and technical assistance, reduced China's opportunities to gain influence in Africa and thus supported U.S. global strategy.

It would be accurate to assert that the United States used Taiwan when China was an enemy and then unilaterally downgraded Taiwan's status in the relationship to court Beijing's favor. But to balance out the story, the important benefits Taiwan (and especially the KMT) gained from its Cold War association with the United States should also be noted. In addition to its rescue from an imminent CCP invasion in 1950, Taiwan received substantial economic and military aid, plus urging to undertake reforms that accelerated the island's development. It is hard to dispute that American discouragement and blockage of the KMT's planned "return to the mainland" was in Taiwan's best interests, at least in the short term. Even after "abandoning" Taiwan, the United States continued to provide weaponry and to help deter PRC military coercion.

For the PRC's Taiwan plans the Cold War was a disaster. The opportunity to mop up the remnants of KMT resistance and speedily unify Taiwan with the mainland disappeared, and the United States reentered the picture as Taiwan's self-appointed protector. China faced frustrating decades of arguing that Taiwan was a Chinese internal issue, attempting to weaken U.S. support for the KMT regime, and working to undermine the U.S. defense commitment and military presence on Taiwan.

Ultimately, of course, the political skills and determination of Chiang Kai-shek, Chiang Ching-kuo, and their lieutenants could not hold back the shifts that downgraded Taiwan from UN Security Council member and frontline state in the containment of communism to diplomatic and strategic backwater. As impossible for Taiwan to control as the weather, the global political winds blew favorably in 1950 but unfavorably in 1971–72. Yet the diplomatic defeats of the latter part of the Cold War contributed to political reform at home, as we will see in the next chapter.

※

The Opposition's Struggle and Breakthrough

Although it called itself a revolutionary party, the KMT had become Taiwan's conservative establishment. The KMT entered the 1970s with a supremacy over domestic politics achieved by few authoritarian regimes. The party exercised control over the government, dictating policies and choosing many key officials, with the National Assembly routinely ratifying decisions made by party leaders. The KMT had influence, if not outright control, over not only the state, but also the military, the media, education, trade unions, much of the economy, and every large civic organization except the Presbyterian church. Kuomintang security agents and informants pervaded schools, workplaces, neighborhoods, and meetings among opposition politicians.

Yet despite its immense power and privileges, the KMT was forced to make concessions to its domestic opponents that led to dramatic changes in Taiwan's political system. Although Sun Yat-sen's writings envisioned China moving in stages toward a constitutional democracy, the KMT leaders who oversaw the process of political liberalization did not appear to be following a blueprint for democratization. There is little indication that Chiang Ching-kuo or other top KMT officials had a deep understanding of either the philosophy or practice of democratic governance. Rather, the KMT's efforts to head off a serious political crisis resulted in reforms that set Taiwan on the path of democratization.

The KMT had to compromise because its monopoly over Taiwan's politics was becoming harder to sustain as time passed. The tenability of the KMT's plan to reconquer the mainland faded, weakening the premise on which were based the president's extraordinary powers and the KMT's lock on the parliamentary institutions. Paradoxically, engineering a climate for faster economic growth enhanced the KMT's prestige but at the same time created threats to its status. Except for the global recession in the early 1970s, Taiwan's people enjoyed an annual growth rate of close to 10 percent. By the late 1980s Taiwan's annual gross domestic product per capita reached U.S. $5,000. While the disparity in wealth between the rich and the poor had grown, Taiwan was more equitable in socioeconomic terms than most other countries. The government undertook the Ten Major Projects program in 1973, including construction of a major highway system, harbor facilities, power plants, and other improvements to the island's infrastructure. With a total cost of U.S. $8 billion,[1] this was an ambitious move given Taiwan's limited resources and weak economic growth worldwide, but the stimulation resulting from the Ten Projects helped Taiwan endure the recession. Through a combination of sound management and selective liberalization of Taiwan's marketplace, the government helped Taiwan's people grow richer, better educated, and more cosmopolitan. This accordingly raised their expectations for participation in the political process, fueling the assertiveness of civil society, particularly a middle class with a long-term interest in further political liberalization.

Furthermore, despite its commanding political position, the KMT faced a relentless challenge from the Taiwanese community. This created a dilemma for the KMT. Mainlanders were a minority on Taiwan, and their party could not govern the island without establishing a minimum level of legitimacy. As Chiang Ching-kuo would admit in 1983, "No political party can maintain its advantage forever if it does not reflect public opinion and meet the people's demands."[2] The KMT could not claim legitimacy while large numbers of Taiwanese were demanding greater empowerment. There were two basic strategies for defeating this challenge: repression and accommodation. Both strategies had drawbacks. Cracking down on dissenters was potentially counterproductive, as it would reinforce the view that the government lacked legitimacy. On the other hand, meeting the opposition's demands for political reform could unleash pressures for further liberalization until the KMT's status and core objectives came under attack. The party leadership used a mixture of these strategies in the 1970s and 1980s but increasingly relied less on repression and gradually submitted to piecemeal demands for democratization.

An important premise of the KMT's vision was that the Republic of

[1] Murray A. Rubinstein, "Taiwan's Socioeconomic Modernization," in Rubinstein, ed., *Taiwan: A New History* (Armonk, N.Y.: M. E. Sharpe, 1999), 373.

[2] "President Chiang Ching-kuo's Interview with an Editor of *Der Spiegel*, May 16, 1983," *Parliament Monthly* 14, no. 6 (June 1983): 3–4.

China was working toward a democratic society based on Sun Yat-sen's Three Principles of the People. The party was ideologically committed to the notion of democracy, even if its leaders had little practical experience with the problems associated with building and managing a democratic system. In the 1970s, even some KMT members joined the growing number of intellectuals and politicians openly criticizing the party for failing to make progress in fulfilling its professed commitment to democratization.

Based on these various considerations the KMT leadership in the 1970s implemented a policy of limited democracy: the government would provide Taiwanese with more access to positions of political power and allow non-KMT candidates to compete for elected offices, but would restrict the power of the opposition and would not permit challenges to the core principles of anticommunism and Taiwan's inseparability from China. By addressing the concerns of the opposition, the KMT would secure its own long-term survival.

Conservatives, who feared liberalization would make Taiwan more vulnerable to separatism or Communist subversion, were more willing to resort to harsh measures against political opponents. But the KMT leadership as a whole became convinced that delaying further progress toward democratization would result in social upheaval that could only be subdued through police and military force. The KMT was averse to a repeat of the February 28 crackdown for several reasons. First, many in the party had concluded that a large-scale, public repression of political dissenters would be self-defeating, leading only to greater antigovernment sentiment and larger protests. Second, as part of its efforts to accommodate Taiwanese demands for a greater share of political power, the KMT recruited more Taiwanese into the party and the government. In 1972 the state appointed Taiwanese Hsieh Tung-min as provincial governor, a post previously held by Mainlander generals. In 1973 the KMT's new general secretary, the relatively liberal Li Huan, began recruiting and promoting Taiwanese as well as younger Mainlanders while encouraging many older party leaders to retire. About half of the sixty students Li selected for a training course for high-level cadres, for example, were Taiwanese. By 1981, Taiwanese made up one-third of the membership of the KMT Central Standing Committee, and by 1985, all officials at the city and county level were Taiwanese, as were 75 percent of those at the provincial level.[3] (Mainlanders still dominated the National Assembly and Legislative Yuan, and the top leadership positions in the party.) Kuomintang membership appealed to many Taiwanese, especially those with government

[3] Alexander Ya-li Lu, "Future Domestic Developments in the Republic of China on Taiwan," *Asian Survey* 25, no. 11 (November 1985): 1088.

jobs, as a means of enhancing their career prospects. With Taiwanese entering the KMT ranks in greater numbers, a heavy-handed crackdown on Taiwanese activists would carry the danger of tearing the party apart. Like the Taiwanese who joined the KMT, members of the party who were younger Mainlanders born in Taiwan (i.e., of Mainlander parents) tended to be critical of the party's conservative leadership, favorable toward reforms, and willing to rethink some elements of the KMT's core agenda. Although they scorned the opposition, they often agreed with some of its proposals, such as a Legislative Yuan with its entire membership elected on Taiwan.

International pressure was a third factor that discouraged the KMT from opting to crush the opposition with overwhelming force. Already diplomatically isolated, Taipei risked losing its few remaining supporters if the government was perceived as a ruthless dictatorship. Americans, in particular, expected "democratic" behavior from "Free China." Unfree China, the PRC, created a different kind of pressure. The KMT plan to make Taiwan a model polity was part of the goal of reunifying China. The party wanted to build up Taiwan as a model that mainland Chinese would envy. Chinese suffering under repressive Communist rule would envy a Taiwan operating a successful constitutional democracy, but not a Taiwan under martial law. As the Chinese Civil War had become more of a political than a military contest, Taiwan needed, as Chiang put it, "to demonstrate clearly that the strong contrast between the two sides of the Taiwan Strait is basically due to the fact that one side has implemented a constitution based on the Three Principles of the People while the other has not." He directly linked terminating martial law with Taiwan's responsibility to "serve as a beacon of light for the hopes of one billion Chinese so that they will want to emulate our political system."[4] By the time the younger Chiang succeeded his father as ROC president, the only chance the KMT had of returning to rule on the mainland was to be invited back after a massive popular revolt against Communist rule. Chiang Ching-kuo, furthermore, was unhappy with the long period of martial law and did not want to die as a dictator.

The decision to accommodate demands for political reform was eased by the belief of many KMT members that liberalization did not mean the death of their political careers. The party was well prepared to remain competitive in a pluralistic system, and its members would continue to enjoy advantages over nonparty candidates and, later, over newly legal-

---

[4] *Chiang Tsungt'ung Ching-kuo hsiensheng yenlun chi* (Taipei: Kuomin Tahui Mishuchu, 1984), 19; the latter quotation is from Chiang's interview with Katherine Graham in *Newsweek*, Oct. 20, 1986, 31.

ized opposition parties. Younger KMT members believed the success of their careers was predicated on a favorable public perception of the party, to which liberalization would contribute. They planned to get ahead by winning elections, not by waiting to move up the party ranks through promotions. Younger KMT members, especially those who were Taiwanese, were also less committed to the principle of recovering the mainland and thus less fearful of the prospect that liberalization would lead to a compromise of that objective.

These two decades thus saw a delicate transition from an authoritarian system to a protodemocracy, during which the KMT tried to carry out enough political reform to generate a sense of progress toward democratization that would contain massive civil disobedience. The KMT implemented reforms in three areas. Along with concessions made to the opposition (which will be the main focus of this chapter), the party itself, built as a Leninist institution run by a small core of elites, allowed lower level cadres more input and responsibility. Chiang Ching-kuo also presided over a shift in political power from the party to the institutions of government, seen particularly in a decrease in the influence of the previously powerful Central Standing Committee of the KMT Central Committee; its powers migrated to various government institutions. At the same time, nonetheless, the party struggled to maintain its own hold on the levers of power and to combat the emboldened advocates of the forbidden cause of Taiwan separatism.

Chiang Ching-Kuo: Unexpected Supporter of Reform

The ascendancy of Chiang Ching-kuo would be a boon to the opposition, although this was not immediately apparent. By 1973 Chiang, ROC premier since 1972, ran the daily affairs of the government and the KMT while conferring often with his father. Chiang Kai-shek had often given his son difficult assignments that reflected a high degree of trust. It was well known that the elder Chiang was grooming his son to succeed him as ROC president

After months of declining health, Chiang Kai-shek died on April 5, 1975, at age eighty-seven while amidst his fifth six-year presidential term. Vice president Yen Chia-kan was sworn in as president the next day and completed the balance of Chiang's term as a caretaker executive. Amidst strong opposition voiced by activist academics and non-KMT politicians, the National Assembly elected Chiang Ching-kuo president on March 21, 1978. He took on the title of KMT chairman (*Chuhsi*) a month later (the elder Chiang's title of *Tsung-tsai* or "supreme leader" was retired after his death). Inaugurated May 20, Chiang chose Hsieh Tung-min, then age seventy-one, as his vice president.

Based on his background—supervisor of the commissar system in the armed forces, head of the internal security network, founder of a youth "anticommunist" organization that indoctrinated and spied on young people, and defense minister (1965–72)—Chiang seemed an unlikely reformer. Yet he was progressive in his desire to give Taiwanese and younger Mainlanders more positions of responsibility in the party and the government and to improve the legitimacy of the KMT and the ROC government through economic development. He quickly earned the disapproval of KMT conservatives who believed he was straying from the party's original agenda. There were hints of interest in reform and conciliation in his record. His pattern of patronage showed Chiang favored technocrats, particularly those with higher education from overseas. Chiang had also expressed a commitment to cleaner government. As premier, he promulgated Ten Rules of Reform designed to combat corrupt relationships between the bureaucracy and the business community. He quickly followed up by sending police to record the names of civil servants found in bars and nightclubs and by firing several officials for hosting excessively costly wedding banquets. In 1972 Chiang prosecuted high-ranking officers in the Taiwan Garrison Command involved in a smuggling operation. Wang Cheng-yi, former secretary of Chiang Kai-shek with close ties to the Chiang family, was sentenced to life in prison in 1973 for corruption. Early in his presidency Chiang, who led a relatively austere lifestyle for a paramount leader, promoted a campaign against the "four evils": gangs, drugs, gambling, and smuggling. Chiang said that he favored human rights—he even proclaimed a "human rights year" in Taiwan in December 1976—but that the need to protect public order under the unusual circumstances of the Communist Chinese threat required the restriction of some civil liberties. In the summer of 1975, under Chiang's direction, the Legislative Yuan had passed a law granting clemency to thirty-six hundred prisoners, many convicted of political offenses.

Politically active Taiwanese, nevertheless, objected to what they saw as the establishment of a Chiang family dynasty, especially since the ROC was officially a constitutional republic. They also emphasized Chiang's fearsome reputation stemming from his former position as head of the ROC internal security apparatus. To mollify Taiwan's public, Chiang moved quickly to set a benevolent tone for his administration. He reduced the jail terms for nonviolent dissidents and allowed the press more freedom to report on the performance of government officials and policies. He cultivated an image as a man of the people. Newspaper and television reports frequently showed Chiang participating in festivals and meeting ordinary people on farms, in factories, and at schools around the island.

The Opposition under Limited Democracy

Under the restricted civil liberties associated with the Communist emergency, the formation of new political parties was illegal. This left the partisan field to the three preexile parties: the KMT and the politically insignificant China Youth Party and Democratic Socialist Party. Politicians who were not members of these parties could compete in elections, but only as independent individuals. In the 1970s political opposition to the KMT became known as the *Tangwai* ("outside the party") movement. This was the first organized political challenge to the KMT since the Lei Chen affair in 1960. The movement included many Taiwanese factions as well as a few prominent Mainlander politicians. Taiwanese politicians Kang Ning-hsiang, who was elected to the Legislative Yuan in 1969, and ex-KMT member Huang Hsin-chieh were the *Tangwai*'s first leaders.

Some prominent and common points of the *Tangwai* agenda were political reforms leading to greater democratization and the discontinuation of martial law. The government's position was that Taiwan needed martial law as long as the island faced an imminent security threat from China. The opposition, however, complained,

> Martial law is not supposed to be used to deal with every type of possible crisis and then become a permanent institution. If martial law is perpetually used, you are trying to change the constitution system. In the case of Taiwan, by 1986, martial law had been in effect for 37 years, which is the longest period that any country in the world has imposed martial law. In democratic nations, martial law is only a temporary provision.[5]

Taiwan was not under the government of the constitution, which had been suspended, but rather was ruled by executive decrees. One of the major complaints of Taiwanese was that this concentration of power in the executive enfeebled local government.

Another issue that defined the *Tangwai* was the demand for Taiwan's self-determination: the people on Taiwan should have the right to choose

[5] Song Jitai, "Cong jingjiquan di fali tan Taiwan jieyan tizhi," *Nuanliu Zazhi* 114 (May 19, 1986): 9.

what relationship they would have with the mainland. *Tangwai* politicians insisted this did not imply advocacy of Taiwanese independence, as independence was only one of the possible choices Taiwan's people might make. The KMT nevertheless understood "self-determination" as a euphemism for independence.

Other goals commonly articulated by *Tangwai* politicians were less spending on the armed forces and more on social welfare services; more Taiwanese in high positions of government; more political liberties for Taiwan citizens, including the right to organize a real opposition party; and discontinuation of the KMT's privileges and advantages.

Beyond these points of agreement, a host of issues divided the various *Tangwai* factions. One of the more important schisms was that between moderates who sought political change by working within the system (e.g., gaining access to power through winning political office) and radicals who advocated forcing the government to reform through large-scale protests and civil disobedience. Some *Tangwai* activists were committed to independence for Taiwan, while others wanted only to protect Taiwan's future options. For some, Taiwan's international status was a central issue; others were more concerned about domestic problems.

There was little coordination between the numerous *Tangwai* factions islandwide until the mid-1980s. Aware of their disadvantages as a nonparty vis-à-vis the KMT, *Tangwai* activists made several attempts to create organizations that would function as de facto parties without openly breaking the prohibition. These included the *Tangwai* Campaign Assistance Corps formed after the 1977 election, the extracurricular activities of the magazine *Meilidao* beginning in August 1979, and the *Tangwai* Research Association for Public Policy established after the 1983 election.

Taiwanese political activists continued to campaign against the KMT from abroad, particularly Japan and the United States. Although Taiwanese lobbyists gained influence with several U.S. congressmen, overseas Taiwanese political groups had little impact on political events in Taiwan. Although hardly representative of overseas Taiwanese as a whole, some activists were implicated in plots targeting high-level KMT officials. A parcel bomb, for example, injured Vice President Hsieh Tung-min in 1976. The next year authorities announced the culprit was a Taiwanese residing in the United States who mailed bombs to three ROC officials with the objective of overthrowing the government. The other two bombs, sent to Li Huan and Huang Chieh, were discovered before they could harm anyone. Another incident occurred when Chiang Ching-kuo, then vice premier, was visiting New York in 1970. Taiwanese activists picketed the sites of Chiang's appearances. One protest-placard slogan, playing on the term "Free China," read, "Taiwan is neither free nor China." When Chiang arrived at the Plaza Hotel to deliver a speech on April 24, 1970, he survived an assassination attempt attributed to two Taiwanese students.

Limited democracy offered the *Tangwai* a combination of opportunity and frustration. To achieve legitimacy, the KMT government had to sponsor competitive elections. Indeed, the KMT did not always assign candidates to contest every available office. By leaving gaps, the KMT in effect set aside a few seats for the opposition. Members of the ROC parliament enjoyed immunity from prosecution for their remarks, a privilege the KMT usually honored. These elected offices provided the opposition a rare forum in which to make its case. *Tangwai* candidates won seats in national government organs in the 1970s and 1980s, but the KMT still dominated these institutions because few seats were open to popular election. Even after capturing 24 percent of the vote in 1986 (with Hsu Jung-shu, the wife of jailed Kaohsiung incident participant Chang Chun-hung, the single highest-polling candidate; see more about the Kaohsiung incident later in this chapter in the section "The Long March from Martial Law to a Multiparty System"), the Democratic Progressive Party (DPP, an outgrowth of the *Tangwai;* see more about this party later in this chapter) still held only 12 of 323 seats in the Legislative Yuan and 11 of almost 1,000 in the National Assembly. The most powerful elected positions available to *Tangwai* politicians were county chief executive and, prior to their conversion to appointed offices, the mayorships of Taiwan's principal cities Taipei and Kaohsiung.

Although heavily regulated, electoral campaigns were lively, especially in the 1980s. The opposition often flirted with forbidden subjects. When the government proscribed the use of the term "self-determination" in *Tangwai* campaign literature, some candidates handed out leaflets with half of the phrase replaced by a black dot. Candidates freely hurled insults at their opponents and even their opponents' ancestors. Some recruited endorsements from celebrities or resorted to stunts such as cutting off the heads of chickens or parading scantily clad women to gain the public's attention.

At the same time, however, the KMT also hoped to keep the opposition weak through means that would not incur serious public disapproval. Kuomintang candidates benefited from several structural advantages. They enjoyed the support, collective strength, and coordination provided by a legal political party, while the opposition did not. The KMT, for example, was able to manage its candidates to prevent party members from losing races because they ran against each other and split the vote. *Tangwai* candidates, in contrast, persistently suffered from this problem because they lacked a party structure to coordinate their campaigns. Kuomintang influence over the mass media ensured that party figures received extensive, favorable, and year-round coverage—in effect, free and abundant political advertising. The KMT's large membership and vast property holdings (largely, as discussed earlier, inherited from the Japanese colonial government) gave its candidates a huge treasury to draw from. With compulsory military service for all young men and the system of political indoctrination of the troops through commissars, the KMT could count on support from a sizable bloc of military votes.

As in years past, the opposition accused the KMT of various forms of electoral abuse in the 1970s and 1980s, including vote buying, stuffing ballot boxes, intimidating *Tangwai* campaign workers and supporters (by, for example, photographing spectators at opposition rallies), and arranging for the registration of military personnel and civil service employees to vote in regions where support for the *Tangwai* was strong. Campaign regulations listed numerous restrictions on the amount of money that could be spent and what kind of activities were allowable during specified periods before an election. *Tangwai* politicians complained their KMT counterparts frequently broke these rules with impunity, while the authorities were quick to punish the infractions of candidates not supported by the KMT. The opposition had an interest in exaggerating or even fabricating such claims, but some of the accusations were well founded.

The KMT's close relationship with the state generated clear cases of the KMT's battle with the *Tangwai* influencing the state's administrative decisions. Opposition politician Henry Kao twice defeated KMT candidates in the election for mayor of Taipei. In 1967, during Kao's second term, the government redesignated Taipei a "special municipality." Thenceforth the ROC president would appoint the mayor. (As a concession, Kao was the first appointed mayor.) Kaohsiung, where the *Tangwai* had strong support, became a special municipality in 1979. The official explanation was that these cities were so large the ROC government had to ensure coordination of their policies with those of the national leadership. The same conflict of interest manifested itself on a smaller scale in police action against particular opposition candidates. In 1975, for example, Pai Ya-tsan planned to run for office, but police arrested him shortly before the start of the campaign. A court sentenced him to life in prison for sedition because he had distributed literature that criticized the government and Chiang personally and called for negotiations with Beijing.

Corruption of local KMT political machines also became increasingly common as the party tried to forge relationships with prominent members of the community. Businesses gave financial support and generated votes for KMT candidates, who returned the favor once in office by helping their businessmen friends get licenses and government contracts and by helping them circumvent regulations and evade taxes. This kind of corruption was less common among national-level KMT officials, who were mostly Mainlanders with few personal connections to the Taiwanese business community.

The KMT typically won about 70 percent of the vote, and its success at the polls was not due solely to the party's structural advantages or alleged cheating. Neither Taiwanese support for the *Tangwai* nor Mainlander support for the KMT was automatic; not all *Tangwai* supporters were Taiwanese, and not all Taiwanese supported the *Tangwai*. Ethnic tensions between Mainlanders and Taiwanese were lower after the 1960s because of intermarriage and the economic success of Taiwanese in the private sector, which ameliorated their resentment over the Mainlander domination of public sector employment. By the mid-1970s, two-thirds of the five hundred most prominent businessmen on the island were Taiwanese. Taiwanese economic success had mixed ramifications for the electoral success of the *Tangwai*. By the late 1970s, Taiwan's general economic prosperity had provided the opposition with a funding base that allowed it to support more candidates and market its message more effectively.[6] But many Taiwanese who had prospered in business became interested in ensuring a stable political environment to protect their gains. Similarly, Taiwan's growing middle class, estimated at 2.5 million in 1985, did not want reforms to threaten economic growth.[7] Thus many Taiwanese voted for KMT candidates for largely economic reasons.

A large percentage of Taiwanese also felt a kinship with the mainland and feared provoking a military conflict with the PRC, and thus were not eager to change the cross-strait status quo. The passion of many *Tangwai* politicians for self-determination (or independence) and democratization were not necessarily shared by the bulk of Taiwan's people. Supporters of formal Taiwanese independence were a minority, if a vocal one. Most of the public preferred keeping martial law and cared less about seeking independence than about other matters such as crime, pollution, and the cost of living. Furthermore, most of the Taiwan public, including Taiwanese who had no particular affection for the KMT, disliked the *Tangwai*'s use of tactics such as disrupting legislative sessions and encouraging street riots. Such behavior created doubts about whether Tangwai leaders could be trusted with the responsibilities of important offices.

On some occasions the authorities appeared to target particular opposition politicians the KMT feared were growing too powerful, even at the

---

[6] Linda Chao and Ramon H. Myers, *The First Chinese Democracy: Political Life in the Republic of China on Taiwan* (Baltimore: Johns Hopkins University Press, 1998), 298.

[7] Lu, "Future Domestic Developments," 1085, 1087.

risk of angering the public. Sometimes the wives of imprisoned opposition politicians stepped in and won electoral office on the strength of sympathy votes.

In many cases, however, KMT leaders did not necessarily order the arrests of particular dissidents. The Taiwan Garrison Command, which had the authority to arrest and try political offenders and to censor the media, operated largely autonomously within general guidelines issued by the KMT. In general, the government drew the lines of acceptable behavior by the opposition at encouraging public disorder, personally criticizing government or KMT figures, and advocating communism or independence for Taiwan. But the boundaries were not always clear, and the military police enforced the political laws inconsistently. To complicate the picture, right-wing vigilantes carried out some of the harassment of KMT enemies by attacking opposition activists and their offices, disrupting opposition activities, and provoking fights between demonstrators and police. Overall, retribution against dissidents was somewhat arbitrary.[8] When public security forces made arrests, they often behaved with brutality. Critics of the government frequently claimed the police tortured detainees to get them to sign confessions. Police and Garrison Command security officers could make arrests without warrants and, until 1982, interrogate detainees in seclusion.

Two cases from this period illustrate how Taiwan's society had few safeguards against abuses of police power. Chen Wen-cheng was a well-known critic of the KMT and a permanent resident of the United States, where he was a professor at Carnegie Mellon University. While he was in Taipei doing research in July 1981, police detained, questioned, and released him. The next day he turned up dead in his office. The government tried to close the case quickly by declaring that Chen's death was either a suicide or an accident. This created suspicion of a cover-up and even led to a hearing by the U.S. Congress.[9] A few activists kept the matter alive for years afterward, and in 2000 the Chen Wen-cheng Incident Investigation Working Group implicated former Taiwan Garrison Commander Wang Ching-hsu, two other high-ranking security officials, and two KMT cadre in Chen's murder.

Another case, this one lacking political overtones, involved the death of Wang Ying-hsien, a Mainlander taxi driver, while in police custody. Police suspected Wang of bank robbery and arrested him and his daughter for questioning. The police claimed Wang had confessed to the crime and

---

[8] Steven J. Hood, *The Kuomintang and the Democratization of Taiwan* (Boulder, Colo.: Westview Press, 1997), 59.

[9] Ibid., 69.

then leapt to his death from a bridge while showing investigators where the money was hidden. But the real culprit, captured a short time later, exonerated Wang. Wang's daughter, waiting in a room next to that in which police interrogated her father, said she heard sounds that suggested he was being tortured. Courts subsequently convicted five policemen for mistreating Wang. The case prompted the Legislative Yuan to pass a law in 1982 requiring the presence of a legal counsel for detainees during interrogation.

The KMT owned or controlled all three television stations and most of the thirty-three radio stations on Taiwan. The government refused to issue licenses for new newspapers until 1988. The opposition therefore relied heavily on magazines, which by law could publish no more than once weekly, to carry its political commentaries to the mass public. To cover their costs, publishers of political commentaries often accepted articles expressing extreme or radical views, which attracted additional readers. This also sometimes attracted the attention of the authorities, leading to bans and arrests. From 1977 to 1979, the government was relatively tolerant of opposition magazines critical of the KMT. There was a crackdown after the 1979 Kaohsiung incident. In 1984–87, with future presidential candidate Soong Chu-yu (James Soong) as director of cultural affairs for the KMT, the government again moved vigorously against opposition magazines when several magazines under new, assertive publishers stepped up their criticism of the KMT. Police banned and confiscated most issues of the opposition press and shut down several publications entirely. During one episode in March 1985, some one hundred police armed with clubs enforced the confiscation of an edition of the magazine *Progress* because it contained an objectionable article. The magazine's three top executives tried to resist, receiving injuries and, later, fines for obstructing the police. According to the watchdog organization Committee to Protect Journalists, Taiwan had the largest number of journalists in prison in 1985–86 of any noncommunist country. Changes in the regulations governing the media greatly reduced censorship beginning in 1988.

The Long Path from Martial Law to a Multiparty System

The ROC's expulsion from the United Nations caused deep national discouragement the government feared would exacerbate Taiwanese domestic political discontent. An immediate effect was to steel the KMT against the idea of an unrestrained opposition movement because the reduction of U.S. diplomatic and military support seemed to weaken Taiwan relative to the Communist Chinese threat. The UN defeat prompted a resurgence of pressure by intellectuals on the KMT to open both party and government bodies to greater input and representation by the population as a whole. The party leadership responded first by publishing a book recounting KMT achievements in building up Taiwan's economy. Soon thereafter the government launched a crackdown on dissident academics, labeling them Communist agitators. Several were arrested and dismissed from their university jobs.[10] The longer-term impact of this diplomatic setback, however, was to accelerate political liberalization, as the government sought to counter demoralization by offering Taiwanese more opportunities for political participation and loosening the restrictions on non-KMT politicians.[11] The UN decision, for example, immediately prompted movement toward additional parliamentary elections to reduce the domination of the three national organs by elderly Mainlanders.

In another case of domestic politics being stimulated from overseas, the U.S. government in 1971 yielded administration of the Diaoyutai (Senkaku) Islands, located northeast of Taiwan and traditionally claimed by China, to Tokyo. The Taipei government came under public criticism for letting foreigners take territory perceived as rightfully Chinese. Public discussion of this issue helped spur some of the opposition activities that followed.

In October 1971, fifteen political commentators associated with the journal *Tahsueh* (*The Intellectual*) published a statement arguing that while reunification with the mainland was Taiwan's ultimate goal, other important intermediate goals included prosperity, respect for human rights, and the rule of law. The government dealt with this challenge subtly by warning the media not to overstep their bounds and arranging the firings of some of the dissidents from their academic jobs. In 1973, a group of political activists organized under the name United Independent Front broke new ground by openly calling for reforms such as making the legislature more powerful relative to the president, strengthening the rule of law, curtailing the KMT's privileges, and electing the mayors of the major cities and the Taiwan governor by popular vote. In 1975 the *Taiwan Political Review* began printing articles critical of the government. After a few months its editor was convicted of sedition and sentenced to ten years' imprisonment.

The election of November 1977 saw Taiwanese frustrations boil over in a street riot. Hsu Hsin-liang, former KMT member of the Provincial Assembly, wanted to run as the party's nominee for Taoyuan County chief

[10] Ibid., 50.

[11] Hung-mao Tien, "Taiwan in Transition: Prospects for Socio-Political Change," *China Quarterly* 64 (December 1975): 617.

executive. The KMT snubbed him, so Hsu ran as an independent against the KMT's chosen candidate. In the city of Chungli on November 19, onlookers accused KMT members of tampering with the ballots at a polling place set up in an elementary school. A crowd estimated at ten thousand gathered and some of its members burned a police station and several police cars. This was the first significant political rioting in Taiwan since Chiang Kai-shek moved the ROC central government to the island. But things had changed since the February 28 incident: police were under orders not to use violence against the demonstrators. Learning of the incident, most Taiwanese disapproved of the destructiveness of the rioters, although they condemned the KMT's attempt to manipulate the ballots. The polls showed Hsu the winner, and the government allowed his victory to stand. Because KMT general secretary Li Huan had urged a conciliatory attitude toward the Taiwanese opposition, the KMT leadership blamed him for the Chungli incident and dismissed him from his post.

Political debate was relatively unrestrained in the lead-up to the island-wide elections for offices at all levels of government scheduled for December 23, 1978, in which the opposition expected to make a strong showing. On December 16, however, Washington announced it would normalize diplomatic relations with the PRC the following month. In reaction, Chiang Ching-kuo cancelled the elections and placed the ROC military on a heightened state of alert. The KMT carried out a campaign to assure Taiwan's public that the armed forces were capable of fending off an attempted Chinese invasion. But the government also encouraged the public to donate money to the military for the purchase of modern weapons. The "Self-Strengthening National Salvation Fund" collected an estimated U.S. $100 million in donations,[12] and public support for the party increased in line with the classic "rally 'round the flag" effect.

Frustrated *Tangwai* politicians split over how to respond. Moderates such as Kang Ning-hsiang argued that postponing the elections was reasonable and that the electoral process remained the opposition's best vehicle for challenging the KMT. The radical faction, generally comprised of younger Taiwanese, favored mobilizing the public in antigovernment street demonstrations. Discontent over the cancelled elections contributed directly to the Kaohsiung incident that would occur a year later.

Proponents of pressuring the government through public demonstrations included Yu Teng-fa and Hsu Hsin-liang. The seventy-six-year-old Yu, who had been elected Kaohsiung County executive, organized a Christmas rally to protest the postponement of the elections. In January the state arrested Yu, who was already on the KMT's bad side for his as-

---

[12] John F. Copper, "Taiwan in 1981: In a Holding Pattern," *Asian Survey* 22, no. 1 (January 1982): 52.

sistance to successful local *Tangwai* candidates and for occasionally making favorable remarks about the CCP in public places.[13] In a military trial condemned by government critics as a sham, Yu was convicted based on the testimony of a confessed PRC agent named Wu Ch'un-fa (also known as Wu Tai-an) that Yu was aware of a Communist conspiracy but failed to report it. Wu was a self-styled but apparently confused and harmless revolutionary. Like many other political activists in the Kaohsiung area, Wu had visited Yu and asked for support. Yu had done nothing for Wu, but he got an eight-year sentence (he was released early due to poor health). Wu was executed.

On January 22, Hsu and other *Tangwai* politicians participated in demonstrations against Yu's arrest in Yu's home village and in Kaohsiung. The government retaliated against Hsu. The Control Yuan considered impeaching Hsu based on charges that he left his post without authorization, libeled the government, and participated in an illegal demonstration. In May, police merely looked on while thousands gathered to hear speeches by *Tangwai* politicians and buy banned political books at a rally in Chungli billed as Hsu's "birthday party." It was the largest peaceful, nonelectoral opposition rally in Taiwan's history. In June, however, the government suspended Hsu from his office for two years.

In August 1979, *Meilidao* (*Beautiful Island*) magazine began publication, featuring many articles critical of the government. Run by Huang Hsin-chieh and Shih Ming-teh, *Meilidao* denounced the government's emphasis on economic development over social justice and advocated democratic reform. Even the magazine's name was subtly defiant. *Meilidao* was a reference to the old Portuguese name for Taiwan, "Formosa," which had become widely used in the English-speaking world. Embracing this international, pre-KMT name suggested a rejection of the notion that Taiwan was part of China, a point not lost on the government. *Meilidao* quickly became the second most popular publication on the island (after the Taiwan version of *TV Guide*).[14]

Meilidao opened twelve offices around the island and took on some of the functions of a political party, including sponsoring meetings to discuss political issues. The authorities permitted the rallies and distribution of the magazine, although in September and November, right-wing vigilantes repeatedly damaged the magazine's offices and the residences of some *Meilidao* staff.

International events emboldened *Tangwai* activists. The U.S. president

---

[13] J. Bruce Jacobs, "Taiwan 1979: 'Normalcy' After 'Normalization,'" *Asian Survey* 20, no. 1 (January 1980): 90–91.

[14] Marc J. Cohen, *Taiwan at the Crossroads* (Washington, D.C.: Asia Resource Center, 1988), 38.

Jimmy Carter's emphasis on human rights seemed to demand circumspection from U.S.-aligned authoritarian regimes. China had seen the emergence of its own democracy movement. *Meilidao* planned a rally for December 10, 1979, in recognition of International Human Rights Day.

The Taiwan Garrison Command rejected the organizers' application, which made the planned gathering technically illegal. The day before the rally, police in Kaohsiung arrested and beat two *Meilidao* employees who were distributing publicity material. Participants who arrived the next day at the park designated as the rally site found it already occupied by riot police. A crowd of several thousand moved to a nearby traffic circle. Police and their vehicles blocked the streets to keep more people from joining the rally, preventing the crowd at the rally site from exiting. The large public security contingent was under orders to block off attempts by the crowd to march, but to refrain from aggressive actions that might later give rise to charges of government brutality. Scuffles broke out between participants (unofficially estimated at ten thousand to thirty thousand in number) and police. The authorities and opposition activists accused each other of instigating the violence. The opposition said the government manufactured a riot to shame the opposition and justify a crackdown on political dissenters, and alleged that some progovernment elements or military policemen dressed in plain clothes mixed into the crowd and attacked riot-control police. The organizers tried to calm the crowd and discourage violence. Observers estimated probably less than 100 people were hurt. The government, however, said 182 policemen and one civilian were injured. Subsequent news reports by the pro-KMT media showed high officials and famous entertainers visiting hospitalized policemen, an effort by the government to turn public opinion against the demonstrators. Police arrested the eight rally organizers and charged them with sedition.

Once out of the public eye, the authorities were less restrained. Police held the Kaohsiung Eight in seclusion and coerced them through sleep deprivation and threats to sign confessions. Lu Hsiu-lien, a prominent women's rights activist, said police showed her a photograph of the bullet-ridden corpse of an executed prisoner, forced her to read the notice sent to the dead man's widow, and told her "this is how you will end up."[15] Having obtained confessions from all eight defendants while hampering their defense attorneys, the state convicted them in a series of courts-martial in March and April 1980. The thrust of the state's case was that the Kaohsiung Eight had advocated Taiwan independence. Actually,

---

[15] John Kaplan, *The Court-Martial of the Kaohsiung Defendants* (Berkeley, Calif.: University of California Press, 1981), 19–31; "The Kaohsiung Incident of 1979," http://www.taiwandc.org/hst-1979.htm, 5, accessed Feb. 21, 2001.

most had called not for independence, but for self-determination. They received stiff sentences, ranging from twelve years to life imprisonment, which drew condemnation by the U.S. State Department in its annual human rights report. (Hsu Hsin-liang, who escaped and fled to the United States, was sentenced in absentia.) KMT hardliners—including Taiwanese vice president Hsieh—had demanded death sentences.

The state held two more rounds of trials for those charged in connection with the Kaohsiung incident. In April and May, a civil court sentenced thirty-three more participants to prison terms of two to six years. A group of Presbyterian church members also went to trial for allegedly helping to hide Shih, whom police arrested twenty-two days after the incident. The Presbyterian church had previously sided with the opposition, publishing a "Declaration on Human Rights by the Presbyterian Church in Taiwan" in August 1977. The church members put on trial included the general secretary of the church in Taiwan, the Reverend Kao Chun-ming, who got a seven-year sentence. Shih himself got a life sentence. His wife Linda Gail Arrigo, an American citizen, was deported.

No one involved in the Kaohsiung incident suffered retribution more terrible than Lin Yi-hsiung. Police severely beat Lin while he was in detention in February 1980. After visiting him, Lin's mother attempted to contact Amnesty International's Osaka office. The next day Lin's mother and twin seven-year-old daughters were stabbed to death and his older daughter badly wounded in his home. The authorities claimed to know nothing about the crime, even though Lin's house was under twenty-four-hour police surveillance when the murders occurred.

The state closed down fifteen publications, including *Meilidao*, but permitted media coverage of the Kaohsiung Eight trial. This strategy had mixed results for the KMT. On one hand, most of the Taiwan public accepted the government's position that the demonstration was a threat to public order that called for police intervention. At the same time, however, most Taiwanese sympathized with the motivations of the rally's organizers, which the defendants and their attorneys gained an opportunity to explain to a large audience throughout Taiwan and the international community. In the long run, instead of discrediting the opposition, the state's show trial had the effect of increasing support among the public for democratic reforms. In the 1980 elections, during which the Kaohsiung incident was a major campaign issue, several politicians who had been jailed after the Kaohsiung incident and subsequently released won political offices. Relatives of the dissidents who remained in jail stood for office in their place and defeated their KMT opponents by large margins. The wife of imprisoned dissident Yao Chia-wen was the leading vote-getter for the available seats in the National Assembly. The government still felt sufficiently pressured that it took further steps toward democratization soon after the trial by increasing the number of parliamentary seats to be filled by residents of Taiwan and by clarifying electoral regulations to promote fair campaigning.

In 1982 jailed Kaohsiung incident figures Huang, Yao, Chang Chun-hong, and Lin Hong-hsuan produced a joint statement arguing that democracy would bring Taiwan greater harmony internally and more security internationally. "In the long-term interest of Taiwan," they wrote, "to carry out democracy on the island is far more urgent and important than unification with China."[16] In 1984 they went on a hunger strike that their captors eventually halted through forced feeding. Shih repeated this tactic in 1985 with a four-month, liquids-only fast that brought him near death before the authorities force-fed him.

Tangwai candidates had previously collaborated to produce a common platform calling for political reforms such as ending the KMT's privileged relationship with the government, reestablishing provisions of the constitution that had been suspended as part of martial law, and allowing greater freedoms of speech and of assembly. The 1983 election, nonetheless, convinced many of the need for a stronger organization to coordinate *Tangwai* activities. The result was the formation of the *Tangwai* Research Association for Public Policy (TRAPP), an attempt to create a new de facto party in circumvention of the ban. In 1984, the minister of the interior warned that the *Tangwai* should disband TRAPP or face the consequences, but TRAPP's organizers did not back down. In May 1986, confronted with opposition street rallies and open discussion of taboo subjects such as Taiwanese independence, Chiang ordered the KMT to open negotiations with *Tangwai* leaders. Although Chiang had reportedly arranged a meeting between KMT officials and *Tangwai* leaders in 1978,[17] this was the first time since 1947 that KMT officials negotiated directly and openly with opposition politicians, whom the KMT previously characterized as "traitors." Mediated by a group of respected academics, the meeting was an important step in the KMT-dominated state's acceptance of a legitimate role for the opposition in Taiwan's political system.[18] Substantively the meeting was less significant. The TRAPP and KMT representatives agreed that political activity should conform to the ROC constitution and that neither side would undermine public order. The KMT agreed TRAPP could establish branch offices, but the question of the TRAPP's legal status

[16] Trong R. Chai, "The Future of Taiwan," *Asian Survey* 26, no. 12 (December 1986): 1319.
[17] Yangsun Chou and Andrew J. Nathan, "Democratizing Transition in Taiwan," *Asian Survey* 27, no. 3 (March 1987): 283.
[18] Cohen, *Crossroads*, 55.

remained unsettled. *Tangwai* members were divided on the question of accepting a compromise with the government that would still give them an organization that could campaign, nominate candidates, and open offices in different cities. Some objected to the KMT's insistence that the new organization register under a law governing civic associations or be considered illegal, when the KMT itself had not so registered.

After a second meeting ended in atmosphere of bitterness, police arrested five prominent opposition politicians. All got sentences that would keep them from participating in the next election. These arrests sparked several protest gatherings around the island, during which speakers often referred to the "people power" campaign that had recently forced Ferdinand Marcos out of power in the Philippines. To maintain momentum, TRAPP moved quickly to open its new offices, and the opposition held a twelve-hour rally May 19, 1986, during which some fifteen hundred police were mobilized.

In another challenge to the authorities, *Tangwai*-affiliated activists founded the Taiwan Association for Human Rights in 1984. This association was illegal because it duplicated the function of the Chinese Association for Human Rights (a right-wing institution that focused on human rights violations on the mainland by the CCP), and the civic organizations law forbid more than one organization per function. Several magazines published by Tangwai activists sharply criticized government officials and policies in 1984. The authorities banned many of the magazines and closed down their offices, and some of the officials criticized in the press successfully sued publishers for libel. The opposition used these convictions as the bases for further demonstrations and denunciations of the regime.

The *Tangwai* had been weakened by the loss of several key leaders to imprisonment after the Kaohsiung incident and by continuing disunity: a clear split persisted between moderates such as Kang, who favored peaceful and gradual political reform and refrained from open calls for Taiwanese independence, and the *Meilidao* faction, which called for cutting political ties with the mainland and using public demonstrations to pressure the government into making reforms. But the KMT had problems as well. A series of embarrassing events in 1984–85 weakened the KMT, including the Henry Liu murder case, a disappointing performance by Taiwan's economy, and a major financial scandal. Tsai Ch'en-chou, chairman of the savings and loan institution Tenth Credit Cooperative, was discovered to have misappropriated company funds for private purposes. Tenth Credit and its affiliate, Cathay Investment and Trust Co., failed. The scandal disgraced several high-ranking government officials and forced the resignation of two members of the cabinet. These humiliations, combined with pressure from the U.S. government, helped prompt the KMT to make a few political concessions, including naming Taiwanese Lee Teng-hui as vice president, handing out life sentences for the culprits in the conspiracy to kill Henry Liu, appointing Taiwanese to the cabinet, releasing the remaining political prisoners jailed during the 1950s, and granting parole to Lin Yi-hsiung, Kao Chun-ming, Hsu Ching-fu, and Lin Wen-chen.

In March 1986 the KMT had promoted Li Huan and some younger Taiwanese to the Central Standing Committee, portending liberal reform. In April, Chiang had formed a twelve-man committee to formulate a plan for lifting martial law, legalizing new political parties, and implementing other important political reforms. Although the government was clearly moving toward legalizing new parties, it warned the *Tangwai* not to jump the gun. In September, Minister of Justice Shih Ch'i-yang reiterated that forming a new party was an illegal act and that the state would not allow it. The *Tangwai* was impatient, however, because it wanted to secure the advantages of a true political party—coordinating the campaigns of individual candidates (to keep them from taking votes away from each other), defining ideological coherence, gathering funds for political campaigns, and legitimizing themselves in the eyes of voters—before the next election. Another impetus was that exiled politician Hsu Hsin-liang had decided to form a party overseas, and *Tangwai* politicians in Taiwan did not want leadership of the movement to pass from their hands to an outside group. On September 28, 1986, *Tangwai* politicians gathered in a meeting room of Taipei's opulent Grand Hotel, which lodged most of the foreign dignities who visited the island. Booked in the name of the Rotary Club, the meeting's original purpose was to determine the *Tangwai*'s slate of candidates for the upcoming election. Acting on a motion by Chu Kao-cheng, the participants decided to use the occasion to form a new party on the strength of two arguments: such a large gathering of *Tangwai* politicians was a rare opportunity, and the participants were at that time official candidates for election, which would make it harder for the authorities to arrest them. Credit for the new party's name, Democratic Progressive Party (Minjintang, DPP) went to Legislative Yuan member Hsieh Chang-t'ing, who said it should include neither "Taiwan" nor "China" to emphasize that the party was not prejudging Taiwan's future relationship with the mainland. The meeting yielded a declaration marking the birth of the DPP signed by 132 participants. Knowing they were in danger of a KMT backlash, DPP leaders privately assured the authorities that the new party would not promote Taiwanese independence or communism and would respect the constitution.

Kuomintang conservatives wanted the DPP's organizers arrested. Chiang disagreed, saying, "At this time it is not good to resort to anger and recklessly take aggressive action that might cause great disturbances in society. We should try to adopt a calm attitude and consider the nation's stability and the people's security."[19] The government's response was therefore restrained. It declared the DPP illegal, but did not send the police to round up its members. Government officials publicly reminded the opposition that advocating communism or Taiwanese independence was still forbidden. On October 11 the DPP gave an oblique public response, saying it would uphold the constitution and would not affiliate with any group that advocated violence.[20] Government print media that mentioned the DPP placed the name of the new party in quotation marks, a practice regularly used when listing the titles of officials in the CCP government on the mainland. In the meantime the state kept working on a new civic organizations law that would make the DPP and other upstart parties legal.[21] Chiang said on October 5, "The times have changed, events have changed; trends have changed. In response to these changes, the ruling party must adopt new ways to meet this democratic revolution and link up with this historical trend."[22] The government allowed the new, illegal party to participate in the election. The DPP had won a historic battle.

The DPP was actually an umbrella organization for several groups distinct enough to be separate parties. The party tended to attract support from younger, better-educated voters than the KMT. The DPP was not completely Taiwanese, but also included a few mainlanders such as Fei Hsi-ping and Lin Chin-chieh (although these two eventually quit the new party).

Some DPP members made all their public speeches in the Taiwanese dialect rather than Mandarin. At its first National Representative Congress in November, the DPP adopted a program of basic goals that included self-determination of Taiwan's political status through plebiscite and rejoining the United Nations (under a name to be determined later). The party platform also called for democratic reforms (such as direct presidential elections), an end to martial law, greater civil liberties, less defense spending and an end to compulsory military service, and more benefits for consumers and disadvantaged groups. The DPP's strong environmentalist bent produced a demand for a moratorium on additional nuclear power plants. The party congress named Chiang P'eng-chien, a member of the more radical DPP faction who was a defense attorney during the Kaohsiung incident trials, as party chairman over the more moderate Fei Hsi-p'ing. The delegates to the congress also chose a DPP flag depicting a

[19] Quoted in Lee Teng-hui's journal; Chao and Myers, First Chinese Democracy, 133.
[20] Chungkuo Shihpao (Taipei), Nov. 7, 1986, 2.
[21] Chou and Nathan, Democratizing Transition, 288.
[22] Li Xiaofeng, Taiwan minzhu yundong sishinian (Taipei: Zili wanbaoshe wenhua chubanshe, 1991), 242.

green silhouette of Taiwan over a white cross against a green background. The use of the color green represented the party's environmentalism, another issue area in which it would frequently clash with the KMT in the future. Depicting the island of Taiwan in isolation obviously could be taken to suggest independent statehood. "We will put the 'rest of the country' on our flag," said Frank Hsieh, "as soon as the government 'recovers' it."[23] Kuomintang concessions to the opposition such as lifting martial law and carrying out electoral reforms would soon create pressure on the DPP to take a stronger position on Taiwanese independence to remain relevant.

Because of its identity as a Taiwanese party, the DDP attracted a coalition of groups with various interests. Partly to contain factionalism, the DPP established recruitment rules requiring that prospective members be nominated by at least three current members. This was to prevent any one faction from attempting to dominate the party by strength of numbers.[24] The party also decided to hold annual national congresses (in contrast to the KMT practice of one congress every five or six years) and to limit the chairman to a single one-year term.

Although still small relative to the KMT with about twelve thousand members, the DPP crossed an important threshold in the 1989 election by gaining 35 percent of the popular vote and winning twenty-one seats in the Legislative Yuan, meeting the minimum standard of twenty seats required to introduce legislation.

A KMT politician summed up his party's attitude toward the newly formed DPP thus: "[They] are trying to use the ideology of separatism to destroy social harmony. Their members also use very aggressive tactics to destroy our society's rules merely to further their political aims."[25] Neither did either Beijing or Washington welcome the emergence of the DPP. Committed to the "recovery" of Taiwan, the CCP was as alarmed as the KMT at the prospect of a Taiwanese separatist party. The U.S. government favored political liberalization on Taiwan, but saw the independence movement as a potential cause of tension in U.S.-China relations.

Working toward the cessation of martial law along with the legalization of opposition parties, Chiang in October 1986 got the Standing Committee to accept replacing martial law with a National Security Law and revising the law on civic organizations to allow for new political parties. There was consensus within the government that if martial law was lifted, Taiwan needed a strong alternative basis of protection against enemies taking ad-

---

[23] Cohen, *Crossroads*, 60.
[24] Chou and Nathan, *Democratizing Transition*, 293.
[25] *Lianhebao*, Nov. 23, 1986, 3.

vantage of political liberties to harm the country. The new National Security Law therefore maintained martial law's prohibitions against communism and Taiwan separatism. Article 2 read, "No person may violate the constitution or advocate communism or the division of national territory in the exercise of the people's freedoms of assembly and association." Opposition politicians strongly condemned the law, arguing that it was so broadly worded as to provide scope for the same type of repression that occurred under martial law. They also demanded specific revisions such as the immediate release of all dissidents imprisoned under martial law rather than selective release after a case-by-case reevaluation. Violence broke out in both the streets and inside the Legislative Yuan before the law was passed on June 23, 1987. The government lifted martial law on Taiwan's territories except Jinmen and Matsu on July 14, 1987. Thus ended an era that had endured nearly four decades.

Critics complained that martial law was continuing under a new name. The Taiwan Garrison Command was still in place. The Temporary Provisions of the constitution designed to strengthen the state against the "Communist rebellion," on which were based the extraordinary powers wielded by the president, remained in force. Nevertheless, the National Security Law defined offenses more clearly, lessened the penalties, and moved the adjudication process from military courts to civilian courts. Some of the civil liberties specified in the constitution were restored, although the state reserved the power to suspend them in defense of the public interest. Arrested dissidents were released more quickly and no longer tortured while in detention. Republic of China security agents ceased monitoring Taiwan students and dissidents in the United States. The military no longer had the authority to vet the media. Censorship of political coverage gradually stopped. Three journalists on trial for unauthorized travel to the PRC were acquitted in 1987. The ROC government would remove restrictions on the press on January 1, 1988. The number of licenses granted for publications was expanded, and the permissible number of pages per newspaper increased. In November 1988, Kang Ning-hsiang's opposition-oriented newspaper received a license despite its title, *Capital*, which implied Taiwan was an independent state. The government's moves to lift restrictions on the media were not fast or thorough enough to please all critics. The pro-KMT state operated Taiwan's first three television stations; a fourth station sympathetic to the political opposition, Formosa Television, did not begin broadcasting until 1997. Most radio programming was also KMT-controlled, and the government did not free up additional broadcast frequencies until 1993. In April 1988, about three thousand people demonstrated against biased coverage of the DPP outside a Taipei TV station. Early in 1989, magazine publisher Cheng

Nan-rong burned himself to death to protest what he called the government's continued infringement of the freedom of the press.

The end of martial law cleared the way for dropping sedition charges against some Taiwanese activists living abroad, releasing some imprisoned dissidents, and reducing the sentences of others. But while some old political convicts were leaving jail, new ones went in. Taiwanese activists continued to challenge the limits of dissent, and imprisonment of political offenders increased again after the summer of 1987. In August, 140 former political prisoners jointly founded the Formosan Political Prisoners' Association (FPPA). The FPPA charter explicitly advocated independence for Taiwan. In October the government arrested two of the group's leaders, Hsu Tsao-te and Tsai Yu-chuan, for sedition. During their trial, which lasted only one day, the defendants spoke in Taiwanese as an act of defiance, requiring translation for Mainlander listeners.

A new Civic Organization Law in 1989 finally granted legal status to the DPP and at least ten other new parties. As expected, the law held that "people's assemblies and associations shall not violate the Constitution, advocate communism or the division of national territory." Over thirty new political parties quickly registered, although only the DPP was large and influential enough to challenge the KMT for control of the government. New parties included the extreme right-wing Democratic Freedom Party and the Labor Party, which focused not just on workers' rights but also on environmental issues and on improving opportunities for women and aborigines.

At the end of the year the attempted return to Taiwan of exiled dissident Hsu Hsin-liang sparked another battle between the KMT and the opposition. Having fled to the United States after the Kaohsiung incident, Hsu became head of the U.S.-based Taiwan Revolutionary Party. He advocated armed uprising to destroy the KMT and bring about "revolution." Not surprisingly, the authorities in Taiwan issued a warrant for his arrest on the charge of sedition. In 1986 he said he planned to form a new party called the Taiwan Democratic Party, but he merged his organization with the DPP after the latter's establishment. Hsu then announced his intention to return to Taiwan and help the DPP prepare for the December 6 election. He brought with him an entourage that included Linda Gail Arrigo and former U.S. attorney general Ramsey Clark. During Hsu's stopover at Narita Airport in Japan, his airline, at Taipei's request, refused to let him fly on to Taiwan. A crowd of several thousand Hsu supporters, including most of the DPP leadership, gathered at Chiang Kai-shek International Airport expecting to greet him on November 30. Clashes broke out between the restive crowd and police. The demonstrators injured several policemen and damaged police and television news vehicles parked at the scene. The police employed tear gas and water cannons. Hsu made it to Chiang Kai-shek Airport on December 2 by traveling under a false name, but airport authorities denied him entry. Once again a crowd of his supporters clashed with police outside. The DPP publicly denounced this violence and pledged to discipline any party members found to be involved. Kuomintang-friendly television news broadcasts replayed selected sections of videotape shot during the first incident, showing members of the crowd throwing rocks at police, to demonstrate the KMT's claim that the DPP and its supporters were an irresponsible mob. In response, the DPP held a press conference to screen their own videotapes showing that the police, as well, threw rocks and that the DPP leaders present tried to dissuade the crowd from violent behavior. Hsu entered Taiwan secretly by boat three years later. He was arrested and imprisoned on the charge of sedition. After his release, Hsu returned to working within Taiwan's political system, serving for two years as chairman of the DPP.

With the beginning of political liberalization, protests and demonstrations became common sights in Taiwan in 1987–88. Democratic Progressive Party members instigated vigorous debate, walkouts, and occasional fisticuffs in the previously sedate Legislative Yuan. In September 1987 the Executive Yuan approved restrictive guidelines on outdoor political gatherings that required three days' advance permission from the government and forbade "insults or slander." The opposition flouted the guidelines, leading to the arrests of three DPP leaders.

The opposition focused much of its attention on the domination of parliament by elderly Mainlanders who were exempt from standing for reelection. These Mainlanders represented provinces of mainland China and had won their seats before the CCP sent Chiang Kai-shek's regime fleeing to Taiwan. So few seats were open to competitive elections that the opposition could not gain a parliamentary majority even if won decisively at the polls. By this time the average age of Mainland-elected parliamentarians was eighty, and on average one died every week. Democratic Progressive Party Chairman Yao Chia-wen demanded new elections for all seats in the parliament. In March 1988, activists demonstrating in support of a general parliamentary election attempted to enter a housing area where several Mainlander lifetime delegates lived. Police blocked their passage and beat one of the group's DPP organizers. Such pressure helped push the government to promulgate a new election law in January 1989. Seats in the Legislative Yuan open to candidates representing districts in Taiwan increased from 100 to 130, most of whom would be directly elected. Second-place finishers from the 1948 elections no longer replaced deceased Mainlander delegates. The government would offer severance pay of about U.S. $130,000 to encourage elderly Mainlander delegates to retire. These reforms, of course, did not go far enough to meet the opposition's demands. Opposition politicians were particularly critical of the retirement payout, arguing that these delegates had already been parasites of public money for decades.

Discontent over issues other than democratic reform also spilled out of Taiwan's society into the streets; these issues included pollution, labor rights, women's rights, aboriginal rights, and protection of Taiwanese fishermen from detention by other governments. Reform of labor laws lagged behind political liberalization. Low labor costs had been one of the pillars of Taiwan's economic success, and many workers felt they had not received a fair share of the new prosperity. Managers often got away with violating the protections specified in the Labor Standards Law. Most trade unions were controlled by the KMT—all union heads were KMT members until March 1988. Emboldened by the opposition's success, workers carried out numerous strikes, almost all of which were illegal under Taiwan's restrictive labor regulations. A railroad strike organized outside union auspices was particularly effective, halting the trains for a day.

Many farmers were unhappy as well. On May 20, 1988, between two thousand and four thousand farmers (with some DPP participation) began a peaceful protest over several issues: lack of health insurance, high prices for government-supplied fertilizer, and allegations that the government was permitting the dumping of U.S. agricultural products. The gathering deteriorated into a series of skirmishes between protesters and police that lasted eighteen hours. About 200 people were injured and 122 arrested, of whom 68 were later convicted and fined or imprisoned. This was a more serious outbreak of public disorder than the 1979 Kaohsiung incident, and it led to follow-on protests over the alleged over-aggressiveness of the riot police and the large number of arrests. It was an embarrassing incident for the new ROC president Lee Teng-hui, especially given his background in agricultural administration. Democratic Progressive Party chairman Yao Chia-wen, a fellow Presbyterian Taiwanese, said the government reaction to the demonstration killed hopes that Lee's presidency would be a break with the past.[26] Lee had, however, rejected the calls of conservative KMT leaders that martial law be reinstituted. Instead Lee said the police handled the incident improperly.

Environmentalism motivated many other protests. Following the pattern of newly affluent people in other countries, Taiwan's people in the mid-1990s became increasingly concerned about pollution. Protecting the environment had been a low priority during the drive for economic development. Studies publicized in 1987 revealed that 15 percent of Taiwan's

---

[26] Cohen, *Crossroads*, 74.

farmland had been contaminated by metal-laden wastewater released from electroplating workshops.[27] Rural areas were particularly vulnerable to pollution because government regulators did not scrutinize small industrial firms in the countryside as closely as their larger city counterparts. Grass-roots activism gave environmentalists an additional avenue for redress. In October 1988, for example, an estimated twenty thousand demonstrators gathered to protest the pollution of water by petrochemical plants in the southern Taiwan district of Lin Yuan, forcing the temporary shutdown of two naphtha cracking facilities and a compensation payment of over NT $250 million.[28]

Lee Teng-hui Succeeds Chiang Ching-kuo

Because Chiang had a power base of unmatched strength, including firm support from the party, the military, and the security agencies, his departure was bound to create a huge hole in Taiwan's politics. Chiang had long suffered from diabetes and its complications, which required him to undergo eye surgery for retinal bleeding and cataracts. He also reportedly had a pacemaker implanted in 1985. By 1984 he had delegated day-to-day leadership responsibilities to his advisers, particularly General Wang Sheng, who headed the ROC military's political indoctrination as director of the General Political Warfare Department. With Chiang becoming more enfeebled, speculation about his successor intensified as the list of aspirants narrowed.

The opposition press was highly derisive of the idea of a continued Chiang dynasty, and most of the Taiwan public agreed. Chiang's relatives, moreover, were not strong candidates for the presidency. Chiang Kai-shek had another son, Chiang Ching-kuo's half brother, General Chiang Wei-kuo, who was himself quite old (seventy-two at the time of Chiang Ching-kuo's death) and had little experience outside of the military. Chiang Ching-kuo's own children included three sons and daughter with his Russian wife Chiang Fang-liang (plus two illegitimate sons he fathered while serving in Jiangsu). Chiang's oldest son Chiang Hsiao-wen was in poor health. His second son Chiang Hsiao-wu was tainted by allegations he was involved in the murder of Henry Liu, and his father posted him to Taiwan's trade mission in Singapore. Third son Chiang Hsiao-yung was a businessman with no interest in politics. On Constitution Day (December

---

[27] Ronald G. Knapp, "The Shaping of Taiwan's Landscapes," in Rubinstein (ed.), *Taiwan*, 22.

[28] Simon Long, *Taiwan: China's Last Frontier* (London: Macmillan, 1991), 201.

25) 1985, Chiang said in a speech that the next president "could not and would not" be a member of the Chiang family.

Wang Sheng visited the United States in April 1983. Observers interpreted this as sign that Wang's hosts either expected or hoped he would soon take over leadership of the ROC. Chiang decided Wang was excessively ambitious.[29] The president derailed Wang's career by appointing him ROC ambassador to Paraguay in November 1983. Chiang's protégé former premier Sun Yun-suan suffered a cerebral hemorrhage in 1984 from which he never fully recovered. Consistent with larger trends within the KMT, Chiang in 1984 selected as his vice president Taiwanese technocrat Lee Teng-hui. Lee, a former minister without portfolio (1972–78), mayor of Taipei (1978–81), and governor of Taiwan (1981–84), had a reputation for administrative competence and loyalty to the party. Originally an expert in agricultural economics, Lee had studied in Japan, earned a Ph.D. from Cornell University in the United States, and served with the Joint Commission on Rural Reconstruction.

Chiang died on January 13, 1988. By the end of his life, Chiang had won widespread respect for his willingness not only to loosen the KMT's authoritarian regime to accommodate the demands of Taiwanese society, but also to mix with ordinary Taiwan people, something that set him apart from his father.

Lee ascended to the presidency and then aimed for the top KMT position. He had strong support from Taiwan's public (in February 1988 he held the first presidential press conference in thirteen years) and from Taiwanese and technocratically oriented party members. Kuomintang conservatives, however, feared that Lee secretly supported Taiwanese independence and were disturbed by his advocacy of liberalization. Chiang Kai-shek's widow Soong Mei-ling and premier Yu Kuo-hwa were among Lee's opponents. The efforts of conservatives to block Lee's ascension to the chairmanship worsened disunity with the KMT and, as news of the intraparty debates leaked out, provided the opposition with evidence to support their argument that the KMT was dominated by Mainlanders who did not have the interests of Taiwan's people at heart.

The dispute forced the postponement of the thirteenth KMT congress, originally scheduled for January 1988, until July. The Central Standing Committee had already nominated Lee as party chairman, but a sufficiently large vote against him during the KMT congress could have overturned his nomination. With the support of ROC armed forces chief of staff Hau Pei-tsun and a large number of reform-minded members of the

[29] John F. Copper, *Historical Dictionary of Taiwan* (Metuchen, N.J.: Scarecrow Press, 1993), 114.

KMT elite, the congress confirmed Lee KMT chairman. To help calm the fears of conservatives, huge portraits of Sun Yat-sen, Chiang Kai-shek, and Chiang Ching-kuo backed Lee while in his opening address he emphasized the need for stability. Soong May-ling made an appearance as well, which suggested Lee had her blessing.[30] James Soong replaced Li Huan as secretary general. For the first time, a majority (sixteen out of thirty-one) of members of the Central Standing Committee were Taiwanese.

The KMT traditionally used an open ballot to help enforce discipline: party leaders could identify those who do not support the leadership's agenda. Some younger, reform-minded KMT members interested in democratizing the party advocated a secret ballot for the election of the new chairman. Lee and his allies, judging that the open ballot would create pressure on voters to honor the wish of the Central Standing Committee, successfully campaigned for retaining the open ballot. This episode, like many others that would follow, demonstrated that Lee's desire to consolidate his power took precedence over his ideological commitment to political liberalization.

A Gradual Revolution

By the time Lee ascended to the presidency, Taiwanese had overcome a good deal of their initial disadvantages, both economic and political, relative to the class of Mainlanders who had replaced the Japanese elite after the war. Despite its privileged position, the KMT could not resist political liberalization indefinitely. Once begun, it created a spiraling effect. Political reforms, mainly undertaken to maintain public support, unleashed a new wave of criticism of the KMT and thus pushed the party to make additional reforms.

International influence was not a decisive factor, but played a significant role. Large, effective public demonstrations during the 1980s by South Koreans against the Roh Tae Woo government and by Filipinos against Ferdinand Marcos's regime emboldened dissenters in Taiwan, and the U.S. government pressured the KMT to protect civil liberties.

Taiwan's political opposition achieved its breakthrough over a long period of sustained pressure with a strategy to capitalize on both international and domestic political circumstances to further the causes of reforming the structure of government, legalize new parties more representative of the Taiwanese community, protect civil liberties, and allow

---

[30] Long, *Last Frontier*, 190–191.

more open discussion of Taiwan's destiny. The collective and increasingly strong pull of a chain of events over nearly two decades produced substantial political liberalization without massive violence by either the agents of change or the forces of resistance. Chiang Ching-kuo also deserves credit for making the decision to gradually reform rather than attempt to crush the political opposition and for steering the process between the vociferous calls for immediate, dramatic changes in policy on one hand and the resistance of strongly entrenched conservative forces on the other.

✳

Taiwan under Lee Teng-hui

A number of initial, yet dramatic political reforms, including the termination of martial law, the legalization of new political parties, and a commitment to greater protection of civil liberties, occurred in the late 1980s. A second phase of reform in the 1990s involved knotty constitutional questions: the relative power of the president versus the premier, the composition and duties of the National Assembly, the procedure for electing the president, and the status of the provincial level of government. With considerable tumult, the politicians settled these issues. Lee Teng-hui's government found it difficult, however, to address what should have been the next phase of reform—rooting out official corruption and government links with organized crime and dismantling the KMT's systemic advantages—because of fears the KMT would lose control of the government.

Lee's agenda could be generally described as a program to expand Taiwanese sovereignty. He continued the push toward further Taiwanization of government, supported direct election of the president and downsizing of the provincial government, and campaigned for greater "international space" for Taiwan in the international community. Lee compared himself to the biblical prophet Moses, who led the enslaved minority Israelites out of Egypt on a journey toward establishing a country of their own. He also drew a parallel between the ethnic Chinese who immigrated to Taiwan in premodern times and the Europeans who settled in America in search of freedom.[1] It is easy to see why Beijing considered Lee a separatist. In fact,

---

[1] Shiba Ryotaro, "Basho no kurishimi: Taiwanjin ni umareta hiai," *Shukan Asahi*, May 6–13, 1994, 44; Lee Teng-hui interview with Maynard Parker, *Newsweek* (Asian edition), May 20, 1996.

however, Lee did not play up Taiwan independence. Instead, he aimed to capture the political middle ground by focusing on economic growth and constitutional reform, and enhancing Taiwan's international opportunities under the status quo. In fact both of the two major parties converged toward the political center: the DPP moderated its stance on independence, while the KMT adopted many of the DPP's positions on political reform.[2]

Lee Teng-hui Consolidates His Power

The KMT's evolution through the 1980s saw the beginning of deep divisions that would worsen during Lee's tenure as party chairman. One of the most important fault lines involved the perennial struggle between Taiwanese and Mainlanders, with Mainlanders generally more sensitive and hostile toward changes that appeared to support independence for Taiwan, while Taiwanese were generally more attentive to local business interests. Divisions could also be identified between older and younger generations, between urban and rural members, and between liberals and conservatives. These divisions were most prominent among the party's central leadership. Locally, factions tended to form around particular politicians based on personality rather than philosophical issues.

Ethnic Taiwanese technocrats inclined toward political reform now dominated the KMT mainstream, epitomized by Lee himself. The KMT mainstream supported Lee mainly because he was Taiwanese rather than for any ideological reason. Mainstream KMT politicians were in turn heavily dependent on the support of business interests in their home districts. As we have seen, even before the political system started to liberalize, Taiwanese KMT members developed close connections with local business people. This led to growing corruption, with KMT officials getting illicit payments or help in marshalling votes in exchange for pulling official strings to benefit businesses. Financial backing from businesses in a candidate's constituency was crucial because the party provided little or no funding for individual electoral campaigns. The perceived corruption of the KMT mainstream would become a major issue to the voting public. In contrast to the conservative Mainlander faction, which believed the KMT's popularity depended on the party's positions on important issues, the party mainstream believed KMT electoral success was based on fulfilling the public's desire to see Taiwanese in high political offices.[3]

[2] Julian Baum, "Loyalist Rebel," *Far Eastern Economic Review*, Jan. 16, 1997, 15.
[3] Steven J. Hood, *The Kuomintang and the Democratization of Taiwan* (Boulder, Colo.: Westview Press, 1997), 108–111.

Many observers expected Lee would be a weak president compared to his predecessors. Lee, however, commanded respect with his strong educational background and a record of successful public service. More important, he proved adept at courting popular approval and gamesmanship against opposing politicians. From the outset Lee displayed an interest in reform, confirming the fears of KMT conservatives that he would steer the party in a direction they thought unhealthy. Along with political liberalization, Lee pledged to meet society's demands in the areas of labor issues, human rights, economic development, and protection of the environment, while talking less than his predecessors about reconquering the mainland. During Lee's first year in office, the government announced it planned to gradually reduce the ROC military by thirty thousand men (to around 400,000—still huge for Taiwan's size) and for the first time allowed soldiers to join political parties other than the KMT. In May 1990 Lee granted another round of thirty-four political amnesties, which restored the eligibility of several top DPP leaders to run for office. Kaohsiung incident convicts Shih Ming-teh and Hsu Hsin-liang were freed. On April 30, 1991, Lee announced the abolition of the Temporary Provisions and the termination of the "Period of National Mobilization for the Suppression of the Communist Rebellion." The ROC was no longer formally at war with the PRC, and the president no longer claimed the extraordinary powers that had precluded full implementation of the constitution. This implied recognition of the legitimacy of CCP rule on the mainland and a weakening of the ROC's claim to jurisdiction over China, with many political ramifications. In August 1992 the government abolished the Taiwan Garrison Command. The Coastal Patrol Command assumed the duty of protecting Taiwan's coasts against illegal immigration and smuggling, while other internal security responsibilities passed to the National Police Administration under the supervision of the Ministry of the Interior.

During the same year the government changed the law to define sedition more narrowly as attempts to violently overthrow the government. The mere advocacy of Taiwan independence or communism were no longer crimes, clearing the way for the release of more political prisoners and for the return of many exiled activists. Lee also moved to satisfy Taiwanese demands for a proper reckoning of the February 28 incident. The 1992 report by a task force he commissioned did not shy away from blaming military indiscipline, Chen Yi's misgovernment, Chiang Kai-shek's failure to punish guilty officials, and the disproportionate political power of Mainlanders in Taiwan as contributing factors and also concluded that the number of casualties was many times higher than the government's original claim, yielding a revised figure in line with independent estimates. Lee and Hau Pei-tsun, ROC premier, attended a meeting with the families of victims and promised the government would pay compensation.

Although these steps were popular with much of the public and among many activists, two groups of opponents to Lee soon emerged within the KMT. High-ranking conservatives such as Hau and a few members of the cabinet and the Central Standing Committee, as well as military veterans and many overseas Chinese, comprised the first group. The other was made of up of younger KMT members who favored democratization of the KMT, opposed Taiwan independence, and criticized what they saw as the excessive concentration of power in Lee's hands. Opponents within the KMT arguably posed a more formidable challenge to Lee than those in competing parties. Much of the criticism of Lee's leadership centered on the assertions that he was a closet dictator and a closet separatist.

Some of Lee's opponents within the KMT organized an informal group known as the New KMT Alliance (Hsin Kuomintang Lienhsien), composed of mostly younger Mainlanders who harked back to the KMT's traditional core agenda and pushed for reform within the party. Another KMT subfaction opposing Lee was the Chinese Democratic Reformers Alliance (CDRA). Its Chinese name, Hsin Tungmenghui, revived the old title of Sun Yat-sen's revolutionary organization. The CDRA emphasized rededication to recovering the mainland and to the Three Principles of the People, which Lee had allegedly abandoned in his drive for personal power. At this group's core were senior KMT members, including Hau, Li Huan, Lin Yang-kang, Chiang Kai-shek's surviving son Chiang Wei-kuo, and prominent overseas Chinese. Labeled the KMT's "underground central committee,"[4] the CDRA claimed it wanted to defend democracy against Lee, but at heart the group appeared less prodemocracy than anti-Lee.

Many of Lee's political battles involved the premiership, seen as a pivotal office that could either counterbalance the president's agenda (if occupied by a member of a rival faction) or greatly augment the president's control over domestic politics (if occupied by an ally of the president). After ascending to the presidency, Lee initially retained Mainlander Yu Kuo-hwa as premier, but mainly recruited younger, U.S.-educated Taiwanese to fill his cabinet. Lee set a precedent by appointing a woman, Shirley Kuo, as finance minister. Lee replaced Yu with Mainlander Li Huan, who while popular became a strong rival to Lee and a supporter of reforms that would weaken the powers of the president. Lee would soon succeed in getting Li Huan to resign as well, but had to avoid overly antagonizing the Mainlander faction. Prior to the 1990 presidential election,

[4] *Tsai Hsun* (Taipei), July 1, 1993, 88.

KMT conservatives who felt political and economic reform was proceeding too rapidly threatened to take the unheard-of step of sponsoring an alternative party presidential ticket of Taiwanese politician Lin Yang-kang and Chiang Wei-kuo to run against Lee. After internal negotiations, they eventually withdrew their challenge and Lee won an uncontested vote by the National Assembly on March 21. To help mollify the Mainlander faction, Lee appointed military heavyweight Hau to replace Li Huan as premier in May 1990. Hau, who had been a commander on Jinmen during the 1958 Taiwan Strait crisis, was known as a strong supporter of the one-China principle and a champion of law and order. Hau's appointment sparked public protests from activists who argued he represented a retrogression toward military rule. Lee countered that he was responding to the public demand for a tougher policy on crime. Within a few months, however, Hau's public approval rating had surpassed not only those of his two predecessors, but also that of Lee himself.[5]

The Lee-Hau pairing did not heal the divisions within the KMT. On the right, the New KMT Alliance accused Lee of autocratic tendencies and complained that his government was excessively corrupt. On the KMT left was the Wisdom Club (Chishihui), established by Taiwanese legislators in 1988. This group had a "Taiwan first" agenda and criticized the one-China principle, arguing that Taiwan was already de facto independent. During the 1992 election campaign, Wisdom Club legislators accused Hau and other conservatives of selling out Taiwan's interests while intimidating Taiwan's people with the threat of PRC military retaliation. They proposed that the KMT adopt the premise of "one China, one Taiwan." The rift led to the expulsion of Wisdom Club leader Chen Che-nan from the KMT and again highlighted the extent of party disunity.

The Lee-Hau relationship, on shaky ground from the start, deteriorated as both philosophical and personal differences between the two leaders became more prominent. Constitutionally, however, while Lee had the power to appoint Hau, he lacked the authority to fire him. The KMT's disappointing performance in the 1992 parliamentary election (a major factor in the resignations of premiers Yu and Li) and the renewal of the Legislative Yuan created pressure for Hau to quit. In January 1993 his supporters demonstrated in the streets of Taipei, but at the end of the month Hau submitted his resignation. He left office raising his fists and shouting into a jeering crowd, "Eradicate Taiwan independence!"[6]

This time Lee appointed a Taiwanese premier, Taiwan's first: Lien Chan,

---

[5] *China Post* (Taipei), July 9, 1990, 12; June Teufel Dreyer, "Taiwan in 1990: Fine-tuning the System," *Asian Survey* 31, no. 1 (January 1991): 60–61.
[6] "Search for Identity," *Asiaweek*, Mar. 17, 1993, 22.

a former governor of Taiwan and foreign minister and holder of a doctorate degree from the University of Chicago. Although Lien was born in the mainland city of Xian, his father had emigrated there from Taiwan. Lee also made an unusually large number of additional personnel changes to strengthen his power by promoting his supporters. The resignation of Hau removed the strongest reason for members of the New KMT Alliance to remain in the KMT. While the DPP was well known as a fractious party, it was the KMT that suffered the first major split. In August 1993, a few days before the KMT's Fourteenth Party Congress, the New KMT Alliance faction broke away to establish the Chinese New Party (later known as the New Party, or Hsintang). The name reflected admiration for the recent success of the Japan New Party against the long-dominant Liberal Democratic Party, Japan's counterpart to the KMT. The New Party would never be a serious contender for control of an important political organ or office, but it could take votes away from the KMT in parts of northern Taiwan with large Mainlander populations. On the other hand, the exit of some of his most powerful opponents increased Lee's control over the KMT. Re-elected as KMT chairman at the Fourteenth Party Congress in the first use of a secret ballot, Lee sought to pacify the Mainlander faction by nominating its members (Hau and Judicial Yuan president Lin Yang-kang) for two of the four KMT vice-chairman positions.

Presidential versus Parliamentary System

The ROC constitution did not clearly define the relationship between the president and the premier and left room for either of them to emerge as the state's most powerful leader. Constitutional revisions made during Lee's tenure settled this contest clearly in the president's favor. Securing these changes was one of Lee's major goals. He argued this would contribute to Taiwan's democratization. His opponents, of course, saw this as part of Lee's plan to strengthen his personal power. Even during what turned out to be Lee's final term, many assumed Lee wanted a strong presidency because he planned to campaign for another term.

Soon after taking office Lee said he wanted to reduce the prominence of the National Security Council (NSC), which was attached to the Office of the President and which some considered an artifact of dictatorship. In late 1993, shortly before the NSC was scheduled to disband, the KMT got the Legislative Yuan to pass a bill retaining it under the president's purview. This prevented Lee from losing ground on the issue of whether the president or the premier was the ROC chief executive. This move also deepened suspicions that Lee's ambition was a threat to Taiwan's democratization.

The president's power expanded with the constitutional amendments the National Assembly approved in July 1994 after a typically raucous session featuring sharp debate, walkouts, and fistfights. The president gained the authority to appoint and fire officials without needing the premier's approval. The balance of power had now swung decisively in the favor of the president and away from the premier.

By 1997, the issue required further attention. The KMT was slipping from its previously dominant position in the legislature, raising the possibility of a divided government. Since the president's nominee for premier required approval by the Legislative Yuan, a legislature split among different parties might preclude the confirmation of a new premier and the formation of a cabinet. The tough battle that preceded the confirmation of Lien Chan as premier in early 1996 was a warning that change was necessary to forestall gridlock. The constitution did not provide for a dissolution of the legislature or other means of breaking a political stalemate.[7] Pending systemic revisions, Taiwan was in a "permanent constitutional crisis," as one commentator observed.[8]

The KMT wanted stronger presidential prerogatives. The DPP wanted to strengthen the legislature. Lacking a sufficiently numerous majority to roll over the opposition, the KMT worked out a compromise with the DPP on the constitutional revisions. The president gained the power to appoint a premier without needing the legislature's consent and to dissolve the legislature and call new elections. To help balance the power of the president, members of the Legislative Yuan could take a no-confidence vote and remove the premier. They could override the cabinet's veto of a bill or resolution with a simple majority. The legislature had the power to bring the president under impeachment, with the final judgment vested in the National Assembly. The Legislative Yuan also took on some of the oversight powers that previously belonged to the Control Yuan. These changes consolidated the presidency's preeminent position in Taiwanese politics. The New Party, excluded from the KMT-DPP alliance, protested in vain that the revisions moved Taiwan toward dictatorship and permanent separation from China.

[7] Tun-Jen Cheng and Yi-Hsing Liao, "Taiwan in 1997: An Embattled Government in Search of New Opportunities," *Asian Survey* 38, no. 1 (January 1998): 55.

[8] The quotation is from Antonio Chiang, editor of *Journalist*, Taiwan's most-read weekly political magazine; Julian Baum, "Rough and Tumble," *Far Eastern Economic Review*, Oct. 31, 1996, 21.

The National Assembly was criticized as a wasteful and redundant body. In additional to the well-founded argument that it was not representative of the people of Taiwan, detractors said the National Assembly was too large to be effective and that it represented a huge sinecure since its members met only once every six years unless called in for a special session. Its members collected an annual salary equivalent to U.S. $43,000, plus up to $250 per diem while the assembly was in session. As indefensible as the arrangement had become, unseating the Mainlanders elected for life was nonetheless a politically difficult task because it weakened the political ties between Taiwan and China.

Against this background of smoldering frustration, the National Assembly session of February 1990 was destined for controversy. During the ceremonial oath of office, DPP members departed from custom by pledging their support to the people of Taiwan instead of the Republic of China. The DPP complained that elderly Mainlanders dominated the body, symbolized in the election of ninety-three-year-old Hsueh Yueh as chairman of the session. In the streets, rioters scuffled and overturned cars. For six days in March, thousands of students (estimates on various days of the protest ranged from four thousand to thirty thousand) occupied part of the square inside the gate of Taipei's sprawling Chiang Kai-shek memorial park. Clearly inspired by the demonstrations in Beijing's Tiananmen Square the previous year, many of the students went on hunger strikes and donned headbands inscribed with political slogans. They demanded the abolition of the National Assembly and the Temporary Provisions, a schedule for further political liberalization, the retirement of Mainlander parliamentarians elected for life, and several constitutional reforms. Lee responded like Zhao Ziyang rather than Li Peng: he visited the students, told them he was sympathetic to their goals, and promised them the government would study their proposed reforms.

This led to the National Affairs Conference (Kuoshih'hui) in June–July 1990, during which a broad range of invitees, including members of the KMT and DPP as well as prominent citizens from academics and other walks of life, discussed most of the important issues of domestic political restructuring. While there was vigorous debate and disagreement on issues such as the importation of foreign labor and whether to amend the old constitution or write a new one, the overall result was a picture of consensus across much of Taiwan's political spectrum both for making substantive changes to the system of governance (such as dropping the Temporary Provisions and allowing direct elections for the highest political offices) and for reevaluating Taiwan's relationship with the mainland.

Points of agreement included the following: (1) all seats in the National Assembly and Legislative Yuan should be opened to competitive elections; (2) the ROC president, the governor of Taiwan, and the mayors of Taipei and Kaohsiung should be popularly elected; (3) the special powers vested in the government due to the "communist rebellion" should be discontinued; and (4) the people of Taiwan rather than the people of mainland China should be the government's primary concern.[9] There was no agreement, however, on a timetable for implementing these changes. Lee used the conference as evidence of widespread support for his agenda. In broader terms, the conference, which saw Lee shake hands across a table with DPP leader and former political prisoner Hsu Hsin-liang, marked another milestone in the legitimacy of the political opposition in Taiwan.

A ruling by the Council of Grand Justices in June 1990 sealed the fate of the mainland-elected members of the National Assembly. The justices ruled that parliamentarians (members of the National Assembly, Legislative Yuan and Control Yuan) elected by constituencies on the mainland had to retire by the end of 1991. This required the National Assembly to convene in a special session in April 1991 to establish the procedures for renewing the membership of the parliamentary bodies, among other revisions. The DPP argued constitutional revisions should wait until after the next National Assembly election. Kuomintang conservatives opposed changing the constitution. Lee's KMT mainstream favored making certain immediate revisions. Democratic Progressive Party delegations walked out during the debate and organized street protests in Taipei that drew thousands of supporters. Lee went on television to appeal for calm, saying "a responsible political party should follow legal procedures in voicing political views to solicit voters."[10] His camp prevailed. The National Assembly passed a constitutional amendment providing for elections for all seats of the parliamentary bodies over the following three years, beginning with the National Assembly itself in December 1991. Similar elections for the Legislative Yuan and the Control Yuan would follow in 1992 and 1993, respectively. The National Assembly reduced its own size and shortened the terms of members from six to four years. According to the new procedures, most members of the National Assembly (225) and Legislative Yuan (135) would be directly elected, each by a particular district. A smaller number of seats (80 in the National Assembly, 20 in the Legislative Yuan) would be reserved for "nationwide representatives" and for overseas Chinese (20 and 6, respectively). The overseas Chinese awarded seats in government organs not only resided abroad, but some were citi-

[9] Hood, *Kuomintang and Democratization*, 101.
[10] *Lianhe Pao*, April 18, 1991.

zens of foreign countries. This practice was grounded in the KMT's claim that the Republic of China was the rightful government of all Chinese, but many in the political opposition argued this arrangement was undemocratic. The national and overseas seats would be distributed among the parties in proportion to the number of district-based seats they won. In the Control Yuan, the Taiwan Provincial Assembly would elect 25 members, the Taipei and Kaohsiung City Councils 10 each, and the National Assembly would choose 5 national and 2 overseas Chinese members.

The election for a new National Assembly coincided with a more assertive DPP position on Taiwan independence. In August 1991 the DPP adopted a draft "Taiwan Constitution." In September thousands demonstrated in the streets of Taipei in support of a DPP call for the "Republic of Taiwan" to apply for admission into the United Nations. Lee faced conflicting pressures. A highly vocal minority of Taiwan society demanded movement away from the one-China principle and toward statehood. Kuomintang conservatives held passionately to the opposite position. Most of Taiwan's public was alarmed at the prospect of openly breaking the theoretical tie with China. To soothe proindependence activists, Lee invited several Taiwanese politicians and scholars for discussions on the issue. During these talks Lee said unification was impossible in the near future, and Taiwan did not need to declare independence because it had already been de facto independent since 1949. This surprised conservatives already sensitive to what they saw as Lee's lack of interest in defending core KMT values. But Lee's statement resonated well with the Taiwan public, most of which was relieved at this indication that the government did not intend to move quickly toward formal independence.

The DPP's Fifth Party Congress in October nonetheless added to its platform the goal of establishing an independent Republic of Taiwan. Another large crowd, estimated at thirty thousand, rallied nonviolently in Kaohsiung to demand a referendum on Taiwan's independence, and both foreign investment in Taiwan and the Taipei stock exchange declined sharply. Pointing to the economic burden West Germans assumed when Germany reunited, advocates of Taiwan independence pointed out that there were sixty poorer mainland Chinese for every resident of Taiwan.

Taiwan independence thus became perhaps the central issue in the December 1991 National Assembly election. During the campaign, DPP candidates publicly advocated statehood, sometimes indirectly (e.g., floating the idea of "Republic of Taiwan passports") and sometimes blatantly, in contravention of a guideline established by the Central Election Commission. The ROC National Security Council decided not to arrest the highest-profile politicians associated with the independence movement, but police rounded up others and the Executive Yuan's Political Parties Screening Committee threatened to disband the DPP over its stated position on independence. The private sector fought back as well, with corporations and other organizations sponsoring advertisements against independence.

In contrast to the DPP, Lee's KMT mainstream aimed to capture the political middle ground by avoiding strong advocacy of either reunification or independence. The inevitable cost of this strategy, of course, was alienation of the KMT conservative wing. The KMT abandoned its previous slogans calling for reunification under the Three Principles of the People in favor of the pragmatic themes of "Reform, security, prosperity" and the motif, signifying a new beginning, of a baby lying on the ROC flag.[11] The KMT countered DPP rhetoric not by articulating an alternative vision of Taiwan's future, but rather by attacking the DPP's vision. Kuomintang politicians predicted, for example, that breaking the connection with the mainland would lead to the rewriting of Chinese genealogies and a ban on the worship of the goddess Matsu, a practice that originated in Fujian Province.[12] Kuomintang campaigns also emphasized the party's past performance in economic development and plans for future projects. Taiwanization of the party made the ethnic element less relevant than in the past; most KMT candidates were Taiwanese, and even in Taipei the Mainlander candidates outnumbered Taiwanese by only twelve to eleven.

Results of the election showed that the DPP had overplayed the independence issue. Voter turnout was substantially reduced from the previous Legislative Yuan election, and the DPP captured less than a quarter of the vote in the election for the new National Assembly, while the KMT got over 71 percent. The KMT would hold 254 seats in the new National Assembly to the DPP's 66. The DPP mainstream took this lesson to heart and thereafter watered down its stance on Taiwan independence. One year later, in plenary elections to renew the membership of the Legislative Yuan, the DPP's campaign focused more on domestic issues and less on Taiwan independence. Democratic Progressive Party politicians summarized their program as "three anti's, three demands": antimoney politics, antimilitary involvement in politics, antiprivilege politics, and demands for sovereignty of the people, direct elections, and lower taxes. The DPP won 50 seats to KMT's 96, a major victory for the DPP and a disappointing showing for the KMT, reflecting the latter's disunity as well as public reaction to the KMT's reputation for cheating and the DPP's promised com-

---

[11] Christopher Hughes, *Taiwan and Chinese Nationalism* (London: Routledge, 1997), 71.
[12] Ibid., 72.

mitment to political reform and social services. Officially endorsed KMT candidates tallied only 53 percent of the vote (the total for all KMT candidates was 62 percent).

The contentious process of revising the constitution continued in another National Assembly special session in March–May 1992. Frustrated at their inability to force compromises from a dominant KMT, the DPP members and most of the independents walked out of the session. The new National Assembly added eight more constitutional amendments, including provisions for popular election rather than appointment of the governor, county chief executives, and the mayors of Taipei and Kaohsiung, and guarantees of legal protection of women, aborigines, and the handicapped against discrimination. The changes also made the National Assembly more relevant, increasing its powers (largely at the expense of the Control Yuan) and requiring it to meet annually. Many of the changes were intended to limit the prerogatives of the president, indicating the strength of fears Lee was amassing too much power.

The issue of direct election of the president was one of the most sharply debated. This was an important objective of the DPP, which employed the slogan, "Be masters of Taiwan, elect your own president." On this issue, unlike independence, the DPP position reflected the desire of the majority of Taiwan's people. Lee and most of the KMT stood ready to accommodate this wish, confident their interests would not suffer as a result. Lee and others argued that a directly elected president would be better able to stand above party politics and serve the entire country. Opponents of direct presidential elections saw them as another step toward independence. Polls in which only voters on Taiwan participated would further erode the winner's basis for claiming to be the president of "China," while consolidating Taiwan's separation from China. Some KMT leaders, mostly Mainlanders, worried that the DPP might run a candidate popular enough to win the presidency and push harder for a "Taiwan first" agenda. Another basis for opposing direct elections was the fear that, ironically, they would move the country toward dictatorship by strengthening the president's mandate.

In May 1992 the National Assembly adopted a constitutional article stipulating that beginning with the 1996 election, "the president and vice-president shall be elected by the entire electorate in the free area of the Republic of China." This wording provided for a practical expansion of Taiwanese sovereignty while at the same time honoring the ROC government's claim to ruling China (if only the "free area"). Some aspects of the presidency were settled: starting with the next presidential election, the term length would be reduced to four years and no individual could serve more than two consecutive terms. With the KMT split on the issue, the assembly left the more difficult matter of electoral procedure for a future session to decide, setting an ultimate deadline of May 1995. The lack of resolution left the public largely disappointed. More than ten thousand citizens signed a condemnatory statement charging that the National Assembly had "failed to improve the Constitution." Further amendments and legislation in 1994 and 1995 worked out the remaining details of the presidential election and campaign. Some aspects remained controversial, such as the onerous requirements that prospective presidential candidates put down a $550,000 deposit and produce a supporting petition with the names of at least 1.5 percent of the electorate (over 200,000 people).

As for the National Assembly itself, the elections invigorated a body some critics wanted to see abolished. A July 1994 amendment further strengthened it by creating the position of speaker. Some National Assembly members wanted to increase the assembly's powers and stature, with the eventual goal of creating a two-house legislature such as those in Britain and the United States. In the meantime, fights and other outrageous antics became common after the opening of all assembly seats to elections, which brought in ambitious younger politicians who needed to make a name for themselves in preparation for seeking a seat in the more prestigious Legislative Yuan. Meanwhile scuffling in the Legislative Yuan decreased after the KMT and DPP reached a compromise on rule changes that made it harder for a small number of opposition politicians to block the passage of bills through filibuster, but benefited the DPP by allowing ordinary bills to be introduced with only ten sponsors.

A Direct Presidential Election amidst the Third Taiwan Strait Crisis

The year 1995 began with signs of a possible thaw in cross-strait relations. In January, PRC president Jiang Zemin presented his "Eight Points" proposal for peaceful unification. The speech was notable for its conciliatory tone and its premise of resolving the Taiwan question through negotiations, to which he welcomed "various parties," not only the KMT. Jiang said Beijing would "fully respect the lifestyle" of people on Taiwan, honor "their wish to be masters of our country," and "protect all their legitimate rights and interests." The PRC could accept Taiwan having economic and cultural exchanges with other countries, Jiang said. While he did not renounce China's right to use force against Taiwan, Jiang said this threat was "not directed against our compatriots in Taiwan but against the schemes of foreign forces to interfere with China's reunification."

Jiang's unsatisfying explanation seemed to reaffirm that Beijing was unwilling or unable to recognize that a large segment of the ethnic Chinese population on Taiwan did not wish to unify with China. In April 1995 some ten thousand Taiwanese marched in downtown Taipei to commemorate the one-hundredth anniversary of the Treaty of Shimonoseki. Democratic Progressive Party legislator Lu Hsiu-lien visited the site in Shimonoseki, Japan, where Chinese and Japanese delegates signed the treaty. Chang Fu-mei, a DPP member of the National Assembly, summarized the point of these activities: "For people who are living on Taiwan who are constantly told by the authorities that their roots are in China, it is important to know that it was China that 100 years ago gave up Taiwan—forever."[13]

In April, Lee responded to Jiang's Eight Points with his own "Six Principles." Lee expressed a willingness for high-level negotiations, but repeated his previous views that such a meeting should take place at an international venue and that Beijing should accept the reality of two separate Chinese governments. Lee's response was disappointing to China, but a meeting in Beijing of the PRC and Taiwanese governmental organizations charged with developing cross-strait relations was planned for July. This meeting never materialized. Lee's visit to his U.S. alma mater, Cornell University, in June led not only to a suspension in cross-strait dialogue, but to a dramatic escalation in China-Taiwan military tensions.

During a trip to South Africa via Central America in 1994, Lee's aircraft had stopped in Honolulu to refuel. The U.S. government refused Lee's request for a transit visa, confining him to the military airfield where he had landed and forcing him to spend the night on his plane. Attempting to minimize the offense to Lee, a U.S. State Department official arranged a reception for Lee and his party in a meeting room at the airfield. The facility and its furnishings were austere. "It was embarrassing," admitted the State Department official on the scene. Forewarned by an advance man from Taipei's Washington office, Lee refused to leave his plane, complaining about Taiwan being treated as a second-class country.[14] This humiliation not only angered Lee, but also caught the attention of influential pro-Taiwan Americans.

Both U.S. secretary of state Warren Christopher and assistant secretary of state for Asia and the Pacific Winston Lord assured the Chinese government Lee would not get a visa to enter the United States for the proposed Cornell visit. Congress, however, intervened on Lee's behalf. Some congressmen pointed out the incongruity of the State Department allowing

---

[13] "100 years since Treaty of Shimonoseki," [n.d.], 2–3, online at http://www.taiwandc. org/hst-1895.htm, accessed Sept. 18, 2001.

[14] James Mann, "Between China and the U.S.," *Los Angeles Times*, Jan. 10, 1999, C1.

alleged terrorists such as the Irish Republican Army's Gerry Adams and the Palestine Liberation Organization's Yasir Arafat to visit the United States while denying entry to the leader of a democratic polity. In May 1995, the House of Representatives passed, by a vote of 396 to 0, a resolution asking the executive branch to allow Lee to visit the United States. The Senate passed a similar resolution by a vote of 91 to 1. These resolutions were not legally binding, but Congress threatened to pass legislation forcing Clinton's hand if necessary. The State Department relented. Lee got his visa partly as a result of efforts by the Washington lobbying firm Cassidy and Associates, which Taipei hired in 1994 and paid $4.5 million for three years of work.[15]

Lee traveled to the United States while the Chinese press viciously derided him as "traitor" and "sinner" who sought to "split the motherland." Equally angry at the perceived broken U.S. promise, Beijing renewed its charges that America was providing the cover for Lee to fulfill his alleged separatist agenda, and that U.S. support for the ROC was the main reason the PRC had not been able to settle the Taiwan problem on PRC terms. Beijing concluded Lee was taking advantage of the PRC's conciliatory posture to move Taiwan toward independence while claiming commitment to the one-China principle. With few options, the CCP resorted to the crude tactic of military coercion.

In July, the PLA test-fired missiles into the waters off Taiwan's coast. Naval exercises in the Taiwan Strait in August were followed by the largest amphibious exercises in the PLA's history during November. The Chinese government admitted the military exercises were a response to Lee's actions. The PRC had not displayed such belligerence toward Taiwan since the 1960s.

The United States' reaction was low-key. In late December, a U.S. aircraft carrier, the *Nimitz*, passed through the Taiwan Strait for the first time in seventeen years. This gesture, however, came well after the PLA military exercises were over, and the U.S. government did not announce it until six weeks after the *Nimitz's* transit. A Chinese general nonetheless warned a U.S. envoy visiting China that the PLA might retaliate against American intervention in defense of Taiwan with a nuclear attack against the west coast of the United States.

Beijing efforts to intimidate Taiwan were successful. During 1995, Taiwan's stock market lost a third of its value and an estimated $10 billion in capital fled the island. More important, in the December 1995 Legislative Yuan election, the prounification New Party greatly improved its repre-

[15] Tim Healy and Laurence Eyton, "Perils of Money Diplomacy," *Asiaweek*, Dec. 20, 1996, 23.

sentation, increasing its seats from eight to twenty-one, while Lee's KMT lost seats and the DPP gained less than expected. The shrinkage of KMT parliamentary representation continued a six-year trend. The KMT's poor showing reflected the sense among many Mainlander voters who held to the traditional agenda that the Taiwanized KMT had fundamentally changed its direction. Many voters also believed that Lee had unnecessarily provoked Beijing in a bid to raise his own historical stature and as a way to insulate himself from the general public disgust with perceived KMT corruption.

The crisis was only half over. Beijing had warned of more pressure in connection with the presidential campaign. This cast a dark shadow over the preparations for Taiwan's first direct popular presidential election. Over 90 percent of the delegates to the KMT's Fourteenth Party Congress in August voted for Lee as the party's presidential candidate after a failed attempt by his opponents to complicate the process by inviting all KMT members, including those overseas, to vote in a closed primary election. In contrast, the DPP adopted a grueling primary system for selecting its first presidential candidate, including two rounds of voting and fifty public debates for the two finalists. Hsu Hsin-liang, Lin Yi-hsiung, Yu Ching, and Peng Ming-min competed for the prize, with the seventy-two-year-old Peng emerging as the winner. Like Lee Teng-hui, Peng was a Presbyterian who studied at a Japanese university (he lost his left arm while in Japan during a bombing raid). He chose legislator Frank Hsieh as his running mate. Peng took a relatively tough stance toward China, arguing that Taiwan should not invest on the mainland until the Chinese agreed to "treat Taiwan as an equal" and guaranteed in writing protection of Taiwan's investments. He provocatively warned that the government's one-China policy might lead to another February 28 incident. Although Peng was the DPP's best-known politician, his opponents said he was too old, not familiar enough with the latest developments in Taiwan because of his long exile in the United States, and lacking in government experience. Both Peng and DPP chairman Shih Ming-teh adopted the relatively moderate position that Taiwan was already de facto independent and therefore did not need to formally claim statehood. Taipei should declare independence, Peng said, only if the PRC attacked. From Beijing's standpoint, Lee and his DPP opponent Peng were "absolutely identical in attempting to divide the motherland."[16]

Recognizing it lacked islandwide support, the New Party decided not sponsor a candidate in the 1996 presidential election after its initial nomi-

[16] Li Jiaquan, "Two Fallacies on Taiwan Independence Are the Same Strain," Beijing radio broadcast, Feb. 6, 1996; FBIS, *Daily Report—China*, Feb. 8, 1996, 70–73.

nee dropped out. Instead the party supported independents Lin Yang-kang, a popular Taiwanese former governor and vice premier with realistic presidential aspirations, and Hau Pei-tsun. Lin and Hau likewise endorsed and even campaigned on behalf of the New Party. In a television interview, Hau blamed the KMT for widespread corruption in Taiwan politics and said demotion from ruling to opposition party would help the KMT put its house in order. Lin and Hau registered as candidates on November 27, prompting about one hundred KMT members to gather in Taichung and demand that the two mavericks be punished. This led to the "cancellation" of their membership in the KMT (a step just short of expulsion) in December on the recommendation of the party's disciplinary committee, which accused the two senior members of "viciously attacking" Lee and "seriously damaging the party's image and prestige."[17] This was the most dramatic and open KMT dispute in its history on Taiwan. In terms of substance, Lin championed the one-China principle and said he favored opening direct links with China to improve cross-strait relations.

A fourth ticket included former defense minister and Control Yuan president and ex-KMT member Chen Li-an and Control Yuan member Wang Ching-feng. Chen had resigned from the KMT and registered as an independent. Lin Yang-kang and Chen Li-an had discussed the possibility of running as a team, but neither man wanted the lesser role of vice president. Son of the former vice president and premier Chen Cheng, Chen Li-an was a devout Buddhist and lay leader of the Fo Kuang Shan order, which boasted several million adherents. Taiwan did not have a tradition of religious-based voting blocs, but Chen's Buddhist credentials reinforced his image as a clean politician. Chen emphasized honest government and the importance of moral purity, drawing additional publicity for his views by walking around the island for eighteen days wearing a straw farmer's hat.

Soon after the presidential campaign formally began February 24, Beijing announced another round of missile firings into the Taiwan Strait. Chen Li-an asserted, "If you vote for Lee Teng-hui, you are choosing war," which was essentially Beijing's message. Lin similarly accused Lee Teng-hui of endangering the lives of Taiwan's people in the pursuit of the president's own political agenda. Lee, however, urged his countrymen to resist China's efforts to influence the election through "state terrorism."

People's Liberation Army tests on March 8–15 sent missiles into two impact areas close to Taiwan's northeast and southwest coasts, near the principal ports of Keelung and Kaohsiung. The missiles were M-9s, variants of

[17] Julian Baum, "Talk the Talk, or Walk," *Far Eastern Economic Review*, Dec. 28, 1995/Jan. 4, 1996, 21.

the Scud missile of Gulf War infamy, and similarly inaccurate. Although the missiles would not pass over Taiwan, the announced target zone near Keelung stretched to within twenty kilometers of the main island, just within the ROC's territorial waters (Taiwan claimed the twelve-nautical-mile limit allowed by international law). Republic of China defense minister Chiang Chun-ling first said that any PLA missile strikes within Taiwan's territorial waters would trigger an ROC counterattack, but later backed away from this threat.[18] Missile tests were well suited to Beijing's purpose. Since the PLA was not capable of undertaking an amphibious invasion of Taiwan with a reasonable probability of success, missile strikes and a naval blockade of the main island's ports were China's most likely tactics in the event of a cross-strait war. The missile shots demonstrated the PLA could (randomly) destroy parts of Taiwan's metropolitan areas with a weapon against which Taiwan had no effective defense. The missile tests also had the effect of a blockade, forcing the temporary closure of sea and air travel routes.

Although the United States was under no explicit, formal obligation to militarily defend Taiwan against a PLA missile attack or naval blockade, the 1979 Taiwan Relations Act established the principle that America would view with "grave concern" any PRC "effort to determine the future of Taiwan by other than peaceful means, including by boycotts or embargoes." Washington was also aware that Asians who harbored doubts about the endurance of American leadership in the Asia-Pacific region would be watching the U.S response to the attempted Chinese coercion.

The U.S. Congress sent several signals of support for Taiwan. More significantly, the Clinton administration announced on March 8 that it was deploying the aircraft carrier *Independence* and its supporting ships to international waters near Taiwan. The next day Beijing announced live-fire exercises near Penghu planned for March 12–20. These naval and air maneuvers came close to the center line both sides recognized as dividing the Taiwan Strait into ROC and PRC zones. On March 11 the United States announced it was deploying a second aircraft carrier battle group led by the *Nimitz* to the area. Sending one carrier in support of Taiwan was a symbolic gesture, but sending two was a much stronger signal that suggested readiness to do battle. Beijing responded on March 15 with the announcement of a third exercise, a simulated amphibious assault, planned for March 18–25. Both the ROC government and the DPP welcomed the gesture of support by the U.S. Navy (although privately some ROC military

[18] "PRC Announces More Missile Exercises," *China Post*, Mar. 6, 1996, 1; "Minister Denies Reprisal Threat," *China Post*, Mar. 7, 1996, 1.

officers complained that this unnecessarily made the crisis more tense[19]), but Lin and Hau joined Beijing in decrying this "foreign intervention." Their New Party allies carried out a campaign suggesting that American troops would again occupy Taiwan and morally degrade Taiwan's society.

As large as the Chinese exercises were, and despite the aggressive rhetoric that accompanied them, the forces mobilized were far too small to attempt an actual invasion. This was clearly no more than a show of force designed to warn Taiwan what might happen in the future. Taiwan's people indeed got a taste of war. Some residents of the Matsu islands close to the mainland coast evacuated their homes. Workers cleaned disused government bomb shelters and schools conducted disaster drills. Taiwan's stock exchange fell 17 percent from mid-1995 to the end of the crisis, forcing the government to spend $1.8 billion in propping it up.[20] Housing and land prices and the value of the New Taiwan dollar fell, the price of rice rose due to hoarding, capital fled the island, and applications for passports and foreign visas jumped. But along with fear, Taiwan's public reacted with considerably more anger than during the 1995 missile episode. From the first round to the second, defiance replaced shock. On March 7, a giant rendering of the character *gan*, an obscene term for sexual intercourse, took up most of the front page of the proindependence *Commons Daily*, the most widely read newspaper in southern Taiwan. This plucky spirit redounded to Lee's benefit. On election day, March 23, he and running mate Lien Chan won with 54 percent of the vote. They also won twenty-four of Taiwan's twenty-five counties and cities, losing only in Lin's home Nantou County. Runners-up Peng and Hsieh got 21 percent, Lin and Hau 15 percent, and Chen and Wang 10 percent. Most analysts concluded that Chinese military coercion increased Lee's share of the vote by at least 5 percent.[21] If so, the PLA enabled Lee to win the presidency with a majority of the vote when he would have otherwise won with a plurality. This strengthened Lee's position domestically with the aura of a national mandate. Democratic Progressive Party chairman Shih Ming-teh pledged to resign in recognition of his party's disappointing performance.

Lee did not immediately employ his mandate to further distance Taiwan politically from the mainland. During his May 1996 inauguration speech, Lee said Taiwan independence was "totally unnecessary and impossible" and offered to make a "journey of peace to mainland China."

[19] Gary Klintworth, "China and Taiwan—From Flashpoint to Redefining One China," Parliament of Australia Research Paper 15 2000–01, Canberra, Australia, November 2000, 14.
[20] Susan Berfield and Alejandro Reyes, "Eye of the Storm," *Asiaweek*, Mar. 29, 1996, 23.
[21] See, for example, Alejandro Reyes, "The Making of a New Taiwan," *Asiaweek*, Apr. 5, 1996, 37.

The latter was a minor concession, given Lee's previous position that a summit meeting should take place in neutral territory.

Viewed as a contest between the PRC and Taiwan, the results of the 1995–96 Taiwan Strait crisis were mixed. Although China apparently failed to sway the election results in the direction Beijing hoped, the Chinese proved they could make Taiwan suffer by applying military coercion and got proindependence candidates to soften their positions. In the court of international opinion, Taiwan scored a clear victory. Taipei laid claim to achieving the first popular election for a national leader in China's long history, while in contrast the troglodyte PRC leadership attempted to militarily coerce a democratic people. Still, most Asians wished Taiwan would stop resisting and accept unification with the PRC under the "one country, two systems" formula.

The crisis had consequences that improved Taiwan's security in the medium-term. It was a major factor in the revision and strengthening of the U.S.-Japan security treaty beginning in April, increasing the potential role Japan might play in support of U.S. military action in the region. Beijing was quick to criticize this as a step toward Japanese armed forces helping to defend Taiwan. The crisis eliminated some of the ambiguity in American strategy, heightening the expectation that Washington would intervene when the PLA threatened Taiwan. The crisis also strengthened the argument for robust U.S. arms sales to Taiwan.

The long-term consequences for Taiwan's security were not clear. Taiwan hoped that the Beijing leadership would draw the lesson that coercing the islanders was counterproductive. From a Chinese perspective, the aversion of all major groups on Taiwan to declare independence was encouraging, but the willingness of the United States to support Taiwan separatism and the continued defiance of Taiwan's people decreased the possibility that China could reclaim Taiwan by a means other than military force. The main question for the future was whether leaders in Beijing would continue to see intimidation as their best or only option, or shift to the alternative strategy of attempting to attract and woo Taiwan.

Harder Times for Lee's Government

Lee's moment of triumph in March 1996 was brief. With only a two-seat majority in the Legislative Yuan, the KMT faced stronger opposition than ever before in the parliament. A new interparty battle developed over the premiership. Both Lee and Lien Chan had promised during the presidential election campaign that Lien would resign from the premiership if elected vice president. But with the KMT's control of the Legislative Yuan greatly reduced, Lee's new premier would face a tough confirmation battle. The expectation of a high-level vacancy also set off politicking among Soong Chu-yu, KMT secretary general Hsu Shui-teh, and Presidential Office secretary-general Wu Bo-hsiung, all of whom sought the premiership as a springboard to the presidency. Lee decided Lien would continue to concurrently hold both positions. The president argued that a second confirmation of Lien was unnecessary. This drew bitter criticism from both within and without the KMT. The Legislative Yuan asked the Council of Grand Judges to rule on whether Lien's occupation of two important positions was consistent with the constitution.

Another highly contentious issue was the government's decision to build a fourth nuclear power plant. Officials argued the new plant, to be located in Kungliao, was needed to ensure sufficient power to meet the growing needs of Taiwan's industries. Antinuclear activists, however, joined with the DPP and the New Party in bitter opposition to the plan. The Legislative Yuan voted against releasing the $4.5 billion in funds the cabinet sought for the project. As Lien Chan arrived at the Legislative Yuan in October 1996 to ask for support, opposition legislators physically blocked his entry. The government resorted to invoking never-before-used Article 57 of the constitution, which allows the executive to disallow legislative action that threatens national security if it can obtain a one-third vote. During the voting, opposition legislators attempted to seize the voting record from the presiding speaker, while KMT members stood near the podium trying to fend them off. The cabinet got sufficient votes to proceed with the plant, a partnership with the U.S. firm General Electric scheduled to take eight years to build.

With the KMT weakened in the Legislative Yuan, DPP and New Party politicians saw value in cooperating to counter KMT initiatives. In judo-like fashion, however, the KMT found a way to exploit ideological divergences within the DPP. The KMT courted individual DPP members, offering them positions in the government. Dismayed that their colleagues were making common cause with both the KMT and the New Party, DPP radicals broke away and formed the Taiwan Independence Party (TAIP). This split mirrored that by the New Party from the KMT, in that the more extreme faction could not abide the movement of the party mainstream toward the middle of the political spectrum. Democratic Progressive Party chairman (since June 1996) Hsu Hsin-liang took a moderate stand on independence and tried to shift the party's emphasis to domestic issues. Peng Min-min, the DPP's defeated presidential candidate, argued that the DPP had become indistinguishable from the KMT on the independence question and quit to form his own strongly proindependence Nation-Building Party.

In elections for mayors and county chief executives in November 1997, the DPP garnered more votes than the KMT for the first time. The DPP now governed more territory and population than the KMT at the county level.

Within his own party, neither Lee's position nor his agenda were seriously challenged. At the KMT's Fifteenth Party Congress in August 1997, Lee ran unopposed and won 93 percent of the votes for reelection as party chairman. Much of the other 7 percent was the result of spoiled ballots caused by voter confusion with a newly introduced computerized voting procedure. Taiwanese representation in both the Central Committee and Central Standing Committee grew, and an aborigine gained membership in the CSC for the first time. Vincent Siew Wan-chang became the first Taiwan-born ROC premier.

Among Taiwan's people as a whole, however, Lee's popularity, previously his greatest asset, was quickly declining. Between the 1996 election and early 1998, Lee's public approval rating dropped from more than 80 percent to below 40 percent. Although Taiwan stood up relatively well against the financial crisis that devastated the economies of South Korea, Thailand, Indonesia, and other Asian states, the business community was unhappy with continued restrictions on trade with China. Taiwan's international competitiveness worsened, as the ROC's global ranking by the prestigious Institute of Management and Development dropped from eighteenth to twenty-third in one year. Lee's diplomacy posted disappointing results: Taiwan's campaign to join the United Nations was a failure, and South Africa switched diplomatic recognition to Beijing. The government's ineffective response to a March 1997 outbreak of foot-and-mouth disease among pigs in southern Taiwan increased public disapproval of the cabinet. The single most important reason for Lee's decline in popularity was that many of Taiwan's people came to believe he was more interested in revising the constitution to enlarge his presidential powers than in tackling the public's greatest domestic concern, crime and corruption.

The KMT finally got a political boost in the elections of late 1998. In the voting for the Legislative Yuan, the KMT halted its electoral decline and ended the DPP's string of gains. The KMT benefited from the participation of popular former members of the Provincial Assembly in the legislative election. The parties representing the political extremes fared poorly; the New Party was left with only eleven seats, and only one of the Taiwan Independence Party's seventeen candidates won. The KMT also captured the mayorship of Taipei, which along with the mayorship of Kaohsiung had again become an elected office in 1994. The incumbent, DPP member Chen Shui-bian, had won by taking a more moderate stance on Taiwan independence than his party mainstream. Chen's record as mayor of Taipei was considered successful, but former minister of justice Ma Ying-jeou narrowly defeated Chen in his bid for reelection. Born in Hong Kong of Mainlander parents, Ma described himself as a "New Taiwanese," employing a term Lee popularized. Ma's victory over Chen demonstrated the increasing capability of politicians to overcome the ethnic division between Taiwanese and Mainlanders. Taipei's results were reversed in Kaohsiung, with the DPP winning another close race.

Corruption, Crime, and the KMT

We saw earlier that as more Taiwanese joined the KMT, their cooperative and sometimes corrupt relationships with various local constituents became a prominent party characteristic. A second trend that became pronounced by the 1990s was a deterioration of party discipline. In the 1992 elections for the Legislative Yuan, for example, a quarter of the KMT candidates on the ballots ran without their party's permission, and another 13 percent were endorsed but not nominated. This KMT infighting helped DPP candidates achieve a higher success rate than their KMT counterparts for the first time.[22]

Rank-and-file KMT members were demanding more of a say in the making of decisions that affected them. As the KMT began to undergo democratic reform, KMT elders had to accept greater influence from local factions in shaping the party agenda.[23] Local leaders were in a better position to judge which candidates or strategies had the best chance of success in a given district. Consequently, local KMT factions, which cared more about getting votes than pleasing party officials in Taipei, often disregarded the wishes of the party's central leadership. Some ran their own candidates against those officially endorsed by the party, or took policy positions that departed from the official platform. Local KMT factions also battled each other, sometimes with violent consequences.

The electoral system of single-vote, multiple-member districts inherited from the Japanese colonial government made it feasible for candidates to win political office with a comparatively small number of votes. This contributed to candidate-based rather than issue-based voting and required candidates to demonstrate their ability to provide services to voters (by handing out gifts during the campaign, for example) to win votes. Gift-giving and clientelism were aspects of Taiwanese culture that predated

[22] Shelley Rigger, *Politics in Taiwan: Voting for Democracy* (London and New York: Routledge, 1999), 164.
[23] Hood, *Kuomintang and Democratization*, 110.

the Japanese occupation. Although open vote buying was an embarrassment to the KMT, the party's central leadership had to tolerate this practice to accommodate local factions. Consequently, the costs of election campaigns rose dramatically, and candidates came to accept that they needed to raise huge sums of money to be competitive.[24]

Corruption thrived in this environment, leading to collusion between politicians and organized crime. Involvement with gangsters was not unique to the KMT, but apparently most widespread within the KMT because of its relative size, wealth, and longevity. The colloquialism "black gold" referred to the intermingling of politics, graft, and organized crime. Gangsters used their influence in certain neighborhoods to deliver votes. Once elected, officials paid the gangs off, sometimes by giving preferential treatment to the gangs' businesses. Public works spending rose greatly during the 1990s, expanding the potential for bid rigging and other types of corruption. Every major Taiwan gang ran construction companies, which became the gangs' single greatest source of revenue. Officials and their business partners allegedly skimmed off much of the funding for Taipei's rapid transit train system, highlighted by serious engineering problems that soon emerged. Despite the legal limit of U.S. $300,000, candidates for public office were commonly spending millions of dollars on their election campaigns to cover the costs of gifts and favors for voters and to pay the fees of consultants. As justice minister, Ma Ying-jeou had to fight hard for the passage of a 1993 "sunshine law" requiring the disclosure of the financial assets of high-ranking officials and their families.

Increasing public resentment over official corruption led directly to growing disaffection with the KMT. The public was well aware of the criticism that KMT officials' cooperation with organized crime left them unable to effectively combat criminal influence in politics. If it aggressively prosecuted organized criminals, the KMT would be undercutting part of its support base. Indeed, with the DPP gaining ground, the KMT's ability to win elections without the help of gangsters was increasingly doubtful.

As a consequence, officials who tried to crack down on criminal enterprises not only received threats against themselves or their families, but they also encountered opposition from fellow officials and politicians who benefited from their links with gangsters. Ma, appointed justice minister in 1993, did his job too effectively: his vigorous prosecution of corrupt officials ate away at the dark heart of the party machine and became intolerable to many KMT legislators and local faction leaders. In 1996 Lee shifted him to minister without portfolio. Many politicians had or were suspected of having such links—according to some claims, between one-third and

[24] Rigger, *Politics in Taiwan*, 39–46, 149.

half of high-ranking officials at the city and county levels. A blatant example was Luo Fu-tsu, who was a prominent legislator despite his links to the Heavenly Way Alliance criminal gang, including his self-description as the gang's "spiritual adviser." Although Luo was an independent, the KMT valued his service, such as the support he helped build for confirming Lien Chan's second term as premier. With only a two-seat majority in the Legislative Yuan, the KMT could not afford to move against Luo and other KMT-friendly legislators with ties to organized crime. In 1997, Luo even won a position as co-chairman of the Legislative Yuan's judicial committee, which opposition politicians decried as a national disgrace. Another indication of the depth of the problem followed elections to fill city and county councils in January 1994. Contests among councilors in March to choose speakers and deputy speakers exhibited obvious improprieties. Pressure from the opposition and public opinion forced the Ministry of Justice to investigate the process for corruption. The probe resulted in charges of vote buying against more than two hundred politicians and their associates, many of whom had connections to organized crime or criminal backgrounds. These prosecutions were a major embarrassment for the KMT, forcing the resignation of party provincial chief Tu Teh-chi.

The corruption of politics by organized crime led to a series of violent crimes against politicians. In one of the less serious cases, in August 1996 legislator Liao Hsueh-kuang was kidnapped and briefly imprisoned in a dog cage in a remote area in Taiwan's mountains after publicly criticizing gang leaders and supporting a tax that harmed gang interests in the city of Hsi Chih. Other victims of 1996 attacks attributed to their public criticism of gang activities were DPP secretary general Chiu I-jen and legislator Peng Hsiao-jing. A gang-related political assassination in November 1996 was the worst mass-murder in Taiwan's history. Taoyuan County chief executive Liu Pang-yu and eight associates were shot in the head while in Liu's home. Liu had been under investigation for corruption and also planned to tear down gangster-operated businesses in Chungli.

Already dismayed over the high level of corruption in government, the public perceived by 1997 that violent and property crime was worsening dangerously. A series of sensational cases fed this sense of crisis and made law and order the top domestic political issue. The murders of Liu and his associates were quickly followed by the rape and murder of prominent feminist Peng Wan-ju, Democratic Progressive Party Women's Affairs Department Chief and a university professor, in Kaohsiung in December 1996. In April, a gang led by Chen Chin-hsing, who would become the most notorious criminal in Taiwan's modern history, kidnapped Pai Hsiao-yen, the seventeen-year-old daughter of television variety show hostess Pai Ping-ping. Demanding $5 million in ransom money, the girl's captors sent photos of her, bound with tape, along with her severed finger. They murdered her while her mother was still trying to raise the money, dumping the body in a drainage ditch. Some of his accomplices were quickly captured or killed, but ringleader Chen remained at large for months. Police had jailed Chen's wife and brother-in-law, who were suspects in the Pai case. While eluding a massive manhunt, Chen wrote to police arguing they were innocent and threatening to commit more crimes unless they were released. In the summer of 1997 Chen and another seasoned felon kidnapped a businessman and collected ransom money. They allegedly forced a Taipei plastic surgeon to alter their appearance and then murdered the surgeon, his wife, and a nurse in October. In November Chen invaded the home of Colonel McGill Alexander, South Africa's military attaché, and held hostage Alexander and his family, including an infant Taiwanese foster child. Chen demanded freedom for his relatives, making his case during an interview with television journalists while hundreds of police surrounded the house. Chen finally surrendered and released his hostages after a twenty-four-hour standoff, including a shootout in which Alexander and his twenty-two-year-old daughter, whom Chen used as a human shield, suffered bullet wounds. Taipei offered the government of South Africa a formal apology after the incident. Chen was finally shot by a firing squad in October 1999. Even then his execution was controversial: Chen was convicted under the auspices of a statute known as the "bandit law" that had technically lapsed in 1945.

Support for Lee foundered with the widespread belief that the government was not responding effectively to the crime problem. Liao Chenghao, appointed justice minister in 1996, oversaw the indictments of hundreds of gangsters and government officials and forced many gangs to disband and their leaders to flee Taiwan or go into hiding, but opposition politicians complained that the government crackdown spared politically well-connected gangs such as the Heavenly Way Alliance and the Bamboo Union. Police often appeared ineffectual, an impression reinforced by their lackluster performance apprehending the Pai culprits. One of the legacies of martial law was that most of the police budget went toward activities such as riot control and protection of officials and government property rather than preventing and solving crimes against ordinary people. With the Pai murder case, the public's simmering sense of fear and outrage over rising crime boiled over. The kidnapping of children was especially worrying, as this crime had become more common in Taiwan than anywhere else in the world except the Philippines. Commenting on the strong reaction of Taiwan's people to the murder, Lee remarked during a meeting with KMT Central Standing Committee that the ROC's foreign relations were more important than the death of a schoolgirl. Reported in the press, Lee's statement evoked angry charges that he was insensitive and out of touch with his people. Tens of thousands of citizens, with particularly strong participation by women's rights groups, took to the streets in protest, demanding that Lien Chan and other officials accept responsibility for the failure to maintain law and order and resign. After one of these protests former justice minister Ma, now one of the KMT's most popular politicians, resigned his cabinet post, saying he felt ashamed to be part of a government that was ineffective against crime. Minister of the Interior Lin Fong-cheng also quit over the Pai case. Lien made an unprecedented appearance on a television talk show to assure the public that the government was doing its best to fight crime. Lien promised he would step down from his post as premier after the National Assembly implemented its constitutional reforms. After several attempts by the legislature to remove Lien, he and his cabinet resigned August 21. New premier Vincent Siew promised to make law and order his top priority.

Downsizing Soong's Provincial Government

The provincial government had jurisdiction over all residents of the main island. Its departments duplicated the functions of the ROC central government in all areas except defense, foreign policy, and Taiwan-China relations. The extra layer of administration obviously helped substantiate the notion that the ROC government was temporarily sheltering on Taiwan and planned to resume governing mainland China in the near future. The economic cost of this redundancy, however, had grown difficult to bear. The provincial government required an annual budget of $13 billion and employed thousands of personnel. Excessive investment regulations generated by the overlap of the central and provincial governments in 98 percent of Taiwan's territory were eating into the island's international competitiveness; Taiwan had acquired a reputation for official inefficiency and excessive red tape. In past years, Mainlanders who controlled the central government could offer positions in the provincial government to mollify and co-opt Taiwanese politicians, but democratization and Taiwanization took away the rationale for this practice. Furthermore, with close (and often corrupt) ties to local business interests, the provincial government was in some ways an obstacle to the national government's efforts to promote economic development. Amidst a campaign for privatization, the provincial government owned controlling stakes in three of Taiwan's largest commercial banks and two large investment banks. It also administered the Taiwan Tobacco and Wine Monopoly Bureau. Corruption was reputedly more widespread in businesses owned by the provincial government than in those under control of the central government. The provincial leadership resisted calls to make the ports of Keelung and Kaohsiung more efficient despite the complaints of shipping companies.

The argument for economic efficiency opened the door to politically motivated opposition to the provincial government. Although the issue of governmental reform involved permanent and major changes to Taiwan's political structure, the players did not necessarily transcend their immediate factional self-interests. Lee needed DPP support to win abolition of the Legislative Yuan's power to confirm the premier. Democratic Progressive Party politicians favored abolishing the provincial level of government because it symbolized a demeaned status for Taiwan. (Similarly, the New Party opposed dismantling the provincial government because this was a step toward independent statehood.) This gave the KMT mainstream an incentive to accede to the DPP's wishes on scrapping the provincial government. Former KMT secretary-general, now provincial governor, Soong Chu-yu, moreover, was a serious rival to the Lee-Lien faction. Public approval ratings indicated he was the most popular politician in Taiwan, substantially ahead of both the president and the vice president, who aspired to succeed Lee. Like Lee, Soong had been elected by a direct, island-wide vote, but Soong's victory was earlier (1994) and by a wider margin (57 percent to Lee's 54 percent). The provincial government organization gave Soong a strong, independent power base. Weakening the governorship was a way the KMT might weaken Soong.

Lee called a National Development Conference (NDC), patterned after the 1990 National Affairs Conference, in December 1996 to develop multipartisan recommendations on constitutional reform for consideration by the next session of the National Assembly. The NDC's 170 delegates included representatives of the major political parties as well as government officials and academics. The KMT and DPP struck a temporary alliance and cooperated in support of the NDC's recommendations when the National Assembly convened. These recommendations included dramatically cutting back the provincial government's size and responsibilities and suspending elections for the office of governor and for seats in the Provincial Assembly. Soong and current assembly members would serve out their terms, after which these offices would convert to a chairmanship and commissioners, all appointed by the ROC president. This time it was the New Party that walked out in frustration over its inability to influence the proceedings. Soong resisted as well, answering that the central government rather than the provincial government should be abolished. Soong submitted his resignation from the governorship in protest and the Provincial Assembly adjourned indefinitely. When Lee and Lien declined to accept Soong's resignation, he boycotted KMT Central Standing Committee meetings for five months. Some KMT assembly members were sympathetic to Soong even though Lee and the party Central Standing Committee supported the NDC's suggested reforms. Some KMT members agreed that the provincial government structure had substantial value. Others used support for Soong, who had a reputation for integrity, to indirectly express their dissatisfaction with Lee's leadership of the party, particularly the KMT's inability to tackle crime and corruption. To get the National Assembly votes he needed, Lee threatened to reduce privileges or conduct surprise tax audits of party members who did not side with him.[25]

Others in the provincial government publicly campaigned against the proposed changes, arguing that the provincial government was better equipped than the central government to perform some essential functions. The National Assembly nevertheless codified the NDC's principal recommendations in July 1997, essentially eliminating a layer of government. Employees of the provincial government organized protests in Taipei. The Provincial Assembly privatized its three large commercial banks to keep the central government from inheriting them. Some newer legislators also resented the change, having won office on the strength of support from local factions rather than the national KMT organization, and having grown accustomed to using provincial government jobs and resources as rewards for those supporters.

With the National Assembly's passage of the constitutional revisions, the provincial government was fated to become an agency of the Executive Yuan at the end of 1998. Over the next two years its staff shrunk from 180,000 to 10,000. Soong called a press conference to complain about the downsizing and demand that the central government accept his resignation. Lee reportedly wanted to avoid adding to Soong's status by making him a "tragic hero."[26] Soong would stay on as governor until late 1998. The KMT did not expel Soong because of his popularity and because this would have worsened party disunity going into the November elections for mayors and county chief executives. Although Soong had strongly supported Lee's ascension to the leadership after the death of Chiang Ching-kuo, the former allies had clearly become bitter adversaries. Soong stopped attending meetings of the KMT Central Standing Committee and skipped the Fifteenth Party Congress in favor of a vacation in California. Despite his absence, he garnered the highest number of votes from dele-

[25] For a detailed analysis of the dismantling of the provincial government, see Gerald A. McBeath, "Restructuring Government in Taiwan," *Asian Survey* 40, no. 2 (March/April 2000): 251–268.
[26] "Lee gives Soong Cold Shoulder," *China News* (Taipei), Aug. 4, 1997, 2.

gates to the congress in the election for members of the KMT Central Committee. According to press reports, Lee nonetheless angrily dismissed a proposal to make Soong a party vice chairman. Soong declined the consolation prizes Lee offered: a position as senior advisor to the government and KMT vice presidential nomination for the 2000 election campaign.

Foreign and Cross-Strait Relations

There was a direct correlation between Taiwan's political liberalization and the deterioration in cross-strait relations. While the KMT was firmly in charge and committed to Taiwan-China unification, Beijing could be patient. But as the KMT opened the system, groups demanding greater Taiwanese sovereignty gained influence over both domestic and foreign policy. With Taiwan seemingly drifting toward independent statehood despite growing economic interaction with the mainland, Beijing saw no effective alternative to using military coercion to rein in the island, ruining the atmosphere for negotiating an accommodation.

Polls showed that about 70 percent of Taiwan's people wanted their government to improve the ROC's international status and opportunities at least as much as they wanted improved cross-strait relations. Many Taiwanese identified themselves as a nation distinct from the mainland Chinese and resented the long-term suppression of their nationalistic impulses. Pride in Taiwan's recent economic and political development only deepened these feelings. At a more practical level, increasing numbers of Taiwan's people ventured abroad for tourism and business, encountering numerous restrictions and inconveniences due to Taiwan's constrained diplomatic status. Society pressured the government to demand better treatment from the international community.

Strategically, international connections and recognition could enhance Taiwan's security. By strengthening its membership in the international community through economic, cultural, and (where possible) political links, Taiwan became more eligible to partake of the protection offered by international norms. At minimum, Taiwan's international enmeshment would raise the costs to Beijing of resorting to military coercion against Taiwan. Paradoxically, however, increased international political recognition of Taiwan signaled to the PRC that Taiwan was moving closer to independent statehood, triggering military countermeasures that would *decrease* Taiwan's security.

These were the basic wellsprings of Lee's foreign policy of increasing Taiwan's "international space" while upholding the one-China principle. This was a difficult balancing act that mirrored Lee's domestic challenge to keep from fatally alienating either the conservative or Taiwan separatist camps. Adapting to an environment the PRC tried to make inhospitable, the ROC employed flexible diplomatic approaches. Taipei sought political and economic interaction with other states regardless of whether they had diplomatic relations with the PRC and tried to gain "substantial relations" through quasi-official institutions where formal diplomatic relations were not possible. Taipei also tried to join international organizations. Lee's diplomacy strengthened his domestic political position by portraying him as a statesman who merited international notice and respect.

On cross-strait relations, Lee's government took a position that could be summarized thus: (1) Taiwan and China could not reunify until China's economic and political development approached the levels achieved on Taiwan; (2) in the meantime the ROC government would allow economic and other kinds of exchange (within certain limits) with the PRC and welcomed semiofficial dialogue between the two sides; (3) to improve relations, the ROC demanded that Beijing renounce the use of force against Taiwan and treat the Taipei government as a political equal. Lee in effect modified the Three No's: government-to-government contact remained proscribed, but private contacts were allowed, and even encouraged. Lee said he was prepared to wait indefinitely for China to attain the preconditions for serious unification plans. By and large, his countrymen as well preferred to wait rather than commit to either unification or independence. As Tun-jen Cheng succinctly observed of attitudes in the 1990s, "Most Taiwan residents have a fluid and ambivalent national identity."[27] A large percentage of the population was amenable to the idea of a Taiwan with the usual privileges of statehood (if this was attainable without provoking hostility from the PRC) *and also* to the notion of unification with China (but only after the mainland became more democratic and wealthy).

Commentators on both sides of the strait abundantly discussed the one-China principle. Since both the ROC and PRC governments accepted it in theory, it provided the starting point for negotiations. Both sides, however, promoted interpretations of the principle that supported their respective agenda, taking advantage of the inherent ambiguity of the term *China*. Beijing described the one-China principle this way: China equals the PRC; Taiwan is a part of China; therefore the PRC has sovereignty over Taiwan. (In the late 1990s a few Chinese officials began to float the idea that the "one China" did not necessarily mean the PRC in particular.) In contrast, Taipei's premise was that "China" was larger than either the

[27] Tun-jen Cheng, "Taiwan in 1996: From Euphoria to Melodrama," *Asian Survey* 37, no. 1 (January 1997): 45.

ROC or the PRC. China was divided and administered by two separate governments, implicitly of equal status. Through the 1990s Lee and other ROC officials offered several versions of their position that held to the basic premise: "one country, two areas;" "one country, two governments"; "one country, two political entities"; and "one country with two areas separately ruled by equal political entities." Lee's book *The Road to Democracy*, published in May 1999, envisioned a federal China comprising seven "fully autonomous" regions, one of which was Taiwan.

Cross-strait relations made little progress during Lee's tenure because nearly every issue invoked the underlying and insoluble dispute over which government had ultimate sovereignty over Taiwan. Even when, for example, Lee said he was willing to meet the PRC president in a third country (which would have subtly supported Taipei's position that the two governments are equals), Beijing responded that such a meeting should be on Chinese territory because the Taiwan question is an internal rather than an international matter. Another obstacle was Beijing's insistence that Taipei negotiate under conditions that denied giving the ROC recognition as an equal of the CCP government in Beijing, such as characterizing proposed talks as between KMT and CCP party leaders or between the Chinese central government and a provincial government. Similarly, Beijing held fast to the argument that using force within its own territory is the right of a sovereign state. Pledging not to use force against Taiwan would therefore compromise China's claim to sovereignty over the island. Beijing also rejected ROC presidential spokesman Cheyne Chiu's 1992 suggestion of an ROC-PRC "non-aggression treaty," similar to the document the two Germanys signed in 1972. Thus both of Taipei's major demands, renunciation of the use of force and acceptance of equal status, were highly problematic for Beijing because each implied the PRC lacked sovereignty over Taiwan. Lee's government, for its part, continued to rebuff China's "one country, two systems" proposal and offers for a negotiated capitulation that would allow Taiwan to choose its own leaders, retain its armed forces, and control its own finances. The fact that Beijing deeply distrusted Lee did not make these problems easier to address. The Chinese were suspicious from the beginning of the ROC's first Taiwanese president, who had studied at Kyoto Imperial University and was on record as saying that during part of his life he felt more Japanese than Chinese. From Beijing's standpoint, this said more about Lee's agenda than his verbal support for the one-China principle. The Chinese soon became convinced that Lee was committed to moving Taiwan toward independence, based on their interpretation of his "deeds rather than his words"—including his campaign to gain membership for Taiwan in international organizations, his attempts to travel abroad and meet with foreign officials, his "state-to-state relations" comment in 1999, and his hosting of a 1997 visit by the Dalai Lama, despised by Beijing (and by many conservatives in Taiwan) as head of the Tibetan independence movement.

At home, Lee was vulnerable on the issue of cross-strait relations from both ends of the political spectrum. Conservatives within Lee's own party were skeptical about the sincerity of his stated commitment to reunification. In 1990 Lee established a National Unification Commission under the Office of the President, saying it proved his dedication to this core KMT goal. The DPP complained the commission's title prejudged Taiwan's destiny. When the government refused to change the name, the DPP boycotted the commission. Desirous to secure DPP participation to give the organization legitimacy, Lee found only one DPP member, Kang Ning-hsiang, who was willing to join it. Kang immediately came under threat of expulsion by the DPP's proindependence wing. Conservative bureaucrats apparently formed a symbiotic relationship with the PRC leadership based on a common opposition to Taiwan independence. To minimize Beijing's pressure on countries hosting Lee, his office tried to keep his itinerary secret prior to his arrival. Typically, however, advance notice of Lee's international travel was leaked to the press. In most cases the Foreign Ministry was the likely culprit. Lee's government tried to combat cooperation between its foreign and domestic opponents by instituting a requirement for high-ranking civil servants to submit reports on all their foreign trips and on any contacts with PRC citizens while in Taiwan.

Lee's government made some early concessions. In 1990 the *Goddess of Democracy*, a ship run by PRC dissidents, sought Taipei's permission to broadcast radio programming into China from Taiwan-controlled waters. The government refused, only allowing the vessel to refuel and resupply at Keelung. In 1992 the Mainland Affairs Council announced that PRC athletes could participate in international sporting contests on Taiwan and that the PRC flag and national anthem, proscribed in the past, would be allowed. Taiwan also welcomed a delegation of Chinese scientists and sent the president of Taiwan's Academia Sinica, a government-sponsored research institution, on a visit to the PRC Academy of Sciences in Beijing. Travel restrictions relaxed so that by 1992, 2.4 million residents of Taiwan had legally visited China, with 22,000 Chinese reciprocating.[28] The most important and significant gesture was Lee's April 1991 proclamation of the end of the "Communist Rebellion." In effect Lee was doing what his government hoped Beijing would do: renouncing the use of force to unify China and accepting the legitimacy of his negotiating partner.

[28] Jurgen Domes, "Taiwan in 1992: On the Verge of Democracy," *Asian Survey* 33, no. 1 (January 1993): 56.

Critics of Lee's diplomacy complained the government was winning small diplomatic battles but losing the big ones. During the 1990s the ROC lost diplomatic relations with South Korea, South Africa, and Saudi Arabia while gaining recognition from states such as Nicaragua, Nauru, Guinea-Bissau, Lesotho, Macedonia, Palau, and the Marshall Islands. Saudi Arabia had been the most important country retaining diplomatic relations with the ROC. The Saudis had awarded Taiwan a large increase in oil sales beginning in 1980 in recognition of Taiwan's technical assistance. Losing relations with the Saudis was more than a symbolic defeat. Taiwan finished the decade sharing normal relations with twenty-nine states. In August 1992 South Korea moved with unexpected swiftness to recognize Beijing. While Taipei had shown a recent willingness to accept dual recognition, it immediately broke relations with Seoul, its oldest Asian ally. Despite South African president Nelson Mandela's friendly relationship with China, his government initially maintained its diplomatic relations with the ROC, for which Taipei rewarded South Africa with economic aid. When Pretoria made the inevitable announcement in November 1996 that it was switching recognition to Beijing, the ROC cancelled thirty-six bilateral agreements, including a commitment to invest $5 billion in a South African petrochemical plant. This was accompanied by a reassessment of Taiwan's "money diplomacy." Recognizing that small, poor countries were extorting greater sums of financial aid from Taiwan by threatening to recognize Beijing, Foreign Minister John Chang Hsiao-yen said his country would "turn down those who want to profit from the situation and make unreasonable demands."

Pressure from the PRC also limited Taiwan's opportunities for participation in international organizations. Taiwan attained observer status in the GATT in September 1992 as the "Taiwan, Penghu, Jinmen and Matsu Customs Territory." This was humiliating treatment considering the strength and development of Taiwan's economy, and it renewed criticism of the one-China principle within Taiwan. Despite Taipei's effort to promote investment in Southeast Asia, the Asia-Pacific Economic Cooperation (APEC) organization did not invite Lee to its leadership summit in Indonesia. For the October 1994 Asian Games in Hiroshima, the Olympic Council of Asia originally invited Lee to attend the opening ceremony. But after PRC pressure on Japan, Taiwan had to settle for an invitation to Vice Premier Hsu Li-teh to attend the games in a private capacity. The biggest single setback came from the United Nations. In a policy that the DPP supported, Lee's government campaigned throughout most of the decade for a ROC seat in the UN general assembly. Taipei argued that each of the two political entities that made up "China" should have a seat. Few UN member states, however (only fifteen by 1998), were willing to endorse

Taiwan's application in the face of countervailing PRC pressure. Taiwan even attempted to buy its way into the UN, pledging to donate $1 billion after admission, but the issue of seating the ROC did not make it onto the General Assembly's agenda. The UN refused to accept an attempted donation of $160,000 that DPP politician Annette Lu Hsiu-lien raised from the Taiwan public.

Even where Taiwan was successful in attaining international connections and commitments, these entailed costs as well as benefits; in the mid-1990s, for example, Taiwan faced the threat of sanctions under the Convention on International Trade in Endangered Species because of its appetite for the body parts of exotic animals such as tigers, elephants, and rhinos, which are traditionally valued for making medicine and tonics.

Lee inherited the problem of capital migrating from Taiwan to the mainland, with its worrisome implications for Taiwan's security. The mainland offered Taiwan business people cheap labor, resources, and overhead costs in an environment of linguistic and cultural familiarity. For its part, Taiwan helped fulfill China's needs for investment capital and expertise in technology, management, and marketing. Industrial heavyweights such as Evergreen chairman Chang Rong-fa and other members of the Taiwan business community lobbied for dropping the restrictions on investment and for direct trade links. The lack of a direct airline route, for example, added hundreds of dollars to a cross-strait commercial passenger flight. While Taiwan's business community pushed, the PRC pulled. One of the concerns of potential investors from Taiwan was legal protection for their enterprises on the mainland. China sought to address this concern with the passage by the National People's Congress Standing Committee of a "Law on Protection of Investment by Taiwan Compatriots" in March 1994. The next month China sponsored a National Economic Working Conference on Taiwan, with the theme of attracting investment by Taiwan's corporate conglomerates.

Lee tried to meet these pressures with a mixture of compromise and persuasion. His government laid out guidelines, often difficult to enforce, that required prior official approval, limited investment on the mainland to a maximum of $50 million, and forbade investment in high-tech or infrastructure projects. The Mainland Affairs Council proposed requiring Taiwan firms to balance their investment on the mainland with comparable investments in Taiwan, but the Ministry of Economics rejected this idea as impractical. Lee asked his countrymen to exercise "patience" in establishing economic ties with the mainland. The government encouraged Taiwan businesses to invest in Southeast Asia as an alternative to China in a "southward policy" (nanhsiang chengtse). Lien Chan visited Singapore and Malaysia in January 1994 as part of his "vacation." Lee followed in

February with trips to the Philippines, Indonesia, and Thailand. Lee secured meetings with Philippine president Fidel Ramos and Indonesian president Suharto. Lien and Lee asked their host governments to offer financial incentives to help lure Taiwan investors away from China. Few Taiwan investors, however, responded. Taipei moved closer to direct trade links by deciding in 1995 to allow foreign-flagged cargo vessels to sail from Kaohsiung to the mainland ports of Xiamen and Fuzhou. In early 1997 Beijing finally said it would begin processing shipping applications. Eventual realization of the "three links" appeared inevitable, but Lee's government hoped to gain a significant concession for them, such as Beijing pledging not to use force against Taiwan. Taipei's security concerns aside, an upside to the cross-strait economic relationship was that Taiwan amassed a hefty trade surplus that helped offset its deficit with Japan and keep its overall trade in the black—not to mention contributing substantially to Taiwan's economic growth.

Economic interaction was one of a variety of issues that made the need for coordination between the two governments inescapable. As noted above, the ROC wanted China to provide stronger formal guarantees of protection for Taiwan's growing investments on the mainland. China was also reluctant to take back its illegal immigrants caught in Taiwan and took a more tolerant view of the small-scale trade in the strait that Taipei characterized as "smuggling." In November 1994 artillery on Jinmen accidentally fired ordnance into a mainland village, injuring several Chinese. Ten airliners were hijacked from China to Taiwan between April and November 1993, raising the sovereignty issue from a new angle. Taipei wanted recognition of its legal jurisdiction over Chinese hijackers within Taiwan's territory. Beijing was unwilling to grant this because it seemed to imply Taipei had equal status with the PRC government. Taiwan therefore prosecuted the hijackers but refused to extradite them to China in the absence of a formal agreement to do so.

A terrible crime in March 1994 highlighted the issue of legal protection for ROC citizens visiting China. Twenty-four tourists from Taiwan were robbed and murdered aboard a boat on Qiandao Lake, a popular resort in China's Zhejiang Province. Word of the atrocity brought an onslaught of demands from Taiwan for information about the crime and the subsequent investigation, to which local officials reacted clumsily and uncooperatively. The Chinese government quickly produced three suspects and summarily executed them, but this failed to halt the outcry and suspicions of a cover-up from across the strait. The incident brought to the surface many of Taiwan's negative feelings about China, highlighting differences between the two systems and suggesting how far the two Chinas stood from political unification. Polls indicated that support for an independent

Taiwan increased. Some Taiwan travel agents quit organizing tours to China. The DPP used the opportunity to criticize the Straits Exchange Foundation (see below) for its inability to secure protection for Taiwanese citizens in China. The ROC government temporarily stopped approving proposals for investment on the mainland and suspended cultural and educational exchanges, although these minor sanctions lasted only a few months.

To provide for direct communication with the Chinese while formally maintaining the ban on official contact, Taipei established the Straits Exchange Foundation (SEF) in 1991. Although supervised by the Mainland Affairs Council (MAC) and funded mostly by the government, the SEF was technically a private organization staffed by ROC officials who were on leave or retired from government service. The SEF answered to the MAC, but their agendas were not identical. The MAC tended to be more cautious and to worry more about the security implications of Taiwan-ROC contacts than the SEF. These differing philosophies resulted in occasional tensions between the two organizations.

In 1991 China formed a counterpart to the SEF, the Association for Relations Across the Taiwan Straits (ARATS). The Chinese government appointed Wang Daohan, the former mayor of Shanghai, as ARATS chairman. The ROC appointed Koo Chen-fu, a tycoon and a member of the KMT Central Standing Committee who had a penchant for Beijing opera, as chairman of SEF.

Disagreement over the one-China principle was an obstacle to cross-strait talks. In 1992, however, negotiators for Taiwan and China agreed to shelve this tough political issue and arrange a meeting between SEF and ARATS representatives to discuss practical matters.

Subsequently a controversy developed over whether the two sides had reached a "consensus" that they could hold differing interpretations of the one-China principle, or merely agreed to go ahead with cross-strait talks despite their differences. In April 1993, to the disapproval of the DPP but with high hopes in most other quarters, Koo and Wang met for discussions in the neutral site of Singapore. They secured agreements on postal service and on verifying documents, and committed to meet again, but achieved no political breakthrough. Two more meetings that year were even less fruitful and exacerbated tensions between the SEF and the MAC. In October 1993 SEF secretary-general Chiu Cheyne resigned, and MAC vice-director Chiao Jen-ho replaced him. In August 1994 ARATS vice-chairman Tang Shubei traveled to Taiwan for talks. A group of DPP supporters met Tang's motorcade near Hsinchu, south of Taipei, chanting proindependence slogans and hurling eggs at Tang's car. The two sides made some progress on the issues of Chinese hijackers, fishing disputes, and rescues at sea, but the only product of the meeting was a joint statement.

Cross-strait talks resumed in 1998 after a three-year lapse following Lee's decision to visit the United States. The combination of American assurances that it would not support Taiwan independence, continued gains by the DPP in Taiwan, and China's large appetite for investment capital from Taiwan helped draw Beijing back to the negotiating table.[29] In October Koo and Wang met in Shanghai. Although producing little more than a mutual commitment to maintain dialog, this was the first such meeting ever on Chinese territory. Koo also traveled to Beijing for a meeting with Jiang Zemin.

Manipulating U.S. support for his government was one of Lee's most important tasks. His overall record in this area was mixed, with the F-16 sale announced in 1992 and the support of the U.S. Navy during the 1995–96 crisis balanced by the Clinton administration's subsequent signals that Taiwan had moved too far from the one-China framework. With the world's largest stock of foreign currency reserves, Taiwan had plenty of cash to pay for advanced American weaponry, but it needed a breakthrough in political will. Such a breakthrough occurred in September 1992, when U.S. president George Bush announced that the United States would sell 150 F-16 fighters to Taiwan for $6 billion. Days later France agreed to sell the ROC sixty Mirage 2000 fighters for $2.6 billion. The Bush administration explained that this move was necessary to help offset recent improvements in the PLA's capabilities, such as the purchase of advanced Russian Su-27 fighters. Bush was also running for reelection and expected to enjoy a boost in domestic popularity from the arms deal, which would benefit thousands of U.S. workers. Taiwan maintained that even with the new Western fighters, the ROC's armed forces would still be weaker than China's. Beijing nevertheless reacted with strong, angry protests that Western countries were impeding the reunification of China. But Beijing did not sever its diplomatic or economic relations with the United States.

Under the Clinton administration, Washington slightly upgraded its relations with Taiwan, allowing the quasi-official U.S. representative (the director of the American Institute in Taiwan) to meet with the staff of the ROC's Ministry of Foreign Affairs. Taiwan's office in the United States also changed its name from Coordination Council for North American Affairs to Taipei Economic and Cultural Representative Office. But Clinton did not invite Lee to the APEC meeting in Seattle, and after the 1995–96

[29] Jean-Pierre Cabestan, "Taiwan in 1998: An Auspicious Year for the Kuomintang," *Asian Survey* 39, no. 1 (January/February 1999): 142–143.

crisis Washington warned Taipei not to expect U.S. military support in the event of a PRC attack provoked by a declaration of independence. During his 1998 visit to China, U.S. president Bill Clinton made a concession to his hosts regarding Taiwan. The U.S. government, he said, did not support "two Chinas," Taiwan independence, or membership for Taiwan in international organizations requiring statehood. Although the U.S. State Department had already spelled out this policy, this was its first articulation by an American president, as Clinton's predecessors had resisted Chinese pressure to further constrain the U.S.-Taiwan relationship. In broad terms, the Clinton administration had stepped back from the Taiwan Relations Act's premise that the people of Taiwan had the right to decide their own destiny. Increased U.S. arms sales to Taiwan and a visit by Energy Secretary Bill Richardson helped balance American moves to accommodate the PRC.

Persistent U.S. pressure on Taipei after the crisis to reach an interim agreement with the PRC might have been a motivating factor in Lee's controversial "state-to-state" comment in July 1999. Lee might also have intended to steal the independence issue from the opposition and improve the fortunes of KMT presidential candidate Lien Chan, then third in opinion polls behind Chen Shui-bian and Soong Chu-yu. Lee said during an interview on a German news program that since 1991, the ROC had "redefined its relationship with Mainland China as being state-to-state relations (*guojia yu guojia guanxi*) or at least special state-to-state relations (*tesude guo yu guo guanxi*)." Lee's statement broke little new ground. The "state" he referred to was the Republic of China, not an independent Taiwan. His government's previous claims that the ROC was a sovereign state and a political equal to the Beijing government were well known. Lee's administration had previously described Taiwan and the PRC as "two governments" or "two equal political entities;" now they were two "states." China, nevertheless, chose to characterize Lee's statement as a disavowal of the one-China principle—that is, two states meant "two Chinas." Although the verbal response from Beijing was sharp, this time there was no military retaliation other than a few incidents of PLA aircraft flying across the centerline of the Taiwan Strait. The fact that Washington expressed disapproval of Lee's statement and reiterated its support for the one-China principle certainly made it easier for Beijing to forbear from taking stronger military action. Lee's government planned to abolish the Unification Council and amend the ROC constitution and other legal documents to implement the "special state-to-state relationship" concept, but held off under heavy U.S. pressure. China's decision to attribute such great consequence to Lee's statement perhaps stemmed from the CCP's perception of increased threats both domestically (with serious economic, political, and social challenges to the Jiang government's leadership) and internationally (with a militarily preeminent United States seemingly hostile toward China). In any case, Beijing indefinitely suspended talks between SEF and ARATS, canceling a meeting planned for autumn 1999. China offered symbolic assistance of $100,000 in cash and $60,000 worth of emergency supplies after a serious earthquake in Taiwan in September, but later squandered the opportunity to foster goodwill by demanding that international aid entering Taiwan be approved by Beijing and by the PRC chapter of the Red Cross.

The Aboriginal Community in Democratic Taiwan

The socioeconomic status of aborigines, who numbered 381,000 in 1999, remained considerably lower on average than that of ethnic Chinese on Taiwan despite new opportunities for political activism and the educational and social welfare programs provided by the government. Farmers made up about half of the aboriginal workforce. Those who moved to the cities usually found only low-skilled, low-paying jobs. Aborigines earned on average less than half the pay of ethnic Chinese in Taiwan. They had low levels of education, with only about half of aborigine children finishing elementary school, and high rates of alcoholism. Aborigines complained of frequent social and economic discrimination. Despite prejudices against the aborigines, the ethnic Chinese generally consider them a handsome people. Beauty and poverty contributed to the frequent sale of aborigine girls into prostitution. Aborigines, many of them minors, comprised up to 20 percent of Taiwan's prostitutes. Aboriginal communities faced the continuous threat of losing title to their land to private developers and government agencies. It was not difficult for the Bureau of Forestry, the Ministry of Defense, or other government entities to expropriate aboriginal land thought to have economic or strategic value. This often led to the forcible relocation of aboriginal villages. The government built a dump for Taiwan's nuclear waste on Lanyu Island, home of the Yami tribe.

Lee's regime carried on the original paternalistic KMT policy toward aboriginal issues: the goal was to help the aborigines catch up in socioeconomic terms with mainstream Taiwan society through education and assimilation. Critics charged the government's policy of assimilation aimed at destruction of aboriginal cultures and language. Aboriginal children (along with non-Mandarin-speaking Chinese) were forbidden from speaking their home languages in school during most of the KMT's rule.

The DPP was relatively sympathetic to aboriginal demands. The party's 1988 platform included a call for aboriginal self-government, and Yi-chi-ang served as director of a Department of Aboriginal Affairs within the DPP Central Committee. Aborigines nevertheless tended to vote KMT. Affected by centuries-old feelings of interethnic antagonism, they generally saw the DPP as a party devoted mainly to furthering the interests of Fujianese.

Aboriginal activists commonly made demands that included the following: changing their official designation from *shantiren* or *shanpao* ("mountain people" or "mountain compatriots") to *yuanchumin* ("original inhabitants"); the right to use traditional names on official documents; the removal of nuclear waste from Lanyu; the return of lost lands; deletion of the Wu Feng story, which activists said was both false and denigrating to aborigines, from elementary school textbooks; opposition to the establishment of additional national parks on aboriginal land; and self-government.

With the impending termination of martial law, 1987 was an eventful year for aborigine activism. In January a large demonstration in Taipei publicized and called for action against the sale of aboriginal girls into prostitution. In April aborigines expressed outrage over the "Tungpu graves incident," in which an aboriginal gravesite was unearthed during the construction of a tourist hotel. Also during the spring, the sentencing of convicted killer Tang Ying-shen, a nineteen-year-old laborer from the Tsou tribe, created a national sensation. The previous year Tang left his home in the mountains to look for work in Taipei. An employment agency found him a job in a laundry, but misinformed him about the pay, promising him triple what he would actually earn, which was five dollars for an eighteen-hour day. Tang's employer lent him sixty dollars to pay off the employment agency's fee and confiscated his identity card. After nine days of work Tang decided to quit and return home. His boss refused to return Tang's identity card, necessary for travel. Tang got drunk and then returned to confront his employer. They quarreled, and Tang murdered the man and his family. Intellectuals and religious leaders appealed for mercy because of the lack of opportunity faced by young aborigine men such as Tang. Despite these appeals Tang got the death sentence. In June an aborigine newspaper published a demand for self-government by aboriginal communities. An organized campaign calling for the return of certain lands to aborigine ownership developed by the end of the year. The "Return Our Land" movement asserted that as the first inhabitants of Taiwan, the aborigines' "right to the land is absolute and a priori. Those lands which have been robbed by violence or deceit by the later occupying Han Chinese, or taken by successive governments by legal force, should by right be returned to us."[30]

In the early 1990s aboriginal members of both national and provincial government organs proposed legislation that would increase aboriginal autonomy. The Presbyterian church of Taiwan, of which aborigines made up 40 percent of the membership, was also heavily involved in aboriginal activism. Aboriginal activists such as Yi-chiang Pa-lu-erh attended the UN Working Group on Indigenous Populations in Geneva and brought back new ideas and strategies for aboriginal empowerment. Yi-chiang wrote that "the collective vitality of Taiwan aboriginal peoples has grown weaker with every passing day" and "only sufficient self-government rights can save their race from extinction." He noted that states had granted national minorities substantial autonomy not only in the democracies, but even in the PRC.[31] In July 1994 Lee met with aboriginal activists, symbolizing recognition of the legitimacy of their campaign. But Lee rejected their call for self-government, instead emphasizing the need for education. Convicted for leading unlawful demonstrations, in 1995 Yi-chiang and Ma-yau Ku-mu became the first aboriginal activists imprisoned in Taiwan.

This activism bore some fruit. A few aborigines attained roles in the political system. The chief executive of Taitung County, elected in 1993 and reelected in 1997, was an aborigine. A 1991 constitutional revision set aside six seats in the Legislative Yuan for aborigines, three from plains communities and three from mountain communities. Some activists argued that six seats amounted to an insignificant token that gave aborigines no impact among an overwhelming Han majority. In 1993 a constitutional revision codified usage of the term *yuanchumin* to refer to aborigines, replacing the terms *shantiren* and *shanpao*. This was no small accomplishment, as the ROC government had resisted the substitution in terminology because of political and legal implications. In 1985, for example, the government refused an application from the Alliance of Taiwan Aborigines, an aboriginal rights advocacy group, to register its publication under the title *Yuanchumin*. The argument was that if the aborigines were recognized as an indigenous people, they could claim much greater rights to land ownership than if they were considered immigrants like the Chinese. The government allowed the use of traditional aboriginal names on legal documents after 1996. That same year the legislature passed a bill

[30] Quoted in Michael Stainton, "The Politics of Taiwan Aboriginal Origins," in Murray A. Rubinstein, ed., *Taiwan: A New History* (Armonk, N.Y.: M. E. Sharpe, 1999), 39.

[31] Michael Stainton, "Aboriginal Self-Government: Taiwan's Uncompleted Agenda," in Rubinstein, ed., *Taiwan*, 425.

establishing an Aboriginal Affairs Commission within the Executive Yuan. This long-standing idea finally got action because the KMT needed to secure the six aborigine votes in the legislature during the fight over Lien Chan's confirmation as premier. Dimming the victory were the facts that the final version of the bill left the commission weaker than the original proposal, and an amendment reclassified aboriginal land illegally occupied by nonaboriginals as ordinary freehold land. Under legislation passed in 1998, the Ministry of Education subsidized higher education and funded aboriginal studies centers to preserve aboriginal language and art. Social workers devoted considerable effort to discouraging aboriginal families from selling their daughters into prostitution.

Lee Teng-hui and Taiwan's Political Evolution

Taiwan underwent further democratization during the 1990s. No development was more important in this regard than the emergence of a bona fide multiparty system. Democratic Progressive Party politicians began making the adjustment from revolutionaries to administrators. There was great underlying significance in the scenes of newly elected DPP mayors and county chief executives removing the portraits of Chiang Kai-shek and Chiang Ching-kuo, which typically hung in every government office, and decrying them as symbols of a personality cult from an age of dictatorship.

Moreover, the government instituted direct popular presidential elections. Elections that all parties acknowledged as generally fair became routine. The elected bodies gained more power and prestige while KMT leadership organs lost influence. The KMT itself continued to evolve as Taiwan's political system liberalized. It became more internally democratic, a departure from its Leninist roots. The leadership of the party's Central Committee and Central Standing Committee became less important, and pleasing voting constituents more so, in determining the fortunes of individual KMT politicians. Furthermore, the political issue of Mainlander versus Taiwanese privileges was greatly reduced as Taiwan-born officials filled elected offices at the national level, with Lee as exemplar.

Taiwan's economic development continued apace under Lee's administration. The ROC finished the century with international currency reserves of more than $100 billion. Taiwan rode out the Asian economic crisis with a 6.8 percent growth in its gross domestic product in 1997 and 4.8 percent in 1998.

Lee enjoyed public popularity through the end of his first full term, which culminated in his strong reelection victory in the ROC's first direct presidential election while he stood up to attempted intimidation by the PRC. Although he was active in promoting constitutional reform, persistent suspicion surrounded Lee's motivations. Eventually Lee's popularity declined as the public grew impatient with his government's lack of progress in curtailing domestic problems such as corruption and crime. Similarly, Lee's foreign and cross-strait policies, intended to upgrade Taiwan's political status and increase its security, showed signs of having reached their limits in the latter years of Lee's tenure. The inherent contradiction became clear: Taiwan indeed raised its international profile, but alarmed Beijing in the process, upsetting the comfortable cross-strait stalemate and prompting Chinese responses that threatened the island's security. Even though he oversaw further steps toward political liberalization, Lee did not necessarily accelerate the democratization process, which in some ways conflicted with his drive for political control. He often took strong measures to maintain discipline within his party. Lee's campaign to increase the powers of his office and his decision to run for reelection in 1996 served his ambition more than the goal of expanding democracy in Taiwan's political system.

✳

CHAPTER EIGHT

The DPP Captures the Presidency

The trends of Taiwanese empowerment and weakening of the KMT political machine culminated spectacularly in the election of DPP candidate Chen Shui-bian in Taiwan's second direct presidential election in March 2000. The presidential campaign and election, again conducted under PRC pressure and with the rest of the world paying close attention, were full of drama: the division of the KMT vote between Soong Chu-yu and Lien Chan, Soong's financial scandal, the closeness of the race up to the day of the vote, and the implications of a DPP presidency for Taiwan-China relations. Chen helped achieve a peaceful change of regime from one party to another, an additional milestone in Taiwan's democratization. Chen's administration, however, initially appeared weak and ineffective as the KMT regrouped and marshaled its still-formidable political resources to block Chen's agenda. Fortunately Chen was more successful in the important area of cross-strait relations, preventing further deterioration despite the burden of Beijing's deep suspicion that Chen's goal was Taiwan independence. Here KMT efforts to undercut Chen nevertheless contributed to his goal of pacifying the PRC.

The 2000 Presidential Election

KMT candidate Lien represented stability and continuity, but otherwise he was a lackluster candidate. Lien came from an upper-class family, and critics charged he lacked empathy for the common people. During the campaign Lien suggested the possibility of deploying long-range missiles to "deter the enemy from invading Taiwan." Although the government later backtracked (an official transcript of Lien's speech omitted the remark about missiles, and Defense Minister Tang Fei said the ROC had no strategic missile development program), the public responded favorably to the idea.

Lien called Chen a "clown" and "impetuous maniac," but the former Taipei mayor had a reputation for cleverness and caution. Chen, who often referred to himself by his nickname "A-bian" in public speeches, grew up a member of a poor family in a village near Tainan. An outstanding student, Chen went into law and passed the bar exam even before graduating from prestigious National Taiwan University law school. As an attorney he helped plead the case of the Kaohsiung incident defendants. In 1985, while Chen ran for office in Tainan County, a truck struck and injured his wife Wu Shu-chen in what appeared to be an intentional attack, crippling her for life. Wu later won a seat in the Legislative Yuan while Chen served a prison term for libel against the KMT.

In May 1999 the DPP passed a "Resolution on the Future of Taiwan" aimed at assuring voters that a DPP president would carry out a responsible cross-strait policy. The resolution accepted the status quo, repeating the argument of DPP moderates that because Taiwan was already de facto independent there was no need for formalization. Chen therefore described his position as Taiwan first, but without declaring independence (disappointing the vocal minority of independence proponents, some of whom went on a hunger strike to demand a referendum on Taiwan's relationship to China). Chen's agenda also included aggressive action against "black gold;" more funding for social services; and "green island" environmentalism, including opposition to nuclear power. Chen called for a "second stage" of reform: building public confidence in the judiciary by establishing an independent agency to fight corruption and by introducing a U.S.-style jury system. This, he said, would help eliminate corruption and the influence of organized crime from politics. Chen finally announced in mid-December that his running mate would be Annette Lu Hsiu-lien, chief executive of Taoyuan County and perhaps Taiwan's best-known female politician. Shortly before the poll Chen got a boost when Lee Yuan-tseh, winner of the 1986 Nobel Prize for chemistry and perhaps Taiwan's most respected scholar, endorsed his candidacy.

Soong, as we saw, had served in the martial law–era KMT government as an official propagandist who portrayed Taiwanese democracy activists in a negative light. Of this period Soong said, "I just did what an obedient official would have done. We should not always look back at the past."[1]

---

[1] Lin Chieh-yu, "Ironies Abound in Current Political Climate," *Taipei Times Online*, Dec. 10, 1999, online at http://taipeitimes.com/news/1999/12/10/print/0000014315.

Soong running as the KMT candidate could have expected an easy victory. His feud with the KMT mainstream, however, pitted him as an independent candidate against Lee's chosen would-be successor, Lien Chan. Both Lee and Lien called Soong a "traitor." The KMT expelled Soong in November along with twenty-one other party officials who had supported him.

In December the KMT began a negative campaign that targeted Soong's reputation for integrity. Party members accused Soong of secretly funneling millions of dollars in party funds to his son and sister-in-law while he was KMT secretary general. Soong belatedly answered that he had acted under Lee's direction as custodian of the money, which was set aside for special KMT purposes, including assisting the family of the late president Chiang Ching-kuo. Soong's story was unpersuasive to many voters, and his popularity immediately dropped. The episode likely cost him the election. It also reinforced widely held beliefs about KMT corruption, negatively affecting other KMT candidates.[2]

Oddly, the former exiled Taiwanese dissident Hsu Hsin-liang paired with New Party legislator Chu Hui-liang to run on a commitment to the one-China principle. While DPP chairman in 1998, Hsu Hsin-liang had espoused a policy of reconciliation with the PRC, urging Taiwan to "courageously go west" and establish direct trade and transportation links (in contrast to Lee Teng Hui's policy of restraint and "patience"). Many in the DPP branded him a traitor, and he lost the chairmanship to Lin Yi-hsiung. Now Hsu advocated negotiated reunification based on a Chinese pledge not to change Taiwan's domestic systems for fifty years. Hsu said a plebiscite on independence would "bring disaster" to the island.[3]

Soong, Lien, and Chen all promised to allow direct air and sea travel across the strait, a position most voters favored. This was particularly important for Chen as a token of his commitment to maintaining stable relations with the mainland. All three major candidates also made efforts to appeal to voters across barriers of ethnicity. Soong tried to shore up his local credentials by choosing Chang Chao-hsiung, a proindependence Taiwanese surgeon and director of Chang Gung University Hospital, as his running mate. Chen traveled to Hsinchu County, which had a high concentration of Hakka residents, to promote a "Hakka policy white paper," which recommended preserving Hakka culture and establishing a cabinet position for a Hakka affairs commissioner. Chen gave a ten-minute speech in the Hakka dialect, a first for a non-Hakka politician. Soong and Lien as

<hr/>

[2] Karl Fields, "All Is Not Gold that Glitters: The Growing Liability of KMT Inc.," online at http://www.gwu.edu/eastasia/events/taiwan-01/Fields.htm, fn 13, accessed Oct. 31, 2001.

[3] Julian Baum, "Fat and Happy," *Far Eastern Economic Review*, Apr. 29, 1999, 28.

well tried to win the Hakka vote, Soong sponsoring Hakka rallies and Lien promising to appoint Hakkas to his cabinet. The candidates made similar appeals to aborigines, with Lien promising a development fund for aborigine communities and Chen releasing a white paper on his plans for a "new partnership" between the government and the aborigines.

In the days leading up to the election, Chinese officials and media again attempted to influence the outcome, warning that "independence means war." This attempt at coercion again failed, however, as victory went to China's least desired of the three major candidates. The final results of polling on March 18 showed that Chen got 39.3 percent of the vote, enough to narrowly defeat Soong's 36.8 percent. Lien's share was an embarrassing 23 percent. Hsu and New Party candidate Li Ao each got less than 1 percent of the vote.

Sufficient voters responded to Chen's promises on fighting corruption and providing social services, while accepting that he could be trusted not to provoke a war with China. As during many other elections in Taiwan, the outcome hinged on domestic issues such as social welfare and the campaign against corruption, not cross-strait relations. Nevertheless, a change of regime in 2000 was hardly preordained. Chen depended heavily on outside help to win. The KMT split made him competitive. Soong's corruption scandal and Lee Yuan-tseh's endorsement gave Chen the crucial edge.

With Lien's decisive defeat, Lee Teng-hui's twelve-year tenure as leader of the KMT came to a sudden and ignoble end. On March 18 protesters gathered outside the KMT's central headquarters in Taipei demanding that Lee resign as KMT chairman. Lee quickly announced he would resign in September during the KMT party congress. This failed to satisfy the crowd, which grew to several thousand and vowed to demonstrate until Lee stepped down. The demonstration was technically illegal. Taipei authorities surrounded the KMT building with police and barbed wire, but did not attempt to break up the protest. Indeed, Mayor Ma Ying-jeou joined the protesters on the first night. At one point the protesters intercepted KMT limousines, damaging the cars and roughing up seventy-year-old Hsu Li-teh, an adviser to Lien and Lee. Most of the demonstrators were supporters of Soong angry that the KMT under Lee's leadership did not allow Soong to run as the KMT presidential candidate, forcing him to run as an independent and splitting the vote of KMT supporters. Some claimed Lee secretly supported the DPP and deliberately helped Chen win by choosing a weak KMT candidate (Lien) and promulgating phony opinion polls that suggested Lien had a comfortable lead going into the election. In a deeper sense, Mainlanders were expressing their frustration over the Taiwanization of politics and the loss of the KMT's old agenda, a reversal of the countless previous occasions when Taiwanese gathered in the streets to protest Mainlander control of the islanders' destiny. The protest succeeded. Lee resigned on March 24 along with the party's secretary-general and vice secretary-general.

Soong founded a new party, the People First Party (PFP), on March 24, 2000. This indicated there was no immediate prospect of Soong reconciling with and returning to his former party. Kuomintang morale was low, and members spoke of the danger the party would soon die out. But as the new president discovered, the KMT had plenty of life left as an opposition party. On many issues politicians of the PFP, which had few philosophical or policy differences with the KMT, would join in the fight against Chen.

The Chen Administration

The first non-KMT president in ROC history entered office pledging to expand social welfare services and fight corruption in government, while promising he would introduce no new taxes. During his campaign, Chen promised to implement a "3-3-3" program: NT three thousand dollars per month to poor citizens over age sixty-five, exemption from medical expenses for children under age three, and loans at an interest rate of 3 percent for first-time home buyers. Making good on these promises would be difficult, however, given that Chen inherited a budget deficit resulting from several years of gradual increases in social services combined with reduced revenues due to tax and tariff cuts, plus the costs of recovering from a serious earthquake that had struck in September 1999. Centered in central Taiwan, the quake was the island's strongest of the century, killing 2,087, injuring 8,711, and leaving more than 100,000 without homes. Several foreign countries earned Taiwan's gratitude by sending aid, while many of Taiwan's people complained the response by their own authorities was inefficient.

Many of Chen's advisers were young, idealistic, and lacking in administrative experience. Only a third of Chen's cabinet members were DPP members, and few of them had been public servants higher than the local level. An even bigger problem for Chen's first year and a half in office was that although he had captured the presidency, his power base was weak. With less than 40 percent of the popular vote, Chen had not won a strong mandate from the public. Kuomintang influence in other branches of the government remained strong. Most important, the KMT controlled the Legislative Yuan, where the DPP held less than one third of the seats. The bureaucracy, as well, remained largely loyal to the KMT. The officer corps of the ROC military, its higher ranks still dominated by Mainlanders committed to reuniting China, expressed misgivings about serving under a commander-in-chief whose party was dedicated to Taiwan independence.

In hopes of securing cooperation from the powerful opposition, Chen gave its members some of the high-ranking positions in his government, including premier, foreign minister, and defense minister. This tactic proved unsuccessful in the case of Premier Tang Fei, a conservative former air force general and defense minister in the previous KMT government. Proindependence politicians from Chen's own party opposed Tang's appointment and continually harassed him during his brief tenure, and his resignation apparently stemmed from a partisan disagreement with Chen.

With his domestic agenda at the mercy of a KMT-dominated Legislative Yuan, Chen would find it difficult to satisfy his supporters, who grew weary of the compromises he was forced to make. A group affiliated with the DPP released a report in August 2000 that harshly criticized Chen both for failing to achieve his campaign promises and for poor management. Aboriginal activists remained discontent, calling on Chen to formally apologize to Taiwan's original inhabitants (citing the precedent of the New Zealand government's apology to its Maori residents), establish autonomous aboriginal regions, sponsor ethnic education for aboriginal children, and restrict exploitation of the island's forest areas. Taiwan's most serious economic recession since the 1970s magnified dissatisfaction with the government. The stock market lost over half its value in a year and unemployment surpassed 4.5 percent, the highest level in decades. The collapse of high-technology stocks in the U.S. economy was clearly an important factor. Chen's detractors also blamed his administration for failing to contain the crisis, while Chen's appointees claimed the opposition was blocking their relief efforts in an attempt to make Chen's leadership appear ineffective.

Internally, the DPP suffered from factional clashes over the question of removing the call for Taiwan independence from the party platform. Some of the president's moves seemed designed to contain the influence of his rival, DDP party chairman Frank Hsieh Chang-ting. Vice president Annette Lu represented another example of Chen's attempt to broaden his support through his political appointments. The outspoken and controversial Lu, however, soon became an embarrassment to Chen. On cross-strait policy in particular, Chen and Lu appeared to be pursuing contradictory China agendas, with Chen sending conciliatory signals while Lu made inflammatory comments. The proindependence Lu often criticized China and its claims to sovereignty over Taiwan, earning her Beijing's condemnation as "the scum of the nation." In June 2000 Lu said publicly that Chen "wants me to play the 'bad cop' in cross-Strait issues." Chen's office immediately denied this. The Chen-Lu relationship began to look like a soap opera storyline when a respected magazine claimed Lu had told a reporter by telephone that Chen was having an affair with a young aide. Lu complained that the media persecuted her, but also that Chen had sidelined her, treating her as a "flower vase."

In July 2000, while hundreds of thousands watched the drama on television, four construction workers surrounded by the rushing waters of a creek in southern Taiwan waited nearly three hours for a rescue helicopter that never arrived. Eventually the currents overwhelmed them and all four drowned. The rescue failed to materialize largely because of squabbling over responsibility between different government agencies. The incident rekindled a longstanding perception that the military and police cared little about ordinary citizens, and also brought embarrassment to Chen's government. Officials up to Premier Tang Fei tendered their resignations, and that of Vice Premier Yu Hsi-kun was accepted.

The biggest defeat of Chen's first year in office, an episode in many ways emblematic of the early part of his presidency, was the political showdown over the fourth nuclear power plant at Kungliao, a multibillion dollar project that was one-third completed. Proponents of the plant warned it was necessary to forestall an energy shortage, economic downturn, and unemployment. The environmentalist DPP, however, strongly objected to an expansion of nuclear power on Taiwan and hoped to keep the plant from opening. Opposition to the Kungliao plant was the only major issue on which Chen had not compromised to maintain a working relationship with the opposition-controlled legislature.

Tang Fei, reflecting the KMT's strong support for the project, had threatened to resign if it was cancelled. On October 3, 2000, Chen accepted Tang's resignation, ostensibly because of poor health. With only four and a half months in office, he was the ROC's briefest-serving premier. The next day Chen appointed Chang Chun-hsiung as Tang's replacement. Paralleling the experience of Lee Teng-hui, who had seen poor results from his attempt to build a political bridge by installing an opposition premier, Chen turned the opposite direction and selected a close political ally. Chang, a former attorney who had served six terms in the legislature, was a DPP veteran and trusted colleague of Chen's. On October 27 Chang announced the government had decided to cancel construction of the plant. Chang said that without it, Taiwan had a sufficient supply of electricity through 2007, which was enough time to find an alternative new source. The premier held up a photo of a woman kissing her child poisoned by the Chernobyl nuclear accident to dramatize his point that the risks of nuclear contamination were too high for Taiwan to increase its reliance on nuclear power. Chang said Taiwan's three other nuclear plants had registered a total of eighty-two minor accidents, and that the island had no solution to the problem of storing a growing quantity of radioactive waste. Less than an hour before Chang's announcement, Chen held a much-anticipated meeting with Lien Chan intended to smooth relations between the DPP and KMT. During the meeting Lien advised Chen to let the Legislative Yuan settle the controversy over the new nuclear plant. The perception that Chen had deceived and insulted Lien sharpened the KMT's anger at the Chen government's decision to cancel the project. Despite Chen's public apology to Lien, KMT politicians began to marshal support for recalling the president. With a two-thirds majority vote, the legislature could force a referendum on the presidential election. Soong's People First Party favored a no-confidence vote against Premier Chang, forcing new parliamentary elections in which the party hoped to gain seats.

While opposition politicians moved forward with the recall process, tens of thousands had demonstrated in Taipei and Kaohsiung in support of the decision to cancel the plant. Intervention by the Council of Grand Justices on January 15, 2001, averted further crisis. The justices ruled that the cabinet could not cancel the project, but rather this power belonged to the Legislative Yuan. The executive branch, having apparently fought a good fight, gracefully accepted the ruling. In February, Chang and the speaker of the Legislative Yuan reached an agreement to continue work on the Kungliao plant. The public was unhappy both with Chen for once again proving ineffective and with the KMT for threatening to unseat the president less than a year into his term. A DPP poll showed Chen's public approval rating had dropped to 25 percent.[4] During his 2001 New Year's address, Chen made the humiliating admission that "the new government has still been unable to function as effectively as it should. Therefore, I must examine myself, and I am willing to humbly learn."

In the months leading up to the Legislative Yuan election, Lee Teng-hui emerged from his brief retirement to take up a new role as a KMT opponent and Chen ally. With Lien Chan succeeding Lee as party leader, the KMT steered toward a more conservative Mainlander orientation, reversing the cross-strait policy Lee had developed. Lien, for example, entertained the notion of Taiwan joining the PRC in a confederation and opened party-to-party talks with the CCP. This angered Taiwan-first KMT members. In a public spat, Lee referred to the KMT government he previously headed as an "alien regime" and "those bastards." Lien called his

---

[4] In another measurement, according to polls conducted by a television station, Chen's public approval rating fell from 77 percent to 34 percent by early 2001. Mark Lander, "Taiwan Chief Fails to Loosen Old Guard's Grip on Power," *New York Times*, Mar. 5, 2001, http://taiwansecurity.org/NYT/2001/NYT-030501.htm.

former benefactor "an old man still talking nonsense."[5] After the KMT's Sixteenth Party Congress decided to reaffirm the Guidelines for Unification instead of endorsing Lee's idea of a "special state-to-state relationship," Lee helped organize the Taiwan Solidarity Union (TSU) in August 2001 and vowed to help Chen resist the pressure to accommodate China. The new party's goal was to create a home for disaffected Taiwan-first politicians who would be willing to support the DPP's cross-strait policy, but who tended to be more conservative than the DPP on domestic social and economic issues. This would create a strengthened "pan-Green" camp to counter the "pan-Blue" camp of the KMT, PFP, and New Party. The KMT quickly kicked out eleven of its members who had joined the TSU. With much hand-wringing in recognition of Lee's popularity and historical importance, the KMT expelled him as well in September. Lee and Chen appeared together in public, their upraised hands clasped, prompting observers in China and conservatives in Taiwan to declare that their suspicions about Lee being a Taiwan separatist were now confirmed.

The DPP enjoyed a substantial victory in the December legislative election, increasing its seats from 66 to 87, with potential coalition partner the TSU winning 13 seats. Soong's PFP also polled well, earning 46 seats and more than doubling its previous presence in the Legislative Yuan. The KMT lost badly, dropping from 110 seats to 68. The New Party, which previously had 7 seats, managed to win only 1. The DPP expected its plurality of seats would make it easier for the Executive Yuan to get its proposed legislation passed. For the KMT, on the other hand, the election marked the party's further deterioration.

Chen's Foreign Relations

Chen faced a huge challenge in his China policy. Cross-strait relations were already at a low point following the 1995–96 missile launches and Chinese reaction to Lee's "state-to-state" comment. Chen needed to stabilize the relationship, and in particular to restore bilateral dialogue. Yet his party was anathema to Beijing, and his election in itself represented a minor disaster for the PRC. From Beijing's standpoint, Chen was the least desirable of the three leading candidates. The official Chinese media even refused to mention Chen by name. Hoping for a weak, one-term Chen presidency, Beijing had ample incentive to hurt Chen domestically by denying him the appearance of success in managing cross-strait relations.

To forestall further military pressure from Beijing and to assure his own

[5] Taipei Times Online, Oct. 1 and Oct. 15, 2001; online at http://www.taipeitimes.com.

countrymen of his responsible statesmanship, Chen took a conciliatory approach. Ironically, this DPP president set out a softer line on cross-strait relations than his KMT predecessor. The new president immediately distanced himself from the DPP's traditional proindependence position. Chen resigned from the DPP in May 2000, saying that as president he would serve all the people of Taiwan. This move helped him achieve an approval rating of over 70 percent. During his inauguration speech that month, Chen said that if China refrained from using force against Taiwan, his government would not declare independence, change the name of the Republic of China, alter the constitution to implement Lee's "state-to-state relations" premise, hold a referendum on Taiwan's political status, or abolish the Guidelines for National Unification (which were based on the one-China principle) or the National Unification Council. Employing a traditional Chinese aphorism, Chen reminded the CCP leadership, "When those afar will not submit, practice kindness and virtue to attract them." In August he said there was no "predetermined conclusion" on the question of whether Taiwan would eventually reunify with China.

From Beijing's standpoint, these were minor gestures. What the CCP wanted was for Chen to recommit to the one-China principle, which the PRC said Lee Teng-hui had disavowed in 1999. Absent this commitment, Beijing refused to resume cross-strait talks. Chen's party affiliation, however, made it extremely difficult for him to make this concession. Even DPP moderates who were willing to refrain from an immediate declaration of independence could not accept permanently forswearing this option, as the one-China principle seemed to imply. Many Taiwanese agreed with Lu that "accepting 'one China' is equivalent to surrender."[6] Chen took the position that the one-China principle could be a subject of negotiations, but not a precondition.

Observers hoped Chen might endorse a version of the one-China principle that did not imply Taiwan was a province of the PRC. A few Chinese officials including vice premier and former foreign minister Qian Qichen and top-ranking arms control negotiator Sha Zukang publicly suggested that "China" did not necessarily mean the PRC, but rather denoted a larger entity of which both Taiwan and the PRC could be considered equal parts. Both Beijing and the KMT called on Chen to return to the "1992 consensus" that both sides accepted the principle of one China but each had its own interpretation. A compromise seemed close in June 2000, when Chen said, "We accept the previous consensus that each side of the Tai-

---

[6] "Taiwan Vice President Rejects Beijing's 'One China' Policy," Reuters, Nov. 24, 2000, online at http://taiwansecurity.org/Reu/Reuters-112400–2.htm, accessed Nov. 5, 2001.

wan Strait can adhere to its own interpretation of the meaning of 'one China,' but mainland China still insists on its cherished 'one China' principle." This drew criticism from the DPP, however, forcing Chen to backtrack. A few days later MAC chairwoman Tsai Ing-wen "clarified" Chen's statement, saying there was no change since his inauguration speech and that "we never accepted Beijing's 'one-China principle.'"[7] Thereafter, Chen and his allies denied the existence of a 1992 "consensus," saying this term had emerged years afterward. Instead Chen's camp promoted the phrase "spirit of 1992," by which they meant a willingness to engage in dialogue, and called on Beijing to resume talks based on this "spirit."

Cross-strait relations remained stagnant, but did not deteriorate. An important reason for China's patience was that cooperation between the Beijing regime on one hand and Taiwan opposition politicians and former KMT officials on the other offered Chen's domestic enemies another avenue for undercutting him while giving the Chinese more confidence they could exercise some influence on Taiwan through a means other than military force. The relative power of conservatives within the KMT increased after the resignation of Lee Teng-hui as party leader, making the party as a whole more willing to coordinate cross-strait policy with Beijing to achieve the shared goal of upholding the one-China principle. Between March and October 2000, the PRC invited about a third of Taiwan's Legislative Yuan members to visit China, including many KMT and New Party politicians but also some of Chen's rivals within the DPP. Some Taiwan politicians who visited China reportedly urged the CCP to avoid resuming dialogue with the ROC, lest Chen's government gain prestige at home.[8] In September 2001 China allowed the KMT to open an office in Beijing. "They are working very hard to sabotage the unity of Taiwan," Chen complained of the Chinese.

In the meantime, Chen offered Beijing economic concessions in lieu of political concessions such as accepting one-China. Loosening the restrictions on cross-strait trade and investment satisfied a long-standing PRC demand while offering the stimulation and confidence that Taiwan's economy (and, by extension, Chen) desperately needed. In 2000 Chen's government approved lifting the ban on cross-strait travel and trade between the mainland and the ROC-held offshore islands, a policy known as the "small three links." On January 3, 2001, with much fanfare on the Taiwan

---

[7] Veronica Lo, "Chen's Remarks Nothing New: MAC," Taipei Times online, June 29, 2000, http://www.taipeitimes.com/news/2000/06/29/story/0000041839, accessed Nov. 2, 2001.

[8] Bonnie S. Glaser, "China's Taiwan Policy: Still Listening and Watching," PacNet Newsletter, No. 33, Center for Strategic and International Studies Pacific Forum, Oct. 19, 2001, p. 1.

side, a boatload of dignitaries from Jinmen inaugurated the new policy by sailing to the port of Xiamen in the first legal civilian voyage from the ROC to China in fifty-two years. Chen convened an Economic Development Advisory Conference in August 2001. The KMT participated, the risk of appearing obstructionist apparently outweighing the risk of improving Chen's domestic prestige. Conference delegates recommended measures to liberalize trade with China. Chen immediately expressed support for the recommendations, while his vice president complained they would doom Taiwan to dependency on the mainland economy. In November 2001 the government announced it would eliminate the $50 million limit on Taiwan investment in individual projects on the mainland, legalize investments in high technology, and permit links between banks in Taiwan and China to facilitate the transfer of funds across the strait. Chen's administration said it was replacing Lee's "no haste, be patient" policy with a new approach termed "active opening, effective management."

The new U.S. administration under President George W. Bush signaled a tougher line on China and greater support for Taiwan than the Clinton team. Bush's White House pleased Taipei with a 2001 arms sale package worth $6 billion. Bush publicly pledged to do "whatever it took to help Taiwan defend herself"—an apparent departure from the previous U.S. approach of "strategic ambiguity," although the White House subsequently denied any basic change in U.S. cross-strait policy. Chen took advantage of the new climate in Washington to secure a visa to visit the United States in May 2001. His trip would of course not help smooth relations with China, but he had already made concessions to show Beijing he did not intend to declare independence, and traveling to America figured to boost his image at home. Along with a stop in Houston, Chen became the first ROC president to travel to New York City, overcoming the U.S. government's unwritten ban on top-level ROC stopovers in either New York or Washington, D.C. In some ways Chen's U.S. trip was not as provocative as Lee's visit to New York State in 1995. This was technically a "stopover" en route to Latin America rather than a "visit," and the ROC Foreign Ministry rather than his own office planned his travel. On the other hand, Chen's meetings with members of the U.S. Congress gave his trip more political substance than Lee's. China predictably protested, but much less stridently than in 1995. Chen Po-chih, head of the ROC Council for Economic Planning and Development, still got a brief meeting with Jiang Zemin while in Beijing the same month. Chen was the first cabinet-level official to visit China since 1995.

Taipei still worried, nonetheless, that after September 11 the United States might trade Taiwan-related concessions for Chinese support in the war against terrorism, prompting U.S. secretary of state Colin Powell to publicly assure Taiwan this would not happen.[9]

On the broader diplomatic front, 2001 saw the failure of Taiwan's ninth attempt to join the United Nations. Taiwan finally won approval to join the World Trade Organization, but only after a forced three-year wait in deference to the PRC's wishes. Taipei had met all the WTO requirements in 1998, but Beijing demanded Taiwan could not join before China did. The WTO approved China for accession on November 10, and Taiwan on November 11. Cross-strait politics marred a summit meeting of Asia-Pacific Economic Cooperation (APEC) members in Shanghai in October. With Taipei already indignant that China would not permit Chen or even former vice president Li Yuan-zu to attend a gathering to which other countries sent their heads of state, the Taiwan delegation walked out in protest after PRC foreign minister Tang Jiaxuan snubbed ROC economic minister Lin Hsin-yi during a press conference.

A Maturing Democracy amidst Cross-Strait Tensions

The DPP's successes as Taiwan entered a new century underscored the two main themes of Taiwan's recent political history: democratization and the persistence of tensions with China. The sense of crisis surrounding Chen's presidency due to divided government, poor economic performance, and prolonged lack of progress in cross-strait relations clouded the long-term significance of the 2000–2001 elections. With a peaceful, institutionalized change of regime in the Executive Yuan and the DPP's replacement of the KMT as the largest party in the Legislative Yuan, Taiwan took another step in the consolidation of its democratic transformation. Taiwan nevertheless faces the continuing challenge of improving its system of governance (as do "mature" democracies such as the United States). As we have seen, changing political structures can be easier to accomplish than doing away with cultural practices and long-established traditions that have negative effects. For example, the KMT's vast business empire and financial assets, conservatively estimated at U.S. $3 billion, remain a spawning ground for corruption and conflicts of interest.

The DPP's gains also appeared to move the island further away from political reconciliation and reunification with mainland China. The eclipse of the Blue camp, if permanent, would leave China with little more than cross-strait economic ties in which to place its hopes of avoiding an

[9] Charles Snyder, "Powell Assures Taipei There's No Deal with China," Taipei Times Online, Sept. 23, 2001, online at http://www.taipeitimes.com/news/2001/09/23/print/0000104133, accessed Oct. 4, 2001.

ultimate choice between the two disastrous options of fighting to keep Taiwan and accepting its independence.

More favorably, Taiwan can look forward to a gradual diminution of the more soluble problem of interethnic tensions. Intermarriage between "yams" (Taiwanese) and "taros" (Mainlanders) has become common. Taiwan's relationship with China is still a divisive issue, but Taiwanese are no longer denied access to political or economic power. Within two generations ethnic tensions may cease to be a significant factor in Taiwan politics.

✳

CHAPTER NINE

Taiwan's History and Taiwan's Future

This survey of Taiwan's political history seeks to aid comprehension of the island's unusual present-day political circumstances. One peculiarity is that two distinct "Chinese" governments claim ownership of Taiwan. We have seen that each of the two Chinese Civil War rivals came to define ownership of Taiwan as vital to regime and state security. Under the interpretation that currently prevails on the mainland, Beijing's acquiescence to Taiwan leaving "Chinese" control would be tantamount to the CCP admitting failure to protect the territorial integrity of "China," a fundamental responsibility of any Chinese government. The PRC's top leaders would not expect to remain in office after allowing this perceived diminution of the Chinese heritage. Taiwan under the ROC has kept the problem within the family and made it possible for Beijing to be patient, limiting the fight during and since the Cold War to a diplomatic and political battle. In recent years, however, Beijing has seen the KMT, originally the party of Mainlander sentiment and commitment to reunification, gradually slide from its position of almost total command of Taiwan's politics, losing control of both the presidency and the legislature.

Beijing of course has characterized the officials in Taipei as illegitimate pretenders, the descendants of defeated KMT holdouts sheltered by the Taiwan Strait and American intervention. The ROC's claim to Taiwan began with the contention, accepted by the Allied high command at the end of the Second World War, that the island was Chinese territory victimized by Japanese imperialism. The KMT government that took control of Taiwan after the Japanese surrender was a Mainlander regime that had formerly ruled China. Beside strong motivations stemming from ideology, ancestral ties, and a sense of historical accountability, the need to bolster its political legitimacy in post–February 28 Taiwan gave the KMT a strong incentive to continue styling itself as the government of a China of which Taiwan was an integral part. If these Mainlander sentiments are a weaker force in Taiwan domestic politics today than during the rule of Chiang Kai-shek, the fear of changing the status quo in a way that would provoke a military response from the PRC has helped preserve both the notion and the legal framework of the Republic of China on Taiwan.

At issue is not only the question of which Chinese government has rightful claim to Taiwan, but also the possibility that Taiwan will reject both and opt instead for political separation from China. Taiwan has not made up its own mind. The identity of Taiwan's people (taken as a whole) remains unsettled, and the island's future relationship with China is one of the major political issues in contemporary Taiwan politics. Taiwan is not only ethnically divided, but the divisions are highly politicized. The descendants of early Fujianese and Hakka immigrants to Taiwan generally accept the notion that Taiwan is and should be politically distinct from China because their ancestors made this break generations ago. Mainlanders arrived more recently and with a dramatically different attitude: Taiwan was unquestionably part of China and would serve as the temporary home of an ROC government destined to reclaim control over the mainland. The bitterly disappointing experience of the return of Chinese rule in 1945, the bloodbath following the February 28 incident, and the White Terror hardened Taiwanese antipathy toward the Mainlanders and their agenda. During its early years of rule, the KMT squandered the considerable good will with which Taiwanese contemplated an incoming Chinese administration. These experiences account for the depth of this parallel ethnic and political division and its persistence into the twenty-first century.

While recognizing their cultural and genealogical roots in China and the vast scope for cross-strait economic cooperation, Taiwanese are particularly reticent toward the notion of rule by mainland Chinese. This is understandable given the Taiwanese community's past experiences with official indifference, incompetence, corruption, and harshness. As we have seen, imperial China did not claim Taiwan, had no desire to colonize it, and forbid or restricted emigration through much of history. The Chinese who settled there were largely economic and political refugees. The Chinese government incorporated Taiwan in 1683 out of concerns for external and internal security and made it a province as a response to growing foreign pressures. The Qing government's administration was weak, and the central government did not even claim jurisdiction over most of the island until the latter part of this period. Much of the infrastructure built on Taiwan during Qing rule came from private rather than public funds.

Chinese took Taiwan's handover to Japan in 1895 as a sellout by the government. When Mainlander rule returned, Taiwanese expected the new government to recognize their relatively high degree of political development. Instead, deeply suspicious of Japanese indoctrination, the Mainlanders saw the Taiwanese as tainted collaborators and in some respects treated them as a defeated enemy. Mainlanders appeared interested mainly in rooting out disloyalty and harnessing Taiwan's resources for the war against the CCP and for personal gain. The violent purges and repression that soon followed inculcated a sense of bitterness and vulnerability among the Taiwanese.

Thus, Taiwanese nurture a sense of distinctiveness and a reluctance to accept mainland Chinese rule, sentiments expressed in Taiwan's unwillingness to commit to political unification with China. Even Beijing's offer to let Taiwan keep its armed forces, maintain its present political and economic systems, and retain a high degree of autonomy while formally uniting with China under the "one country, two systems" concept appeals to few of Taiwan's people. Conversely, many in Taiwan, principally those of Mainlander background, oppose political independence, which would make them permanent sojourners. The threat of force from Beijing herds most of Taiwan's people into a noncommittal middle ground and prevents the resolution of this question through a natural domestic political process. For the time being, Taiwan harbors a split identity.

The United States and China face the prospect of a war over Taiwan that neither side wants. China is committed to attack Taiwan under certain circumstances, while the United States is committed to defend Taiwan under certain circumstances. For both, failing to fulfill these commitments would likely be more costly politically than honoring them. The PRC has defined the reincorporation of Taiwan as a vital national interest and core national value. For its part, the United States has been deeply involved in the Republic of China's history since the Second World War. The United States assisted Taiwan's economic and political liberalization through advice and education while protecting Taiwan from seizure by a menacing Communist power. Taiwan has been a shining example of successful American internationalism, and a test case affirming American hopes for China. It would be excruciatingly difficult for America to stay on the sidelines while "the butchers of Beijing" made war on this small, nascent democracy. American strategists would also fear their failure to intervene might lead Asian governments to lose confidence in U.S. leadership and move toward accommodation with Beijing.

In the meantime, however, U.S. support for Taiwan is the largest single impediment to a stable working relationship between Washington and Beijing. Based on American assistance to Chiang Kai-shek's government immediately after World War II, the Seventh Fleet's neutralization of the Taiwan Strait in 1950, the U.S.-ROC alliance during much of the Cold War, and the continuation of U.S. arms sales to Taiwan as well as Washington's demonstrated willingness to commit U.S. forces to Taiwan's defense, China considers American intervention the root cause of the Taiwan "problem." Given the value and importance of this relationship, based on China's vast economic potential and growing strategic weight, Washington pays a substantial price for standing by the ROC. United States support for the ROC raises Chinese suspicions about overall American policy in Asia and thus makes Sino-U.S. accommodation on other issues more difficult; motivates Chinese retaliation on other fronts (e.g., transfers of technology for weapons of mass destruction to countries such as Pakistan, linked to American arms sales to Taiwan); and makes area denial against U.S. forces off the Chinese coast the chief mission to which PLA modernization is pegged.

Unlike some wars of the past, a Sino-U.S. conflict over Taiwan could not justifiably be termed a "tragedy of miscalculation." China has explicitly laid out the criteria under which it would use force. Although American foreign policy is notoriously fickle, signals such as the dispatch of aircraft carrier battle groups in 1996 and President George W. Bush's 2001 pledge to "do whatever it takes" to defend Taiwan make clear the U.S. government's intention to get involved in the case of perceived PRC aggression without reasonable provocation.

History has bequeathed dilemmas to both Taiwan and China. Moving toward independent statehood is in many ways an appropriate course of action that would address the Taiwan people's craving for full recognition and respect from the international community, but in the short term this move would likely result in a devastating war. The PRC realizes that left to its own devices, Taiwan would drift farther from Beijing politically. China's only influence over Taiwan has come through trade and the threat of force. That China and Taiwan are drawing closer together economically is undeniable. A total of $60 billion from Taiwan is invested on the mainland. Perhaps half a million ROC nationals reside in China, and Taiwanese make 3 million visits to the mainland every year. Vibrant trade, however, may not solve China's Taiwan problem. Chinese hopes notwithstanding, these growing economic and social ties will not necessarily lead to political ties; the former can exist happily without the latter. If cross-strait economic interchange is not the answer, China is left with the threat of force. The PRC's dilemma is that military coercion has prevented formal independence, but in the long-run it is counterproductive, hardening the Taiwan people's resolve and solidifying their perception of Beijing an as enemy government. Rigid and lacking in creativity, Jiang Zemin's government failed to produce initiatives for stimulating among Taiwan's people a desire to politically unify with the mainland.

What will become of this tense stalemate? Taiwan's history offers a few suggestions about the future of the Taiwan-China relationship. First, Taiwan has strong, abiding cultural ties with China. In this sense Taiwan will always be, to a large degree, "Chinese," as it has been from ancient times. This cultural affinity does not, however, translate seamlessly to political integration. Taiwan has followed a distinct path of social, economic, and political development. Taiwan's people are proud of their society and wish to preserve it.

Second, Taiwan has proven difficult for outsiders to govern, as the Dutch, Qing, Japanese, and postwar KMT administrations discovered. It is a country brimming with rugged individualists with a record of successfully fighting for concessions from their rulers. This suggests that a strategy of forcing Taiwan to submit to political unification is a losing policy. A blockade, missile bombardment, or cyber-warfare are likely to make Taiwan's people more defiant, not coerce them into surrender—not to mention the fact that these tactics allow ample time for U.S. forces to intervene. Even if Chinese forces manage to capture and control the key organs of government, they will have done so at the cost of profoundly angering and alienating the local population, putting true integration even further out of reach.

Third, Taiwan's experience suggests that the CCP will come under increasing pressures to politically liberalize, as did the KMT in the 1980s. In Taiwan's case, economic development and minor political reforms by the state increased society's demands for greater liberalization and empowerment, while attempts to suppress the opposition had no lasting effect. The eventual results were legalization of new opposition parties, greater tolerance of political discussion on previously forbidden topics, reform of governmental institutions, and transfer of political power from the party leadership and the military to the organs of government. The KMT gradually became what it originally opposed: a Taiwanese party and an agent of political liberalization and movement toward independence from the mainland.

Conditions in China today exhibit some parallels with the beginnings of democratization in Taiwan. Expectations among the Chinese public for transparency and responsiveness in their government are growing as living standards rise. The authorities have recently implemented democratic elections at the village level. Although some areas of political reporting remain off-limits, the Chinese press is more open than ever. To the dismay of party conservatives, Jiang favors admitting business people into the CCP. The state is barely able to contain the demands of various groups for reform and redress.

Democratization in the PRC would not automatically remove cross-strait tension. It might, however, facilitate a process of reevaluation and conceptual reconstruction in the mainland's attitude toward Taiwan. At present, the PRC misleadingly associates expression of the popular will of the ethnic Chinese inhabitants of Taiwan with the exploitation of China by the imperialist powers during the Century of Shame. But with the passage of more time and freer discussion of sensitive topics, a future generation of mainland Chinese might realize that whether as a province or an independent country, Taiwan offers China bright prospects for a fulfilling economic and cultural relationship, and that the absence of formal governance by Beijing over the island does not significantly undercut the security or prosperity of Chinese living on the mainland. Then Mainlanders can join with the international community in celebrating Taiwan's accomplishments, viewing the island's progress with pride instead of foreboding.

INDEX

Chiang Ching-kuo, 78, 88, 91–92, 127–128, 131, 136, 138–140, 145, 151, 182, 229
    assassination attempt in New York, 159–160
    ascension to presidency, 156–157
    background, 156–158
    death, 180
    national Security Law and, 174
    on public opinion, 153
    potential successors, 179–180
    responses to PRC diplomatic overtures, 148
    restrained reaction to founding of DPP, 172–173
    vision for Taiwan, 155
Chiang Chun-ling, 200
Chiang Fang-liang, 179
Chiang Hsiao-wen, 179
Chiang Hsiao-wu, 179
Chiang Hsiao-yung, 179
Chiang Kai-shek, 6, 9, 17, 87–88, 92–93, 96
    before relocation to Taiwan, 55–56, 60–61, 66, 67
    Cold War politics and, 105–107, 112–116, 118–130, 136, 150–151
    death, 156
    February 28 incident and, 69–71, 185
    plans for Taiwan after 1949, 78–84
Chiang P'eng-chien, 173
Chiang Wei-guo, 179, 186
Chiang Wei-shui, 47
Chiayi, 22, 71
China and Taiwan (prior to 1945):
    Ancient China, 11–15
    Chinese settlers in premodern times, 12–15
    Ming Dynasty, 12, 17, 21
    Qing Dynasty, 8, 18–30, 33–34, 242
    Sino-Japanese War settlement, 32–33
China and Taiwan (postwar):
    attacks by ROC forces against China, 117
    attitudes of Taiwan's people toward China, 242–245
    diplomatic overtures to Taiwan during the 1970s and 1980s, 146–149
    hijacking of airliners, 149, 218
    Qiandao Lake murders, 218–219
    relations after Chen's election, 236–239
    Taiwan Strait crises, 118–123
        1995–1996 crisis, 195–202
    trade and investment across the Strait, 149–150, 217–218, 237–238

China Democratic Party, 87
China Youth Party, 83–84
Chinese Anticommunist National Salvation Youth Corps, 92
Chinese Association for Human Rights, 171
Chinese Communist Party, 9, 56, 73, 78, 83, 107–108, 113–114, 126
    attitude toward DPP, 174
    prospects of winning the stalemate with Taiwan, 245–246
    Taiwan's significance to, 241–244
Chinese Democratic Reformers Alliance, 186
"Chinese Taipei," 137
Ching Chuan Kang air base, 128
Chiu Cheyne, 219
Chiu Huo-tu, 72
Chiu I-jen, 207
Chow Shu-kai, 116, 135–137
Christopher, Warren, 140, 196
Chu Hui-liang, 229
Chu Kao-cheng, 172
Chu Yi-kuei, 21–22
Chungking, 82
Chungli, 167, 207
Chungli incident, 166
Chungshan Institute of Science and Technology, 143
Civic Organization Law, 176
Clark, Ramsey, 176
Clinton, Bill, 200, 220–221
Commissar system, 91–92
Committee of One Million, 108
Commons Daily, 201
Control Yuan, 84, 167, 189, 191, 194
Constitution, ROC, 83–84
    revision, 194–195
Coordination Council for North American Affairs, 140
Council of Grand Justices, 85, 191, 203, 234
Cultural Renaissance, 144
Cultural Revolution, 116, 144, 146

Dachen Islands, 120
Dalai Lama, 215
Democratic League, 83
Democratic Progressive Party (DPP), 160, 176–177
    1996 presidential election and, 198, 201
    aboriginal policy, 223
    constitutional revision and, 194–195

ABOUT THE AUTHOR

Denny Roy is a senior research fellow at the Asia-Pacific Center for Security Studies in Honolulu, Hawaii. He specializes in international security issues in Northeast Asia. Roy earned a doctorate in political science from the University of Chicago in 1991 and has held teaching and research positions at the Naval Postgraduate School, Australian National University, the National University of Singapore, and Brigham Young University. He is the author of *China's Foreign Relations* (Macmillan and Rowman & Littlefield, 1998) and coauthor of *The Politics of Human Rights in East Asia* (Pluto Press, 2001). His analyses of Asia-Pacific security matters also appear in several academic journals.